AF531343

GUIDANCE AND COUNSELLING

GUIDANCE AND COUNSELLING

By

Singamaneni Nageswara Rao
M.Sc., M.Ed.
Lecturer
Andhra Kesari College of Education
Ongole, Prakasam Distt, (A.P.)

Murugudu Sri Hari
M.Sc., M.Ed.
Lecturer
Acharya N.G. Ranga College of Education
Chilumuru, Guntur Distt., (A.P.)

General Editor
Dr. Digumarti Bhaskara Rao
M.Sc., M.A., M.A., M.Ed., Ph.D.
Reader
R.V.R. College of Education
Srinivasa Nagar Colony
Guntur–522 006
Andhra Pradesh
India

DISCOVERY PUBLISHING HOUSE
NEW DELHI-110002

Published by:
Namit Wasan

DISCOVERY PUBLISHING HOUSE PVT. LTD.
4383/4B, Ansari Road, Darya Ganj
New Delhi-110 002 (India)
Phone : +91-11-23279245; 23253475; 43596065
E-mail : discoverybooksindia@gmail.com
discoverypublishinghouse@gmail.com
namitwasan9@gmail.com
web : www.discoverypublishinggroup.com

***First Published:* 2004**

***Reprinted:* 2023**

ISBN: 978-81-7141-840-4

Guidance and Counselling

© Authors

All rights reserved. No part of this publication should be reproduced, stored in a retrieval system, or transmitted in any form or by any means: electronic, mechanical, photocopying, recording or otherwise, without the prior written permission of the author and the publisher.

This book has been published in good faith that the material provided by authors/editors is original. Every effort is made to ensure accuracy of material, but the publisher and printer will not be held responsible for any inadvertent error(s). In case of any dispute, all legal matters are to be settled under Delhi jurisdiction only.

Printed at:
Infinity Imaging Systems
Delhi

Preface

Guidance is as old a practice, as our social traditions and values.Since time immemorial, the elders of the community and seniors in all walks of life have been acting as leading lights for the youngers and the generations to come. However, counselling is relatively, a new phenomenon. It comes after guidance and along with it as well.

In modern times, guidance and counselling is the part and parcel of the discipline of education. Now, it has further been specified. There are experts and specialists to offer their sound advice on all matters coming under Guidance and Counselling.

Today, the teachers are expected to act as counsellors also. They guide their pupils regarding further studies and as well as the career to be pursued. Hence, they need expertise in this area. This book is meant to fill that vaccuum in our textbooks of teaching series.

This comprehensive book on Guidance and Counselling is bound to help teachers, teacher-students and students in course of their training in the art of teaching.

Author

Contents

1
Introduction

Guidance is practical since ancient times. In those times, guidance was offered to the young by elders in the family and to persons in distress by the family priest or the medicine men who conjured up the spirits of the dead or supernatural forces to help the client. Even today, in India, guidance, whether in personal, educational, vocational or political matters, is sought from the family priest, palmist, astrologer or numerologist.

Guidance—unorganised and informal—has in all places and at all levels been a vital aspect of the educational process. Good teachers have always been interested in providing understanding assistance to students to help them overcome problems of speedy learning and optimum adjustment. They have been generally sagacious and wise in their handling of students. The guidance given was informal and incidental, more akin to 'advising' and sometimes amounted to 'ordering' and 'prescribing'. The process succeeded as the contact between the teacher and students was intimate, the courses of study simple, and occupations less taxing.

Guidance, as a personalised assistance made readily available by a sympathetic, mature, experienced and professionally qualified person, which gives it the status of a separate field of endeavour with adequate sophistication and specificity separate from teaching, is a twentieth century concept. In view of the tremendous increase in the number of students, their wants and aspirations, a need is being felt everywhere for a nucleus of an organised programme of professional help in the form of guidance and counselling in the educational institutions.

Basic Concept

The intellectual climate, out of which guidance emerged as an essential activity of education, can be traced back to the time of Comenius—when the intellectual and social precursors of the modern world were uncertainly established. The development of science was a potent force in this direction. The technological advance of the Industrial Revolution brought in its wake increased division of labour and occupational complexities which made real the need for vocational guidance. The Revolution also brought changes in the way of life. The development of democratic values and the utilitarian emphasis on education gave an impetus to two things—freedom of the individual and a feeling of need for practical education. Thus, the Industrial Revolution, with the changes it introduced in modes of working, living and thinking, made this supposedly family problem of guidance assume wider importance.

Guidance, as an organised professional activity, dates back to 1905 and the credit for the same goes to Frank Parsons of Boston, U.S.A. At the end of his career, Parsons actively engaged himself in social work in a Boston settlement house where he worked directly with young people struggling to find work for themselves. He helped found the Vocation Bureau and wrote his classic ***Choosing*** a ***Vocation***. These two achievements, in the last years of a varied and eventful career made him pioneer in the guidance movement in America.

Parsons was followed by a number of social reformers like Jessie B. Davis, Anne Reed and Eli Weaver who advocated social reforms and stressed the necessity for the school to prepare youngsters to meet the rigours of a competitive and materialistic society. David S. Hill, another guidance pioneer, considered guidance as a means of developing human beings who could build a better society.

World Scenario

Since 1910 a number of professional organisations made significant contributions to the development of guidance movement in America. The National Education Association helped a lot in giving adequate recognition to guidance during annual conventions of this association. The National Society for the Promotion of Industrial Education conducted and published vocational surveys and urged legislation to promote vocational education. The efforts of these agencies were rewarded through the passage of an Act in 1917 which provided federal aid to certain types of vocational education in public schools.

The first national conference on vocational guidance was held at Boston in 1910 when the National Vocational Guidance Association came into being to meet the educational needs of guidance at the higher secondary level.

During the next twenty-five years, a large number of independent guidance associations were formed. The number of these associations was so large that a Council of Guidance and Personnel Associations was set up in 1934 to co-ordinate their work. In 1951, it was felt necessary to co-ordinate separate associations specifically and exclusively interested in the guidance movement and to form another association of guidance workers. This was the beginning of the American Personnel and Guidance Association with the Personnel and Guidance Journal as its official magazine.

The World War I indirectly made a significant contribution to the development of guidance movement. It necessitated scientific selection and training of men. Intelligence tests had to be devised for use with many people at a time. A large section of the male population was given intelligence and other tests. Later, a number of studies were conducted which had significant implications for guidance. After the War, there was the problem of rehabilitation of ex-servicemen—particularly the disabled veterans. A number of aptitude tests were devised which further streamlined the guidance movement. Besides these, the measurement movement, introduction of cumulative records, the interest in improvement of.personnel in their respective fields and the federal government assistance helped the guidance movement.

The emphasis in the beginning was on the vocational guidance and training and it did not take too long for the leaders to recognise the importance of educational guidance and training in preparation of a career. In 1914, Kelley made an analysis of the values of tests in helping a student to select a high school curriculum. He also stressed the role of educational guidance in vocational choice. Gradually, the concept of guidance expanded to include civic guidance, social guidance, religious guidance, recreational guidance and health guidance.

Today, there is a network of guidance clinics of different types and innumerable centres for the training of guidance personnel in U.S.A. The review and revision of guidance techniques and procedures are clear indications of the increasing popularity of guidance work in America. The guidance movement, in fact, has been the greatest single force in improving the educational practices in America where it has assumed the shape of an educational, social and cultural movement.

From America, the movement spread to other countries including Australia, Britain, Canada, Sri Lanka, France, Germany, India, Japan, Norway and Switzerland. The people in France, Belgium, Norway, Denmark are becoming guidance-minded. In most of these countries, adequate guidance services are available in nearly every major town. In Britain, counselling centres, guidance clinics and bureaus have been doing useful work and the guidance services are undergoing a rapid process of improvement, refinement and expansion. The remarkable progress made during the present century by people in the west in the fields of education, science, arts and industry is, to a large extent, the result of proper organisation and utilization of their guidance services.

Indian Scenario

As far as India is concerned, the techniques of guidance—informal and incidental—can be traced far back to ancient times. The ***Panchatantra*** and ***Jataka*** tales are well known for their moral stories, parables and question-answer techniques in learning. Even before the time of Socrates, these were used in India. The teacher-taught relationship was that of Guru-Shishya—the word guru meaning 'the one who guides'.

Guidance, as an organised professional activity, is more than four decades old in our country. While in America the guidance movement started as an attempt to fulfil the practical needs of employers and teachers, in India it began as an academic discipline. Calcutta University enjoys the privilege of being the first Indian university to introduce guidance as a section of its department of Applied Psychology in 1938 to conduct research in the field of educational and vocational guidance. Later, the Department also started the work on occupational information when jobs were classified into four categories according to the level of intelligence and the type of abilities required for then.

In 1941, Batliboi—a retired accountant working in Calcutta—realised the practical implications of guidance and with the help of a Calcutta University psychologist set up the Batliboi Vocational Guidance Bureau in Bombay, with the sole purpose of providing guidance services to the community. During its short life of six years, the Bureau made a significant contribution to guidance and offered an orientation course to the teachers and workers interested in the guidance of young people. This was the beginning of the courses for career masters and guidance counsellors.

The movement received impetus when the Trustees of the Parsi Panchayat Funds and Properties decided to establish a guidance services bureau—Parsi Panchayat Vocational Guidance Bureau— for the Parsi community in Bombay. The remains of the Batliboi Bureau, which had closed, were amalgamated with this set-up. This bureau worked on meagre resources and scanty staff, but with the help of the devoted workers it was able to do pioneering work in guidance. It organised a career conference for the first time to disseminate occupational information. This became a popular feature of guidance programmes in all states and institutions. It was also the first institution to organise a course for career masters and started publishing the ***Journal of Educational and Vocational Guidance*** which provided the guidance workers with a professional organ of communication and interchange of ideas and information regarding research and practice in the field.

In the early stages, the programmes offered by the Parsi Panchayat Vocational Guidance Bureau were confined to the Parsi schools only. Later, these were thrown open to other city schools as well. Guidance programmes were started in a few selected schools. After a few years of successful work, the bureau was forced to close down, but it re-opened in 1963 and conducted a number of interesting programmes of guidance for the Bombay schools.

In 1947, the Government of Uttar Pradesh officially recognised the movement by setting up a Bureau of Psychology at Allahabad. One of the reasons for establishing such an institution was the demand made by the people for an education suitable to Indian conditions and needs, and one of the aims of the Bureau was to provide educational and vocational guidance to the school-going children of the state as well as other young people in need of help. Besides the main bureau at Allahabad, five district bureaus were organised at Varanasi, Lucknow, Kanpur, Meerut and Bareilly for organising psychological programmes for district schools.

Bombay (now the State of Maharashtra) was the next to give official recognition to the guidance programme for the school-going children. The Bureau of Vocational Guidance, Bombay was set up in 1950. It emphasised occupational information rather than testing which enjoyed priority with the Bureau at Allahabad. In 1957, the Bureau was renamed and is functioning as the Institute of Vocational Guidance, Bombay. Guidance has now been given a wider interpretation – guidance with functions of research, test construction and adaptation, individual guidance, selection and training of guidance personnel, and collection and dissemination of occupational information. This was the first institution to provide occupational information service in the country and to conduct training programmes.

In 1952, the Vocational Guidance Association of Bombay was formed to help co-ordinate the work done by individuals in Bombay. Later, at the initiative of Dr Barnette, effort was made to co-ordinate the work being done all over the country. Barnette brought all the guidance workers together during a seminar in 1952 at the Central Institute of Education, New Delhi. An opportunity was provided to guidance personnel to exchange ideas and discuss problems with their colleagues and others interested in guidance. The decision to form an All India Educational and Vocational Guidance Association affiliated with the International Association for Vocational Guidance was taken at a seminar held in 1954. Two years later, in 1956, the association was formed during a meeting held at the M.S. University of Baroda.

An important factor which influenced the development of guidance movement in India was the appointment of the Secondary Education Commission in 1952. As a result of the recommendations of this Commission, the old education system which was unilateral in character, was replaced by a scheme of diversified courses. The Commission provided for seven streams at the secondary stage—humanities, science, agriculture, commerce, technical, fine arts, and home science. The students were supposed to choose the courses at the Delta stage, hence the need for guidance at this stage. The Commission found that, "the secret of good education consists in enabling the student to realise what are his talents and aptitudes and in what manner and to what extent he can best develop them so as to achieve proper social adjustment and seek right types of employment." The Commission recommended the introduction of educational and vocational guidance "...not to be regarded as a mechanical process whereby the advisers and teachers sort out boys and girls as a grading machine sorts out apples! It is not a question of just deciding that one boy should stay in the farm, another work in an aeroplane factory, a third become a teacher and the fourth take to the management of a garage. Guidance involves the difficult art of helping boys and girls to plan their own future wisely in the full light of all the factors that can be mustered about themselves and about the world in which they are to live and work—it is not the work of a few specialists, but rather a service in which the entire school staff must cooperate under the guidance of some person with special knowledge and skill in this particular field. Guidance— is not confined to the vocational field only. It covers the whole gamut of youth problems and should be provided in an appropriate form at all stages of education through the co-operative endeavour of understanding parents, headmasters, principals and guidance officers.

For the implementation of these recommendations, the Commission provided guidelines, both for the Centre and the States, and the result was the creation of an infrastructure of guidance programme in the multipurpose schools. The nationwide guidance and counselling programmes during the first decade following the publication of the Report of the Secondary Education Commission was the result of this progressive national policy on secondary education.

Following the Commission's recommendations, the Government of India established the Central Bureau of Educational and Vocational Guidance at Delhi in 1954, to give technical advice and help in the organisation of the guidance movement. It also offered assistance to the State Governments to establish their own State bureaus and to provide guidance services in their secondary schools. With the setting up of the All India Educational and Vocational Guidance Association in 1956, the guidance movement assumed an All India character.

Soon private agencies and universities started evincing interest in the field and the *Journal of Educational and Vocational Guidance* was started by a private agency in 1954. This was later taken over by the All India Educational and Vocational Guidance Association. Some universities also began to offer courses in guidance as optional papers for Master's degree in education and psychology.

The guidance movement received a further fillip during the Third Plan period. Financial assistance and technical advice were given to the States by the Government of India under a Centrally-sponsored scheme of the Ministry of Education. The scheme provided for:

(i) The establishment of State Bureaus of Guidance in the States where they did not already exist;

(ii) The strengthening of the existing State Bureaus;

(iii) The establishment of guidance services with a full-time counsellor in 170 multipurpose schools; and

(iv) The establishment of an occupational information service in 2500 schools.

The financial assistance offered being meagre, the scheme had little impact on the development of guidance services. By the end of third Plan, the number of secondary schools offering some kind of guidance was about 3,000 which constituted only 13 per cent of the total number of secondary schools and again in a majority of these schools a career master gave a semblance of guidance and very few schools had the services of a full-time or part-time counsellor. The Education Commission (1964-66) considered that the "guidance services have a much wider scope and function than merely that of assisting students in making educational and vocational choices. The aims of guidance are both adjustive and developmental; it helps the student in making the best possible adjustments to the situations in the educational institution and in the home and at the same time facilitates the development of all aspects of his personality. Guidance, therefore, should be regarded as an integral part of education and not a special psychological or social service which is peripheral to educational purposes. It is meant for all students, not just for those who deviate from the norm in one direction or the other. It is also a continuous process aimed at assisting the individual to make decisions and adjustments from time to time."

The Commission emphasised that educational and vocational guidance could play a significant and useful role in the qualitative improvement of educational standards at all levels and suggested a new policy on education from the primary to the university stages. It scrapped the recommendations of the Secondary Education Commission as a result of which the multipurpose system gave place to the traditional system of a unitary type. The scheme bade farewell to the objective of vocationally oriented education envisaged in the previous system.

After having made a strong case for guidance as contributory to a student's all-round development, the Commission recommended that it was not counsellors but teachers who would have to take the responsibility for guidance for the next twenty years. The Commission had thrown cold water on the hopes and aspirations of guidance workers. The Draft National Policy on Education of the Ministry of Education, Government of India (1979) is silent on the guidance and counselling service and the words 'guidance' and 'counselling' are nowhere mentioned in the National Policy Note.

At present two major establishments are developing guidance programmes for school-going children in our country – government organisations and private agencies. The government agencies include the Department of Educational Psychology and Foundations of Education, the National Council for Educational Research and Training, State Bureaus of Guidance and the guidance units (561) of the National Employment Service. Private agencies include Vocational Guidance Society at Calcutta, Gujarat Research Society at Bombay, Y.M.C.A. of Calcutta, the Rotary Club of Bombay, the Lions Club and the Junior Chamber of Baroda.

According to the information collected by the Department of Psychology and Foundations of Education in 1976, out of 30,328 secondary schools in the country, 8,732 (29 per cent) have a programme of guidance. Only 37 schools in the country have full time counsellors, 258 schools have part-time counsellors and the rest of the schools have career masters. As the impact of guidance is not immediately perceptible, effective guidance service is rare in schools. Bureaus are functioning in all the States except Jammu and Kashmir, Nagaland, Sikkim and Tamil Nadu. Among the Union Territories, only Chandigarh and Delhi have guidance bureaus. In most of the States, the bureaus are ill-equipped. The requisite personnel are not available and sufficient funds are not provided to carry on the programme effectively. In most of the States, the programme is considered a frill and a luxury. Teachers and headmasters shirk responsibility and the guidance master cannot work under a management where the guidance programme does not figure in the time schedule. The trained career masters with their normal teaching load are unable to give guidance in the schools and the pupils remain ignorant.

The State Guidance Bureaus have no administrative control over the district/school counsellors and career masters who are generally found doing odd jobs for the District Education officer responsible for writing the annual confidential reports of these counsellors. Thus, the district counsellors are unable to carry out the duties for which they are appointed. School counsellors are also found to be doing teaching work and neglecting actual guidance.

The State Guidance Bureaus are not consulted even for the transfers of district counsellors, school counsellors or Career Masters. Thus, due to the lack of administrative control over the guidance personnel in the state, the guidance work has not made much headway. Besides, occupational and guidance literature is neither available in sufficient quantity nor in the latest and attractive form which dampens the enthusiasm of guidance personnel. It is time to evolve a clear national policy for introducing guidance and counselling in schools.

2

Scope and Sphere

Guidance is defined in many ways. Crow and Crow write, "Guidance is not direction. It is not the imposition of one's point of view upon another. It is not making decisions for an individual which he should make for himself. It is not carrying the burden of another's life. Rather, guidance is assistance made available by competent counsellors to an individual of any age to help him direct his own life, develop his own point of view, make his own decisions, carry his own burdens". Hamrin and Brickson define guidance as "that aspect of educational programme which is concerned especially with helping the pupil to become adjusted to his present situation and to plan his future in the line with his interests, abilities, and social needs."

Mathewson believes that "guidance is the systematic professional process of helping the individual through education and interpretative procedures to gain a better understanding of his own characteristics and potentialities and to relate himself more satisfactorily to social requirements and opportunities in accord with social and moral values". Traxler considers guidance as a help which enables "each individual to understand his abilities and interests, to develop them as well as possible and to relate them to life-goals, and finally to reach a state of complete and mature self-guidance as a desirable member of the social order."

According to Jones, "Guidance involves personal help given by someone, it is designed to assist a person to decide where he wants to go, what he wants to do or how he can best accomplish his purpose; it assists him to solve problems that arise in his life."

An analysis of the above view-points shows that guidance has the following main characteristics:

(i) It is a process: It helps every individual to help himself, to recognise and use his inner resources, to set goals, to make plans, to work out his own problems of development.

(ii) It is a continuous process: It is needed right from early childhood, adolescence, adulthood and even in old age.

(iii) Choice and problem points are the distinctive concerns of guidance as here the individual's unique world of perceptions interacts with the external order of events in his life context,

(iv) It is assistance to the individual in the process of development rather than a direction of that development'. The aim is to develop the capacity for self-direction, self-guidance and self-improvement through an increased understanding of his problems and his resources as well as limitations to solve the problem.

(v) Guidance is a set-vice meant for all. It is a regular service which is required at every stage for every student, not only for awkward situations and abnormal students. It is a positive programme geared to meet the needs of all students.

(vi) It is both generalised and a specialised service: It is a generalised service because every one—teachers, tutors, advisers, deans, parents—play a part in the programme. It is a specialised service because specially qualified personnel as counsellors, psychiatrists and psychologists join hands to help the individual to get out of his problem,

Basic Ideas

Very few terms have been more loosely or interchangeably used than the terms 'guidance' and 'counselling'.

According to Tolbert, "Guidance is the total programme or all the activities and services engaged in by an educational institution that are primarily aimed at assisting and individual to make and carry out adequate plans and to achieve satisfactory adjustment in all aspects of his daily life. Guidance is not teaching but it may be done by teachers. It is not separate from education but is an essential part of the total educational programme. Guidance is a term which is broader than counselling and which includes counselling as one of its services."

Butler makes a logical separation of the counselling process discerned as having two phases called 'adjustive' and 'distributive', In the adjustive phase, the emphasis is on the social, personal and emotional problems of the individual; in the distributive phase the focus is upon his educational, vocational and occupational problems.

According to Arbuckle, Butler's distributive phase can be most aptly described as 'guidance' whilst the adjustive phase can be considered as the description of 'counselling'.

Principles of Guidance Philosophy

According to Hollis and Hollis, there are eight principles on which any guidance programme should be based. They can be modified to fit locally accepted beliefs. The principles are;

(i) The dignity of the individual is supreme.

(ii) Each individual is different from every other individual.

(iii) The primary concern of guidance is the individual in his social setting.

(iv) The attitudes and personal perceptions of the individual are the bases on which he acts.

(v) The individual generally acts to enhance his perceived self.

(vi) The individual has the innate ability to learn and can be helped to make choices that will lead to selfdirection consistent with social improvement.

(vii) The individual needs a continuous guidance process from early childhood through adulthood.

(viii) Each individual may at times need the information and personalised assistance best given by competent professional personnel.

System at Wrok

Guidance and counselling have three-fold functions: adjustments, orientational and developmental.

Guidance and counselling are adjustmental in the sense that they help the student in making the best possible adjustment to the current situations in the educational institution and occupational world, in the home and the community. Professional and individualised aid is given in making immediate and suitable adjustment at problem points. At the same time, the adjustive attitude in the spirit of Reinold Neibuhr is to be developed in the individuals:

God grant me the serenity,

To accept the things, I cannot change.

The courage to change the things I can

And the wisdom to know the difference.

Guidance and counselling have orientational function also. They orientate the students in problems of career planning, educational programming and direction towards long-term personal aims and values. Awareness of the need to plan in the context of the complexity of the world of work is an essential prerequisite of going through education and preparation for after-education career. Guidance and counselling have another important function-developmental function. They should try not only to cure when the problems have occurred and done their damage, rather they should begin before the problems arise and maladjustments occur. If unsolved problems are allowed to accumulate, their total effect may lead the student to the point where his capacity for growth is blocked. In such cases, guidance and counselling have a very important developmental function for helping the students achieve self-development and self-realisation. Guidance and counselling also have to discharge the

important function of furthering the welfare of the society and be important instruments of national development.

Area of Influence

The scope of guidance and counselling is extremely comprehensive. As the life is getting complex day by day, the problems for which expert help is required are increasing proportionately. The scope of guidance, per necessity, is extending horizontally to much of the social context, to matters of prestige in occupations, to the broad field of social trends, and economic development. Guidance is assuming more and more responsibility for the individual in every direction—it helps in the selection of educational courses, and profitable occupation, in job placement; placement in the next stage of education and training, occupational surveys; improvement of study skills, maintenance of mental health; counselling regarding personal adjustment problems; identifying the gifted, the backward and help them achieve the maximum. In short, educational, vocational, avocational, social, personal, moral and even marital problems of individual are the concerns of guidance and counselling. Their scope is indeed very vast.

A cursory glance at our seats of higher learning will show the imperative need of instituting in them a well-organized programme of guidance and counselling. Education is expanding its frontiers making it well-nigh impossible for an individual student to make a choice of courses and careers without expert guidance. Occupational scene too is changing so rapidly that yesterday's rocket circuitry electronics specialist who was once considered as highly prized as a marks-man on the old frontier is to-day's part of the unemployment statistics. One of the great stories in out midst is the dramatic increase in jobs.

Not only that, quite a big number of students at the threshold of a college or university are in for compelling and difficult life situations-they are shy, fearful, gullible, not skilled in managing their own affairs. They lack self-awareness which may enable them to form realistic life-goals and plans. They lack both focus and meaningful direction. Occasionally they lose their way in the dark labyrinths of adolescence and do not know how and when to act. They have to grapple with complex social problems-living with and sharing facilities with peers, such as living in hostels and sharing extra-curricular experiences, adjustment to heterosexual relationships, etc. Surveys of Indian students and alumni document the widespread feeling of dissatisfaction with college and university life.

A survey was conducted by the All India Educational and Vocational Guidance Association for gauging college student's needs. Three thousand students from seventeen Indian universities responded. The survey revealed student's felt needs. Eleven problems were marked by more than 50 percent of the respondents;

1. I cannot do as well in my studies as other people expect me to do.
2. I do not know enough about the qualifications needed for different kinds of works or careers.
3. I worry too much about what my future will be after I have finished my studies.
4. Even though I force myself, my attention will not remain on my assignments long enough to finish them.
5. I do not know how to make frieds among the opposite sex.
6. I do not have sufficient information about matters on sex.
7. I do not know enough about my aptitudes and abilities for different kinds of work or careers.
8. It is difficult for me to get the books I need for study.
9. I cannot read fast enough to complete my studies in time.
10. I do not know proper methods of study.
11. I have more difficulty in forgetting my mistakes than I believe I should have.

The eleven areas may be summarised under four headings Study habits and skills, Career choice, Knowledge of aptitudes and abilities and Sex education.

The respondents reported that their parents were the only source of help they received, if any, along these lines and practically no help had been forthcoming from college personnel!

Eighty per cent of respondents expressed the need of such assistance from their non-parental source. The bigger the college, the bigger the campus, the more the need for personalised student services, else the student will merely feel a small cog in a huge machine!

Another survey of the educational, vocational and personal problems was conducted by Umrudin and Gadri. Widespread maladjustment was rated among hostel residents who showed much concern over problems connected with study habits, vocational choice, family relationship and mental hygiene.

All these emerging issues and problems make it obligatory for our educational planners and administrators to build into our higher education an appropriate guidance and counselling programme for the development of the individual student into an adult personality, imbued with social and occupational awareness, intellectual and functional proficiency, discipline and confidence. The classroom activities, however well-conducted and well-organised, alone are not in a position to accomplish all this.

It is true that provision of guidance and counselling services in the colleges and universities cannot be seen as a panacea for all our educational ills nor can a counselling officer hope to give students a trouble-free or problem-free life, but where possible, he can help them to resolve their difficulties, or if that is not possible, to live with them. To help them resolve the stresses and strains does not require a nosey-parker intrusion of privacy but the response of an understanding and empathic person and an atmosphere of understanding, faith and sincerity. And this is what is needed.

Guidance and counselling programme needs to be introduced in our colleges and universities to meet the varied needs of the educational system, administration and students:

To help in the total development of the student: The emphasis on intellectual development through the teaching of subjects alone cannot help in the total development of the students. We have to evolve some method of helping students understand themselves and helping teachers understand the students. There has to be a basic and fundamental change in our entire system of education, change which recognises that no matter how well a human being is educated in chemistry, physics, economics, history or literature, he remains a barbarian unless he knows something about himself. Self-knowledge in depth which has been the forgotten factor in our educational system must become its primary focus-and this is what can be done through a programme of guidance and counselling. Total development of the students are expected, accepted, understood and planned for and all types of experiences in an institution are so organised as to contribute to the total development of the student. That, all that a student needs in an educational institution is good teaching, is an exploded myth. Something much more and beyond this is needed to produce competent, mature and well-rounded citizens.

The problem is grave in another way also. In his article on 'Unrest on Campus', Piloo Modi, M.P. once wrote, "Our student population reaches the university level, having made up their mind broadly about the courses that they may have-a decision, which in almost all cases, is taken by unthinking and unsympathetic parents and relatives with an eye on a more lucrative profession. It is great tragedy when a potential poet becomes a chemical engineer.. Many a mute inglorious Milton is languishing in the dark engineering world." This entire process of herding our youths into educational disciplines unconnected with their aptitudes needs to be checked through a scientific process of guidance and counselling for the best development of individuals and growth of society.

To help in the proper choice of careers: We are living in a highly complex and rapidly changing world of work. There are changing requirements in industrial jobs, altered market conditions for professional manpower, the development of para-professional has rendered occupational selection more difficult than ever. The young students in colleges and universities need to be informed about various jobs and openings available to them and the requirements, responsibilities and the nature of work involved in them so that they could measure themselves up to them and develop and crystallise their occupational goals. They need to be helped in making meaningful occupational selection and preparation for an entry into them to have a fulfilling and rewarding career.

The need for helping the students in the choice of a proper career is further enhanced due to the fact that majority of our students in colleges and universities are the first generation learners. In their family, they have no one with an experience of college or university education background to guide them in the choice of a career. With a right to the best education available, and a wide range of jobs open to them, these students need mature help in making a judicious occupational choice. Hence the need of adequate guidance and counselling arrangement in our colleges and universities.

To help the students in vocational development: The process of vocational development covers almost the entire span of life of an individual. It begins quite early in one's life and continues till sometimes after retirement. In this process, the individual passes through various stages— growth, exploration, maintenance and decline. Guidance services need to be provided to the colleges and universities to help the students in the process of vocational development—particularly the stage of growth and exploration, by making it possible for them to gain knowledge about themselves—their abilities, interests and needs, on the one hand, and knowledge about the world of work, on the other. By providing them opportunities for self-exploration as well as exploration of the world of work while they are still in an educational institution, their transition from education to work can be facilitated.

To develop readiness for choices and changes to face new challenges: In a paper entitled The Need for counselling in Higher Education, presented at the Third International Round Table of Educational Counselling and Vocational Guidance, Miss Newsome, Counselling Officer at the University of Keels, North Strafford

Shire, England, writes, "For the students of higher education the demands of life are likely to be great, in a most different way from the exacting demands of education itself. On graduating he will be called upon to make use of the kind of person he has become as much if not more than what he has learnt in his course of study—not only to make an initial choice of what he is to do on graduating but will be called upon to change his occupation several times in a life time. Readiness for these choices and changes is essential, not only to the student himself but to the society as a whole. To the extent to which he is able to capitalise on his experience and face new challenges with a realistic expectation of success, to that extent he will benefit society. If he is unable to meet the changing demands, not only of the working world but also of his other roles of life, to that extent he will be a liability and will fail to fulfil the expectations which society has for its most able people." Guidance services are needed to develop in the students the ability to cope with their new problems and concerns in such a way that they become more competent to meet the demands which will continue to be made upon them in the future.

To minimise the mismatching between education and employment and help in the efficient use of manpower. The latest analysis done by Planning Commission reveals that the educated youth between 15 and 29 years of age constituted 11.5 per cent of the corresponding labour force at the same time they accounted for 33.2 per cent of the total unemployment in the country. According to the Planning Commission's labour force projections, the total number of educated unemployed at the beginning of 1980 was estimated at 3.47 million. If there is no further deterioration in the unemployment rate, this number is likely to go upto 4.66 million in 1985. And this is the challenging situation we have to face.

It needs to be pointed out that the hiatus between education and employment has rarely been as wide and as disturbing as it is today. Higher academic education, as very well pointed out by Mr. L. K. Jha, Chairman of the Economic Administration Reforms Commission, is far too general and diffused to be of practical value to the vast majority of youngmen and women. Most of our young men and women have no clear objectives or career targets.

They amble through university courses of learning without acquiring much knowledge of preparing themselves for an uncertain future.

Every 12 months, our colleges and universities release thousands of hopeful youngsters into the labour market who are virtually unemployable-despite their fancy degrees and diplomas. In fact, employers often complain that of the hundreds of applications that come in response to a single vacancy, at least 80 per cent have no relevance to the job specifications whatsoever. Few students pursue their education with a clear idea as to what they would eventually like to become. People even register at the employment exchange with scant idea about the sort of work they would like to be employed at. No wonder while jobs go abegging the youth go begging for jobs. Not only that, the employment of workers ill-suited to their jobs generally leads to a higher rate of labour placement or to the retention of persons who are inefficient. All this is a huge wastage of our scant resources. Guidance facilities can help in reducing this wastage and thus ensure efficient use of manpower.

To motive the youth for self-employment: Considering the magnitude of educated job-seekers flowing into the job market in India every year, it is essential that a sizable fraction of enterprising youth is initiated into careers of self-employment. Some arrangement needs to be instituted in the colleges and universities to identify the deserving cases fit to take up self-employment, educate them on how to proceed about the job of setting up a venture, help them through the cooperation of the concerned agencies in this sphere to prepare technically sound and economically viable projects; sponsor their cases to the banks for loan assistance and guide them to overcome the teething troubles effective follow-up after the commencement of the venture.

To help freshers establish proper identity: In our country the youngmen entering colleges and even universities are comparatively young in years. These young adolescents are passing through a stage between childhood and adulthood, between the morality learned as a child and the ethics to be developed by the adult. They find it extremely difficult to establish a satisfactory identity. Such failure or delay leads to what can be called "role diffusion". This crisis in role identity is perhaps very acute today. The uncertainties of the future, the conflicts in languages, culture, regions, castes, etc., and the erosion of traditional values has rendered Indian youth rootless.

Fuster did a small study with Bombay college students, both men and women. The strongest needs, as reported by the students themselves where they were requested to indicate rank orders, were for achievement in life, self-reliance and a sense of security, success in college and university, to have an understanding friend and (for the males) money.

Guidance and counselling programme is needed to help students deal effectively with the normal developmental tasks of adolescence and face life situations boldly.

To identify and motivate the students from weaker sections of society: Students from weaker sections have their own problems and needs. They experience difficulty in adjustment with the peers, teachers and the environment. To communicate, make friends, utilise the time profitably, make the best use of lectures, make an effective use of library and other facilities available, all pose problems for them. Guidance facilities are urgently needed for such type of students to enable them to adjust and utilise the available facilities properly.

To help the students in their period of turmoil and confusion: The students undergo a great deal of turmoil and searching to give meaning to their lives. They have their conflicts and anxieties. They feel disillusioned regarding higher education. They find that colleges and universities, instead of imparting them education, just enable them to pass examinations – they feel sunk and cheated. When this education does not enable them to get immediate employment, they feel lost and bewildered.

Similarly, they have their personal conflicts and anxieties. They have the problems about their parents and family, their relations with boy and girl friends. They have the problems of adjusting their personality to the world of people, of ethical ideas and of goals and situations. For tacking all these situations successfully, they need someone to sort out the strands-they need, some strong, tactile presence of a hand guiding the anxious and enabling them to develop realistic expectations.

To help in checking wastage and stagnation: The average pass percentage at the graduate and post-graduate level is about 50 to 60. Thousands of our students, unfortunately, drop out, get pushed out, and fall out of the system. This problem is becoming more serious day by day.

There is another unfortunate side of this problem-majority of our students pass in third division, which is a low qualification for the world of work.

This poor achievement may be due to so many reasons—lack of proper study skills and effective study habits, lack of the knowledge for making full use of the facilities provided, and so on.

Also, the majority of our students do not fulfil the promise indicated by the Secondary School leaving examinations and do not utilize their professional qualifications after graduation.

A study of the years 1950 and 1954 alumni of Delhi University where approximately 1800 alumni were interviewed revealed;

(i) In general, these students did not fulfil the promise indicated by secondary school leaving examinations, since about 45 per cent received a lower university rating at graduation.

(ii) Many graduates do not use their training occupationally.

A study conducted by D.G.E and T., Ministry of Labour, 1962 on the graduates of the year 1950 revealed the percentage of graduates in clerical work-commerce 67 per cent; B.Sc. Pass 63 per cent; B.A. Pass 64 per cent; Proficiency in Law Certificate 48 per cent; M.A, Arts 31 per cent; B.A. Honours 25 per cent, etc. It is obvious that sizable percentage of alumni obtaining professional qualifications have to work as clerks. The report also gives evidence of much aimless and unrealistic vocational choice.

Higher education is a very costly enterprise. Much of the

money wasted on these poor and low achievers could be saved by a policy of prevention. Just as preventive medicine is sounder economically and more humane than remedial medicine, so too is preventive education more sound economically than remedial education. There is thus a clear need for developing better professional services of a counselling kind to check the huge wastage of student time and money and also l.uge state expenditure on education. Miller, in this connection, said so well, "If one counsellor could prevent the wastage of only four student years each costing - 800 to -1200, he would be earning his keep. Similar savings of graduate salaries foregone as a result of failure or delay would benefit student as well as the taxpayer."

To Identify and help students in need of special help: There are such students as the gifted, the backward, the handicapped who need special opportunities. Some arrangement needs to be provided in our colleges and universities to identify them and provide them with help according to their requirements.

To ensure the proper utilization of time spent outside the classrooms: It is common knowledge that students in the colleges and universities spend two to three times as many hours outside classrooms as in them. And the manner in which students spend their non-class hours clearly affects their success in achieving both academic competence and personal development of all types. It is, therefore, essential that institutions of higher learning provide positive direction to students by influencing how they can use those non-class hours. The programme of guidance and counselling can meet this need.

To help in tackling problems arising out of student explosion: Increased demand for higher education is outstripping the growth of facilities in the seats of higher learning. Resultant unfortunate qualitative changes in the nature of entire educative experiences are creating innumerable problems. The students population is highly affluent and extremely poor, educated in convents and ordinary schools and colleges, rural and urban areas, moveover, students from our own country and different foreign countries are attending colleges and universities. When students from a broad range of families and educational and social backgrounds meet in classes for instructions, in hostels for housing, in cafeterias and mess halls for eating, numerous problems crop up. Guidance and counselling facilities need to be provided for helping them tackle these diverse and complex problems.

To check migration: There is an unhealthy trend of migrating from rural to urban areas and from our own country to foreign countries among the youth. Unless migration is checked by proper guidance and counselling, cities will continue to swallow the rural talent and foreign countries the national talent and thus render both unproductive.

To make up for the deficiencies of home: A large number of students come to institutions of higher learning from homes which are not able to assist them adequately in dealing with their life problems. Because of various factors such as rapid industrialisation, political and social changes in the occupational structure of the country and the growing complexity of life there are greater pressures and strains in the family. The home is not able to provide the kind of support and help it did in earlier days. Also, there is a gap in the range of sympathetic adults who could be turned to in need, which formerly was filled by adult brothers and sisters, friendly aunts and grandparents when communities and families were more intimate.

Also our homes are not equipped to be the source of information concerning the qualifications required for different kinds of courses or careers. Such information can come from agencies which make a full time job of supplying adequate and up-to-date materials. Similarly, home is not equipped for studying future labour shortages and the labour supply and demand situation. Besides, many parents are not trained for helping their grown up children to develop sound study techniques, and obtain reliable information in matters of sex etc. Seth collected a sample of students at Allahabad University. The parents were indicated as the most usual source of help. Forty per cent of student respondents said that they could not discuss their problems with their parents. There is a strong evidence that professional help could be well-used.

***To minimise the incidence of indiscipline*:** Majority of our students lack a sense of direction, a sense of purpose and a sense of fulfillment. They indulge in destructive activities which lead to social damage and loss. This educated proletariat, so to say, is a time bomb in the heart of the nation that can explode any time if immediate care is not taken to inactivate it. Adequate guidance and counselling facilities is the only answer-to help and guide the youth to worthwhile channels and help them realise the goal of optimum academic, personal and social development.

3

Salient Features

Crow and Crow Define guidance : Guidance is not direction. It is not the imposition of one's point of view upon another. It is not making decisions for an individual which he should make for himself. It is not carrying the burden of another's life. Rather, guidance is assistance made available by a competent counsellor to an individual of any age to help him direct his own life, develop his own point of view, make his own decisions, carry his own burdens". Hamrin and Erickson define guidance as "that aspect of educational programme which is concerned especially with helping the pupil to become adjusted to his present situation and to plan his future in the line with his interests, abilities, and social needs,"

Mathewson believes that "guidance is the systematic professional process of helping the individual through education and interpretative procedures to gain a better understanding of his own characteristics and potentialities and to relate himself more satisfactorily to social requirements and opportunities in accord with social and moral values". Traxler considers guidance as a help which enables "each individual to understand his abilities and interests, to develop them as well as possible and to relate them to life-goals, and finally to reach a state of complete and mature self-guidance as a desirable member of the social order."

According to Jones, "Guidance involves personal help given by someone; it is designed to assist a person to decide where he wants to go, what he wants to do or how he can best accomplish his purpose; it assists him to solve problems that arise in his life."

The Significance

(i) It is a process: It helps every individual to help himself, to recognise and use his inner resources, to set goals, to make plans, to work out his own problems of development.

(ii) It is a continuous process: It is needed right from early childhood, adolescence, adult-hood and even in old age.

(iii) Choice and problem prints are the distinctive concerns of guidance as here the individual's unique world of perceptions interacts with the external order of events in his life context.

(iv) It is assistance to the individual in the process of development rather than a direction of that development: The aim is to develop the capacity for self-direction, self-guidance and self-improvement through an increased understanding of his problems and his resources as well as limitations to solve the problem.

(v) Guidance is a service meant for all: It is a regular service which is required at every' stage for every student, not only for awkward situations and abnormal students. It is a positive programme geared to meet the needs of all students.

(vi) It is both generalised and a specialised service: It is a generalised service because everyone-teachers, tutors, advisers, deans, parents-play a part in the programme. It is a specialised service because specially qualified personnel as counsellors, psychiatrists, psychologists join hands to help the individual to get out of his problem.

The Distinctions

Very few terms have been more loosely or interchangeably used than the terms 'guidance' and 'counselling'.

According to Tolbert, "Guidance is the total programme or all the activities and services engaged in by an educational institution that are primarily aimed at assisting an individual to make and carry out adequate plans and to achieve satisfactory adjustment in all aspects of his daily life. Guidance is not teaching but it may be done by teachers. It is not separate from education but is an essential part of the total educational programme. Guidance is a term which is broader than counselling and which includes counselling as one of its services."

Butler makes a logical separation of the counselling process discerned as having two phases called 'adjustive' and 'distributive'. In the adjustive phase, the emphasis is on the social, personal and emotional problems of the individual; in the distributive phase the focus is upon his educational, vocational and occupational problems. According to Arbuckle, Butler's distributive phase can be most aptly described as 'guidance' whilst the adjustive phase can be considered as the description of 'counselling'.

Fundamental Rules

According to Hollis and Hollis, there are eight principles on which any guidance programme should be based. They can be modified to fit locally accepted beliefs. The principles are:

(i) The dignity of the individual is supreme.

(ii) Each individual is different from every other individual.

(iii) The primary concern of guidance is the individual in his social setting.

(iv) The attitudes and personal perceptions of the individual are the bases on which he acts.

(v) The individual generally acts to enhance his perceived self.

(vi) The individual has the innate ability to learn and can be helped to make choices that will lead to selfdirection consistent with social improvement.

(vii) The individual needs a continuous guidance process from early childhood through adulthood.

(viii) Each individual may at times need the information and personalised assistance best given by competent professional personnel.

Nature and Functions

Very few terms in education have been more loosely or interchangeably used than the terms 'guidance' and 'counselling'. According to Tolbert, "Guidance... is the total programme or all the activities and services engaged in by an educational institution that are primarily aimed at assisting an individual to make and carry out adequate plans and to achieve satisfactory adjustment in all aspects of his daily life. Guidance is not teaching but it may be done by teachers. It is not separate from education but it is an essential part of the total educational programme. Guidance is a term which is broader than counselling and which includes counselling as one of its services".

Butler makes a logical separation of the counselling process with two phases called 'adjustive' and 'distributive'. In the adjustive phase, the emphasis is on the social, personal and emotional problems of the individual; in the distributive phase the focus is upon his educational, vocational and occupational problems.

According to Arbuckle, Butler's distributive phase can be most aptly described as 'guidance' whilst the adjustive phase can be considered as the description of 'counselling'.

Guidance is not compulsion, prescription, domination, cut and dried planning and regimentation. It is not making decisions for the one 'guided'. It is not advice. It is the child who makes the choice of a course or career; the guidance worker just helps the child make that choice as intelligently and as wisely as possible.

Guidance does not mean pampering the student—it tries to provide a more suitable programme for him, out of some which may be easier than the average, while others may be difficult. Efforts are made to provide an especially tailored programme for every individual.

There are certain fundamental facts which justify the foundation of the guidance concept:

1. The differences between individuals in native capacity, abilities and interests are significant, that is, every person

is a complete individual of his own patterns. Native abilities are not usually specified.

2. Varied type of educational, vocational and social opportunities are available in the real world out of which the individual has to make a selection.
3. Individual development and progress can be predicted to a great extent with the help of intelligence, aptitude, interests and achievement tests.

Guidance is adjustive in the sense that it helps the students in making appropriate adjustment to the current situations in the educational institution and occupational world, in the home and the community. Professional and individualised aid is given in making suitable adjustment at problem and choice points. Simultaneously, the adjustive attitude in the spirit of Reinold Niebuhr is to be developed in the individuals:

God grant me the serenity, To accept the things I cannot change, The courage to change the things I can. And the wisdom to know the difference.

Guidance has an orientational function. It orients the students in problems of career planning, educational programming and direction towards long-term personal aims and values.

Guidance has developmental function also. It tries not only to help get rid of problems but helps check their emergence and maladjustments. It contributes to the self-development and self-realisation of the student while furthering the welfare of the society. It is thus an important instrument of national development.

Area of Work

As the life is getting complex day by day, the problems for which expert help is needed are rapidly increasing. The scope of guidance is extending horizontally to much of the social context, to matters of prestige in occupations, to the broad field of social trends and economic development. Guidance is assuming the responsibility for the individual in every direction – it helps in the selection of educational courses and profitable occupations; in job placement; placement in the next stage of education and training; occupational surveys, improvement of study skills; maintenance of mental health; counselling regarding personal adjustment problems; identifying the gifted, and the backward and helping them achieve the maximum. Educational, vocational, avocational, social, personal, moral, physical and even marital problems of individuals are the concerns of guidance. Its scope is indeed vast.

The Requirements

There is an urgent case for introducing and strengthening the guidance service in the schools of our country to meet the varied needs of the students; administration and the educational system for the following reasons:

1. *To help in the total development of the student:* The emphasis on the intellectual development through teaching one cannot help in the total development of the student. Some method needs to be evolved for helping students understand themselves and helping teachers understand the students. The students need to know themselves so that they may seek experiences which harmonise with their abilities, interests and values and may develop their potentialities. They also need to have self-knowledge so that they form life goals and plans which are realistic—neither too high nor too low—and which may enable them to find satisfactory outlets for their talents.

The need for the total development of the students necessitates that individual differences among students are expected, accepted, understood and planned for and all types of experiences are organised to contribute to their total development.

2. *To enable students to make proper choices at various stages of their educational career:* In the new pattern of education, popularly known as 10+2+3, the lower secondary stage will cover classes IX and X. At the end years of general education, there are three possible courses open to students: (i) they can enter the working forces; (ii) they can take vocational courses; and (iii) they can take higher level academic courses of study to prepare for entrance into the first degree class in the college or university. It is obvious that after the ten-year school, there will be a choice point

when the students will need help in making decisions. Students who wish to continue in school up to class XII, either in the vocational or academic courses, will need guidance to enable them to choose the course of study which suits them best.

As the choice of a course at this stage will influence the future of the students and determine the kind of jobs they will find as well as the degree of satisfaction they will derive from them, they will not only need to be provided with information about various educational and vocational possibilities but will also need to be helped in developing a realistic self-concept. Self-knowledge as well as knowledge about the courses and jobs which a good guidance programme envisages, will help in achieving the objective.

3. ***To help students choose, prepare for, enter upon and progress in a career:*** We are living in a highly complex and rapidly changing world of work. There are changing requirements in industrial jobs, altered market conditions for professional manpower, the development of para-professional occupations and many other labour market trends. These make occupation selection more difficult than ever and the students in schools need to be informed about various jobs and openings available, the requirements, responsibilities and the nature of work involved in them so that they measure themselves up to them and develop and crystallise their occupational goal. They need help in making meaningful occupational selection and preparation for entering a rewarding career.

The need for helping the students in the choice of a proper career is further felt by the fact that the majority of our students in schools are the first generation learners. In their family, they have no one with an experience of school education or the background to guide them in the choice of a career. With a right to the best education available and a wide range of jobs open to them, these students need mature help in making a judicious occupational choice.

4. ***To help the students in vocational development:*** An individual passes through various stages of vocational development— growth, explanation, establishment, maintenance

and decline. Guidance services need to be provided in schools to help the students in the process of vocational development, particularly the stages of growth and exploration by making it possible for them to gain knowledge about themselves, their abilities, interests and need, on the one hand, and knowledge about the world of work, on the other. By providing them opportunities for self-exploration as well as exploration of the world of work while still in school, their transition from education to work can be facilitated.

5. ***To help students make the best possible adjustments to the situations in the school as well as in the homes:*** Students have to face situations both in the school and home which, if not tackled properly, lead to problems of adjustment. For example, many students do not know how to study, how to prepare for examinations, adjust properly with peers, siblings, parents, etc. A well organised programme of guidance can help them in these situations. Problem solving skills, if cultivated during school days, will enable the individuals to tackle the problems when they crop up. The individual will then have fewer problems at a later stage in life and will be better equipped to deal with them.

6. ***To supplement the efforts of home:*** Today, a large number of students come to school from homes which are not able to provide, them adequately in dealing with their problems caused by rapid industrialization, political and social changes in the occupational structure of the country and the growing complexity of life, and pressures and strains in the family. The home is not in a position to provide the child the kind of support and help it did in earlier days. Also, there is a gap in the range of sympathetic adults who could be turned to in need which formerly was filled by adult brothers and sisters, friendly aunts and grand parents, when communities and families were more intimate.

Also, our homes are not equipped to be the source of information concerning the qualifications required for different kinds of courses or careers. Such information can come from agencies which make a full time job of supplying timely and adequate materials. Home is also not equipped for studying future labour shortages and the labour supply and demand situation.

Besides, the majority of our parents are not trained for helping their children to develop sound study techniques.

7. ***To minimise the mismatching between education and employment and help in the efficient use of man-power.*** The hiatus between education and employment has rarely been as wide and as disturbing as it is today. Every year, our educational institutions disgorge thousands of hopeful youngsters who, despite their fancy diplomas and degrees, are virtually unemployable. In fact, employers often complain that of the hundreds of applications that come in response to a single vacancy, at least 80 per cent have no relevance to the job specifications. Few students pursue their education with a clear idea as to what they would eventually become. People even register at the employment exchange with scant idea about the sort of work they would like to be employed in. No wonder, while Jobs go abegging, the youth go begging for jobs.

The employment of workers ill-suited to their jobs generally leads to a higher rate of labour placement or to the retention of persons who are inefficient. This is a huge wastage of our scant resources which guidance facilities can help reduce and ensure efficient use of manpower.

8. ***To identify and motivate the students from weaker sections of society:*** Students from the weaker sections of the society have their own problems and needs. They experience difficulty in ajustment with the peers, teachers and the environment. They find it difficult to communicate, make friends, make best use of classroom lessons., and other co-cumicular facilities available. Guidance facilities are urgently needed for such students to enable them to adjust and utilize the available facilities properly.

9. ***To help in checking wastage and stagnation:*** There is an alarming incidence of wastage and stagnation at the school stage. On an average only 17 out of every 100 pupils complete their education. Thousands of our students, unfortunately, drop out, get pushed out, and fall out of the system. The two evils – wastage and stagnation – are in fact, eating into the vitals of our education system, rendering it ineffective. There is another side of this problem. A majority of our students pass in third division

which is a low qualification for the world of work. The poor achievement of the students may be due to many reasons—lack of proper study skills, and effective study habits, lack of knowledge for making full use of the facilities provided, and so on. Good guidance services can help stem the tide of wastage and stagnation at different levels of school education.

10. ***To identify and help students in need of special help:*** There are a large number of students—the gifted, the backward, the handicapped—who need special opportunities in our schools. Some arrangement needs to be provided to identify them and provide them help according to their requirements. Guidance services can fill the bill here.

11. ***To ensure the proper utilization of time spent outside the classrooms :*** The manner in which students spend their non-class hours clearly affects their success in achieving both academic competence and personal development. It is, therefore, essential that some positive direction be provided to the students by influencing them on the use of the non-class hours. The guidance programme is eminently suited for this purpose.

12. ***To increase the holding power of schools:*** Compulsory primary education has posed many problems. It brings to the school not only those who want to join it, but also those who, left to themselves, would not come. To make the second category of children stay in the school, education has to be made meaningful and relevant. Special guidance services can make the school attractive for them so that they continue with it.

13. ***To make secondary and higher secondary education successful:*** In the new pattern of education which the country has decided to adopt, the curriculum has been made comprehensive. It includes social sciences, life sciences, mathematics, work experience, languages, arts, music and other aesthetic activities. The multiplicity of subjects and the making of mathematics and sciences compulsory, is likely to give rise to a number of difficulties. It has been observed that neither are all the students interested in all the subjects, nor do they possess ability to grasp all of them. It becomes imperative that efforts be made to enhance the educability

of the students through an organised programme of educational guidance to ensure their satisfactory progress.

Similarly, at the end of class X, students should have obtained enough knowledge and skills to decide whether to choose the academic or the vocational stream, and also the courses or vocations to be studied in detail. Organised guidance services are needed to make a success of the new pattern.

14. *To minimise the incidence of indiscipline:* Indiscipline is a canker in our educational system wherein something is missing. Students lack a sense of direction, a sense of purpose, and a sense of fulfilment. The educational institutions, in fact, are littered with the shattered dreams of those who entered with high hopes. Guidance programmes can guide the youth to worthwhile channels. The introduction of this programme on a universal scale in our educational institutions may well prove a panacea for the ills of indiscipline and an antidote to the emergence of angry young men and women on the campus as well as outside it.

Today, as never before, the country needs successful doctors, educators, engineers, lawyers, technicians, craftsmen, farmers, inventors, writers, business executives. It is essential that students in the educational institutions are helped and guided to take up courses and careers suited to their needs and aspirations, interests and aptitudes so that they become efficient workers. For optimum individual, social, and national development, guidance needs to be made a regular and continuous activity woven in the educational fabric. No educational programme from the primary to the university stage can be complete without a well-planned, systematic, scientific and comprehensive student guidance service.

What is the significance of guidance and counselling, particularly educational and vocational, in an economy where labour is abundant and jobs and opportunities are too few? What is the utility of this service in a country which is groaning under the strain of unemployment of the educated? These are the apt and oft-repeated questions asked when a case is built up for the introduction of guidance and counselling in our educational institutions.

The logic in these arguments against the introduction of guidance and counselling is too simple to be true. It needs to be remembered that guidance and counselling have a challenging role to play in every developing economy, much more so if it is a labour surplus one. The selection of a job from a multitude of alternatives, although a very important objective of guidance, is not the be-all and end-all of guidance. The core aim of guidance is to help our job-seeking youth form, realistic career notions, in conformity with their capacities, aptitudes and social settings, so that they do not, in their adult life, end up as career 'failures'. The fact that wrong career decisions eventually make a big drain both on the emotional health of the individuals and the productivity of the society can hardly be disputed. Helping the youth to build up a true self-concept, to achieve ever larger measure of self-appraisal, and choose a proper career line is, therefore, the need of the hour and provision of guidance service is our immediate requirement. A guidance and counselling service should enlighten the job-seeking youth on "new" careers coming up on the job horizon. Whether the economy is a labour surplus one or the one characterised by over all manpower dearth, so long as it continually organises developmental endeavours and strives for economic self-sufficiency, it will bring about inevitable, permeating and permanent changes in the occupational matrix. In a developing economy, such as ours, new explanations are constantly attempted; social values gradually change; scientific breakthrough eventually revolutionises consumption and productive patterns; new industries spring up; technological applications modify production processes; consumer tastes are shaped and cultivated. All these growth-induced changes in the society accelerate the demand for the hitherto 'unheard' skills, at the same time eclipsing certain traditional occupations. A device is necessary in our educational institutions to keep track of these changing facets in the occupational matrix and to educate the youth appropriately and adequately. Hence the need for guidance and counselling even in a surplus economy as ours.

The Dimensions

Surveying the faults and conflicts in society obscures many

strengths and advantages and seems to put undue stress on the negative. But these are the factors that must be highlighted. There are shortcomings that demand immediate and comprehensive remedies. Guidance and counselling obviously cannot solve everything alone, but they can play a major role. Guidance workers can reach individuals who need assistance, help modify conditions that call for improvement, change institutions that are failing in their missions, and take steps to reverse destructive trends.

Problems and needs in society are nothing new, but today they seem to be proliferating at an unprecedented rate. Problems once hidden have become visible; new ones arise. All are given extensive coverage by media. No area of life is taboo. But rapid and unexpected local, national, and international changes give rise to needs and challenges qualitatively and quantitatively different from those of the past.

The changing family: On nothing has there been so great an impact as on the family. A recent feature article in *Newsweek* raises the question, "Who., is raising today's childern?" and cogently points out that parents lack time and commitment to serve as models for their children. But these are not the only family problems. The home, once regarded as the ideal setting for bringing up children, is being disrupted by divorce and separation. The institution of the family is being attacked by critics who decry its deficiencies and suggest alternative lifestyles. Working parents face hectic schedules. Another *Newsweek* article concludes that "the emotional demands in a two-career family are profound."

Geographic mobility, changing housing patterns, and the establishment or retirement communities have contributed to the erosion of the extended family. Far fewer grandparents and other relatives live in the home or nearby and now baby-sitters and day centers give children the personal attention once provided by relatives.

Cities in upheaval'. The plight of cities is becoming commonplace. Financial pressures are accelerating the decline of the quality of life in large urban areas.

Cities were once favourable environment for education and personal development, but social conflict, economic crises, loss of family ownership of property, street crime, and deteriorating neighbourhoods have spoiled many of them, Vandalism in schools has increased, and in some areas teachers and pupils alike are assaulted by youth gangs. The inner city has been hit hardest, but crime has also been moving to the suburbs. In many regions, the stabilizing effects of work are missing; unemployment rates are high, particularly among minority youths.

Family and community life exert a reciprocal influence on each other, as the neighbourhood deteriorates, the positive contribution of the family diminishes. Even though efforts are being made to rehabilitate blighted communities, many families move out, thus accelerating the negative trend.

Conflicts in values, attitudes, and morals: The un-precedented spread of therapies points to a widespread sense of life as meaningless and deep conflicts of values. Psychiatry has been called the new religion.

Much of the present unease and uncertainty began in the 60s, a decade in which traditional morals, ethics, and values were profoundly challenged. The 70s is a period of searching for meaning and purpose, and is marked by a new media-wide openness about changing patterns of values. The cover of time shows a sergeant in the Air Force saying "I am a homosexual.' A few years ago, the topic could not have been discussed in the general press. This new frankness reveals issues that must be faced, and confronts young people with complexities once relatively known.

There are other equally striking examples. The daily newspapers carry frequent reports on the behaviour of government officials that would have been called sensationalized, improbable fictions only a few years ago. Stories about cheating scandals on college campuses appear with almost monotonous regularity. Drinking has increased among the young. Studies reveal that one out of every four 13-year-olds is a "moderate" drinker. Cohabitation is a widely accepted life style for many college students. Many high school students drop out because of unwanted pregnancies.

But traditional values have strong supporters. In the search for ways to build moral awareness, schools and professional colleges are introducing new courses in ethics. Secondary schools stressing traditional standards of discipline, dress, and manners have waiting lists, A well-known psychologist has advanced the point of view that the ethical and moral values that have evolved in human societies have a scientific basis.

The new cynicism about politic: Distrust of politicians and the political system is not new, but in the previous and current decades they have reached unprecedented intensity.

The Vietnam War threw the issue of credibility into sharp belief. In this decade Watergate, revelations about CIA and FBI intrigues, and invasions of privacy have multiplied the questions. Lurid sex episodes have surfaced about members of Congress. National government, however, has not been alone in provoking distrust Governors, judges, and legislators have been convicted of minor and major violations of the law.

People have grown doubtful and cynical about the sincerity of the government's concerns for the welfare of the individual. Social services, education, and programs for those in need have been cut back. Moreover, the public is convinced that the government is more keenly aware of the problems and needs than at any time in. the past and that ignorance is not the reason for neglect. As a result, many feel overlooked and powerless to take action in matters that deeply affect their lives.

Economic factors: Much of what constitutes the "good life" is tied to the state of the economic. Inflation erodes resources for education, travel, and improved living conditions. Unemployment and underemployment caused by economic slowdowns wreak havoc on family life, particularly for women, minority group members, and people who are just catching up in the job market.

The very economic conditions that aggravate social problems also necessitate reductions in services rendering several affected. An enormous burden rests on helping agencies and educational institutions, which must cope with long waiting lists and overcrowded classrooms.

The most destructive effects, however, are psychological-the feelings of apprehension, uselessness, and selfishness generated by depressed economic conditions. Capable people with much to offer give up looking for work. Students spoil each other's experiments to improve their own chances of getting into highly competitive medical schools. Only a few businesses and industries agree to reduce wages so that no one is laid off.

The changing role of work: Many young people are uncertain and confused by the conflicting attitudes about work. They hear that the work ethic is disappearing, that most jobs are demeaning and destructive, that technology will replace large numbers of workers, and that in many specialties a flooded market will cause unprecedented unemployment. But they also hear the unemployed asking for a chance to work, that work is the path to equality for minorities, and that you have to develop saleable skills to meet the demands of a technological society.

Many young people worry about the future. Realistic and accurate occupational information is lacking and rumours of shortages and overcrowding proliferate. Career plans can change in a day. In case after case, individuals who have spent years preparing for a specific occupation suddenly realize they must find employment in an unrelated field. Many programs are restricted to avoid projected worker surpluses. Freedom of choice dwindles.

Automation and technological advances have reduced the number of low-skill entry jobs, and have also lessened the worker's pride in his share in producing a finished article. Efforts to establish new procedures to give employees more status and control have met with limited success.

New pressure and demands on school: Problems, issues, and trends in public education figure prominently in this book. They are in fact often the same as those in guidance and counselling. The most pressing are listed below; others will be covered later. The list touches on aspects of all the problems previously mentioned; school problems reflect the problems of society.

1. Writing skills and achievement in science are declining.
2. The quality of preparation of entering colleges students is declining.
3. New workers can except considerable difficulty in finding jobs.
4. There is a growing concern about pupils moral development.
5. The rights of pupils are being violated.
6. School vandalism is costing taxpayers over half a million dollars a year.
7. Violence in schools is increasing.
8. Lack of discipline is considered a major school problem; many parents would prefer stricter schools.
9. Schools have taken over responsibility after responsibility and raised unrealistic expectations in the minds of the public.
10. Questions are raised about the value of increased funds for schools.
11. Schools do not provide an effective learning environment. As much as 95 per cent of current educational practice is of questionable value.
12. Schools need to be dejuvenilized. Break down the isolation of the school subculture, treat pupils more like adults, and make the educational institution more integral a part of life.

Problems of young people: Difficulties for school-age youth and young adults are inherent in the conditions already described. But some particularly pressing ones need to be emphasized. Social and academic pressures on youth have caused increased drug use, running away from home, emotional disturbance, and suicide. Lack of involvement and commitment to meaningful work, education, and social activities leads to isolation and alienation. Difficulties in role identity arise, as typified by expressions like "I don't' know who I am"; "I've got to find myself. Family mobility generates feelings of rootlessness and lack of community identification among the young, some of whom seek a sense of belonging in allegiance to strange or destructive cults and groups. By the end of high school, the typical teenager has watched 15,000 hours of TV, and TV is acknowledged to breed a fascination with violence and a craving for instant success.

Changing sex roles pose problems for all ages, but particularly for the young experiencing conflicts about work, sexual freedom, and family responsibilities. For example, the girl or boy who has learned the traditional sex roles with respect to careers may, because of both personal values and societal pressures, find it difficult to choose a nontraditional occupation.

The increasing average age of the population will also affect the young. More concern is being expressed for problems and needs of older Americans. Major changes in social, economic, and political policy that will touch young people include, for example, increased taxes for services. The proportionally fewer young persons will wield less influence and therefore receive, for example, less attention from consumer markets.

This is only a sampling. Other changes could be listed; and it is likely that even more pressing ones are just over the horizon.

A report of the contemporary status of guidance coming after a review of societies' need might seem to suggest that the profession will supply all answers. But although the guidance profession is a powerful force, its focus must necessarily be limited to appropriate high-priority targets. Trying to do everything for everybody will result in frustrations for workers, gaps in coverage, and thin or invisible effects. The following description of guidance today will help identify priorities and outline the most important factors to weight when considering the occupation and the lifestyle it involves.

The prospective counsellor should be aware that counselling is at a crossroads. Demands of the people served and developments within the profession have led to differences of opinion about strategies, needs, roles, priorities within the population, work certification, and degree of support. Each issue is complex; all defy a brief summarization. In chapters that follow, they will be examined in depth, but at this point, it is important to note a handful that have major implications for opportunities and limitations in the field. First, there is the issue of serving as an agent of change-how actively should the counsellor be involved in altering customs, laws, and established patterns of society? Some want to help the individual adjust to what exists; others want to taken an active role to alter prevalent conditions, for example, current attitudes towards minority groups. Second, there is a trend towards developing large-scale programs and strategies; small-group counselling is being replaced by training and preventive activities. Third, new standards for preparation are emerging. Finally, among other issues and dilemmas, two related matters stand out—accountability and the limitation of resources. Counsellors, like other educators, are being required to demonstrate the difference they make in the lives of others, even though financial support may not match needs. There is a definite trend to require services for all sorts to prove their effectiveness; support is based on evidence. Moreover, counsellors will be expected to produce more without increased support or to prove that higher levels of support will result in measurable and desirable change.

Still, it is apparent that counselling and guidance are well established in public educational institutions, community agencies, colleges, and universities. An impressive number of practitioners are currently employed in public schools. In 1970-71 there were more than 40,000 counsellors in more than 90 per cent of the schools. This is up from a little over 2000 in the 1930s. The mission of providing developmental and remedial help to all pupils during the critical formative years is ambitious. The profession has enjoyed a position of prestige and status in time of critical national needs; its services are sought when human resources must be developed, social conflicts eased, and destructive behaviour eliminated.

Relatively new on the helping scene, it has matured to the point where hundreds of graduate preparation programs are offered; standards, ethics, and local guidelines have been developed; and strong national organizations have emerged with an impressive, stimulating array of professional publications.

Guidance is longest-established and most prevalent in secondary schools. At latest count, nine out of ten school counsellors were working at this level. Development at the elementary-school level has been more recent, but expansion has been rapid. From 1967 to 1971, the number of counsellors more than doubled, reaching almost 8000 in 1971. Growth in the middle/junior high school, post high school, community, and rehabilitation settings has also been substantial.

Guidance and counselling, grades K through 12, are characterized by common major themes. Among them are concern for the total person, the importance of collaborative work, similarities in helping procedures in all settings, and emphasis on development.

The chief theme is the importance of looking at the total person, rather than fragmenting services as if each need existed independently. Help is provided for educational, career, and personal development, thus the work of the counsellor extends to all aspects of school, home, and community life. Emphasis varies with grade level. Parents play a larger role during the elementary years, but increasingly counsellors in all grades are extending services to include work with the pupils' whole environment and with other significant persons in their lives. Help must be more comprehensive than that provided by individual conferences; consultation, coordination, and training are being added to the direct, face-to-face assistance of counselling.

A second theme of guidance is the use of a team approach. Counsellors in elementary, middle, and high schools participate with a team of teachers, social workers, psychologists, and medical personnel to provide a comprehensive help system. The counsellors are unique members and occupy a key position. Being school-based, they can maintain close contact with teachers, pupils, and administrators and emphasize a truly developmental approach. The counsellor is the logical person to coordinate the work of all team members.

A third theme is establishing a common core of helping approaches and rationales applicable on all educational levels. There are differences due to pupil's ages, but theoretical concepts, human relations, skills, and other helping procedures are being developed and tested to build a body of professional knowledge of use to all guidance workers. A degree of specialization is needed, but the bases of guidance at different educational levels are more alike than not.

A fourth major theme with emphasis on development, is visible in the effort to facilitate pupil development rather than concentrating on remediation, and by the trend to link services at all educational levels. It has, for example, recently been recognized that the choice of an occupation is not a single event that takes place at the end of school or college-preparatory. Decisions are made as early as the first years of school, and each year confronts pupils with related new decisions and tasks. The developmental view has given rise to a sequential approach to guidance The total K-12 program is integrated rather than broken down into elementary, middle/junior, and senior high school.

In addition to these four themes, a trend toward increased work with pupils with special needs has been set off by recent state and federal legislation. The new responsibility is mostly diagnostic and could have the long-range effect of blending the roles of the school counsellor and the school psychologist.

Within the fields of guidance and counselling there is an ever-increasing professionalization. Statements by guidance organizations articulate roles and responsibilities. Ethical codes are formulated and put into effect. Preparation standards are upgraded to guarantee quality services. Licensure issues have recently arisen, and guidance organizations are striving to insure that counselling is represented in the formation of school policy. Taking over the destiny of the profession is an uphill battle, but leaders are making substantial progress. Much more needs to be done, but there is no doubt that guidance has established itself as a major helping profession.

A cursory glance at our seats of higher learning will show the imperative need of instituting in them a well-organized programme of guidance and counselling. Education is expanding its frontiers making it well-nigh impossible for an individual student to make a choice of courses and careers without expert guidance. Occupational scene too is changing so rapidly that yesterday's rocket circuitry electronics specialist considered as highly prized as a marks-man on the old frontier is today's unemployment statistic. One of the great stories in out midst is the dramatic increase in jobs. Not only that quite a big number of students at the threshold of a college or university are in for compelling and difficult life situations-they are shy, fearful, gullible, not skilled in managing their own affairs. They lack self-acknowledge which may enable them to form realistic life-goals and plans. They lack both focus and meaningful direction.

Occasionally they lose their way in the dark labyrinths of adolescence and do not know how and when to act. They have to grapple with complex social problems-living with and sharing facilities with peers, such as living in hostels and sharing extra-curricular experiences, adjustment to heterosexual relationships, etc. Surveys of Indian students and alumni document the widespread feeling of dissatisfaction with college and university life.

A survey was conducted by the All India Educational and Vocational Guidance Association for gauging college student's needs. Three thousand students from seventeen Indian universities responded. The survey revealed student's felt needs. Eleven problems were marked by more than 50 percent of the respondents:

1. I cannot do as well in my studies as other people expect me to do.
2. I do not know enough about the qualifications needed for different kinds of worked or careers.

3. I worry too much about what my future will be after I have finished my studies.
4. Even though I force myself, my attention will not remain on my assignments long enough to finish them.
5. I do not know how to make friends among the opposite sex.
6. I do not have sufficient information about matters on sex.
7. I do not know enough about my aptitudes and abilities for different kinds of work or careers.
8. It is difficult for me to get the books I need for study.
9. I cannot read fast enough to complete my studies in time.
10. I do not know proper methods of study.
11. I have more difficulty in forgetting my mistakes than I believe I should have.

The eleven areas may be summarised under four headings Study habits and skills, Career choice. Knowledge of aptitudes and abilities, Sex education.

The respondents reported that their parents were the only source of help they received, if any, along these lines and practically no help had been forthcoming frcm college personnel!

Eighty per cent of respondents expressed the need of such assistance from their non-parental source. The bigger the college, the bigger the campus, the more the need for personalised student services, else the student will merely feel a small cog in a huge machine!

Another survey of the educational, vocational and personal problems was conducted by Umrudin and Gadri. Widespread maladjustment was rated among hostel residents who showed much concern over problems connected with study habits, vocational choice, family relationship and mental hygiene.

All these emerging issues and problems make it obligatory for our educational planners and administrators to build into our higher education an appropriate guidance and counselling programme for the development of the individual student into an adult personality, imbued with social and occupational awareness, intellectual and functional proficiency, discipline and confidence. The classroom activities, however well-conducted and well-organised, alone are not in a position to accomplish all this.

It is true that provision of guidance and counselling services in the colleges and universities cannot be seen as a panacea for all our educational ills nor can a counselling officer hope to give students a trouble-free or problem-free life, but where possible, he can help them to resolve their difficulties, or if that is not possible, to live with them. To help them resolve the stresses and strains does not require a nosey-parker intrusion of privacy but the response of an understanding and empathetic person and an atmosphere of understanding, faith and sincerity. And this is what is needed.

In an article on 'Unrest on Campus', once Piloo Modi, M.P. wrote, "Our student population reaches the university level, having made up their mind broadly about the courses that they may have-a decision, which in almost all cases, is taken by unthinking and unsympathetic parents and relatives with an eye on a more lucrative profession. It is great tragedy when a potential poet becomes a chemical engineer. Many a mute inglorious Milton is languishing in the dark engineering world." This entire process of herding our youths into educational disciplines unconnected with their aptitudes needs to be checked through a scientific process of guidance and counselling for the best development of individuals and growth of society.

To help in the proper choice of careers: We are living in a highly complex and rapidly changing world of work. There are changing requirements in industrial jobs, altered market conditions for professional manpower, the development of para-professional occupational selection more difficult than ever. The young students in colleges and universities need to be informed about various jobs and openings available to them and the requirements, responsibilities and the nature of work involved in them so that they could measure themselves up to them and develop and crystallise their occupational goals. They need to be helped in making meaningful occupational selection and preparation for an entry into them to have a fulfilling and rewarding career.

The need for helping the students in the choice of a proper career is further enhanced due to the fact that majority of our students in colleges and universities are the first generation learners. In their family, they have no one with an experience of college or university education background to guide them in the choice of a career. With a right to the best education available, and a wide range of jobs open to them, these students need mature help in making a judicious occupational choice. Hence the need of adequate guidance and counselling arrangement in our colleges and universities.

To help the students in vocational development: The process of vocational development covers almost the entire span of life of an individual. It begins quite early in one's life and continues till sometimes after retirement. In this process, the individual passes through various stages -- growth, exploration, maintenance and decline. Guidance services need to be provided to the colleges and universities to help the students in the process of vocational development-particularly the stage of growth and exploration, by making it possible for them to gain knowledge about themselves – their abilities, interests and needs, on the one hand, and knowledge about the world of work, on the other. By providing them opportunities for self-exploration as well as exploration of the world of work while they are still in an educational institution, their transition from education to work can be facilitated.

To develop readiness for choices and changes to face new challenges: In a paper entitled The Need for Counselling in Higher Education, presented at the Third International Round Table of Educational Counselling and Vocational Guidance, Miss Newsome, Counselling Officer at the University of Keels, North Strafford Shire, England, writes, "For the students of higher education the demands of life are likely to be great, in a most different way from the exacting demands of education itself. On graduating he will be called upon to make use of the kind of person he has become as much if not more than what he has learnt in his course of study-not only to make an initial choice of what he is to do on graduating but will be called upon to change his occupation several times in a life time.

Readiness for these choices and changes is essential, not only to the student himself but to the society as a whole. To the extent to which he is able to capitalise on his experience and face new challenges with a realistic expectation of success, to that extent he will benefit society. If he is unable to meet the changing demands, not only of the working world but also of his other roles of life, to that extent he will be a liability and will fail to fulfil the expectations which society has for its most able people. Guidance services are needed to develop in the students the ability to cope with their new problems and concerns in such a way that they become more competent to meet the demands which will continue to be made upon them in the future.

The latest analysis done by Planning Commission reveals that the educated youth between 15 and 29 years of age constituted 11.5 per cent of the corresponding labour force but they accounted for 33.2 per cent of the total unemployment in the country. According to the Planning Commission's labour force projections, the total number of educated unemployed at the beginning of 1980 was estimated at 3.47 million. If there is no further deterioration in the unemployment rate, this number is likely to go upto 4.66 million in 1985. And this is the challenging situation we have to face.

It needs to be pointed out that the hiatus between education and employment has rarely been as wide and as disturbing as it is today. Higher academic education, as very well pointed out by Mr. L. K. Jha, Chairman of the Economic Administration Reforms Commission, is far too general and diffused to be of practical value to the vast majority of young men and women. Most of our young men and women have no clear objectives or career targets. They amble through university courses of learning without acquiring much knowledge of preparing themselves for an uncertain future.

Every 12 months, our colleges and universities disgorge thousands of hopeful youngsters into the labour market who are virtually unemployable—despite their fancy degrees and diplomas. In fact, employers often complain that of the hundreds of applications that come in response to a single vacancy, at least 80 per cent have no relevance to the job specifications whatsoever. Few students pursue their education with a clear idea as to what they would eventually like to become. People even register at the employment exchange with scant idea about the sort of work they would like to be employed at. No wonder while jobs go abegging the youth go begging for jobs. Not only that, the semployment of workers ill-suited to their jobs generally leads to a higher rate of labour placement or to the retention of persons who are inefficient. All this is a huge wastage of our scant resources. Guidance facilities can help in reducing this wastage and thus ensure efficient use of manpower.

Considering the magnitude of educated job-seekers flowing into the job market in India every year, it is essential that a sizeable fraction of enterprising youth are initiated into careers of self-employment. Some arrangement needs to be instituted in the colleges and universities to identify the deserving cases fit to take up self-employment, educate them on how to proceed about the job of setting up a venture, help them through the cooperation of the concerned agencies in this sphere to prepare technically sound and economically viable projects; sponsor their cases to the banks for loan assistance and guide them to overcome the teething troubles effective follow-up after the commencement of the venture.

In our country the youngmen entering colleges and even universities are comparatively young in years. Young adolescents as they are, they are passing through a stage between childhood and adulthood, between the morality learned as a child and the ethics to be developed by the adult. They find it extremely difficult to establish a satisfactory identity. Such failure or delay leads to what can be called "role diffusion". This crisis in role identity is perhaps very acute today. The uncertainties of the future, the conflicts in languages, culture, regions, castes, etc., and the erosion of traditional values has rendered Indian youth rootless.

Fuster did a small study with Bombay college students, both men and women. The strongest needs, as reported by the students themselves where they were requested to indicate rank orders, were for achievement in life, self-reliance and a sense of security, success in college and university, to have an understanding friend and (for the males) money.

Guidance and counselling programme is needed to help students deal effectively with the normal developmental tasks of adolescence and face life situations boldly.

To identify and motivate the students from weaker sections of society: Students from weaker sections have their own problems and needs. They experience difficulty in adjustment with the peers, teachers and the environment. To communicate, make friends, utilise the time profitably, make the best use of lectures, make an effective use of library and other facilities available all pose problems for them. Guidance facilities are urgently needed for such type of students to enable them to adjust and utilise the available facilities properly.

To help the students in their period of turmoil and confusion: The students undergo a great deal of turmoil and searching to give meaning to their lives. They have their conflicts and anxieties. They feel disillusioned regarding higher education. They find that colleges and universities, instead of imparting them education, just enable them to pass examinations-they feel sunk and cheated. When this education does not enable them to get immediate employment, they feel lost and bewildered.

Similarly, they have their personal conflicts and anxieties. They have the problems about their parents and family, their relations to boy and girl friends. They have the problems of adjusting their personality to the world of people, of ethical ideas and of goals and situations. For tacking all these situations successfully, they need someone to sort out the strands-they need some strong, tactile presence of a hand guiding the anxious and enabling them to develop realistic expectations.

To help in checking wastage and stagnation: The average pass percentage at the graduate and post-graduate level is about 50 to 60. Thousands of our students, unfortunately, drop out, get pushed out, and fall out of the system. This problem is becoming more serious day by day. There is another unfortunate side of this problem-majority of our students as the Table ·2 shows pass in third division, which is a low qualification for the world of work.

This poor achievement may be due to so many reasons—lack of proper study skills and effective study habits, lack of the knowledge for making full use of the facilities provided, and so on.

Also, the majority of our students do not fulfil the promise indicated by the Secondary School leaving examinations and do not utilize their professional qualifications after graduation.

A study of the years 1950 and 1954 alumni of Delhi University where approximately 1800 alumni were interviewed revealed:

(i) In general, these students did not fulfil the promise indicated by secondary school leaving examinations, since about 45 per cent received a lower university rating at graduation.

(ii) Many graduates do not use their training occupationally.

A study conducted by D.G.E and T. Ministry of Labour, on the graduates of the year had revealed the percentage of graduates in clerical work—commerce 67 per cent, B.Sc. Pass 63 per cent, B.A. Pass 64 per cent, Proficiency in Law Certificate 48 per cent, M.A. Arts 31 per cent, B.A. Honours 25 per cent, etc. It is obvious that sizeable percentage of alumni obtaining professional qualifications have to work as clerks. The report also gives evidence of much aimless and unrealistic vocational choice.

Higher education is a very costly enterprise. Much of the money wasted on these poor and low achievers could be saved by a policy of prevention. Just as preventive medicine is sounder economically and more humane than remedial medicine, so too is preventive education more sound economically than remedial education. There is thus a clear need for developing better professional services of a counselling kind to check the huge wastage of student time and money and also huge state expenditure on education. Miller, in this connection, said so well, "If one counsellor could prevent the wastage of only four student years each costing - 800 to -1200, he would be earning his keep. Similar savings of graduate salaries foregone as a result of failure or delay would benefit student as well as the taxpayer."

To identify and help students in need of special help: There are such students as the gifted, the backward, the handicapped who need special opportunities. Some arrangement needs to be provided in our colleges and universities to identify them and provide them with help according to their requirements.

To ensure the proper utilization of time spent outside the classrooms: It is common knowledge that students in the colleges and universities spend two to three times as many hours outside classrooms as in them. And the manner in which students spend their non-class hours clearly affects their success in achieving both academic competence and personal development of all types. It is, therefore, essential that institutions of higher learning provide positive direction to students by influencing how they can use those non-class hours. The programme of guidance and counselling can meet this need.

To help in tackling problems arising out of student explosion: Increased demand for higher education is outstripping the growth of facilities in the seats of higher learning. Resultant unfortunate qualitative changes in the nature of entire educative experiences are creating innumerable problems. The students population is highly affluent and extremely poor, educated in convents and ordinary schools and colleges, rural and urban areas, students from our own country and different foreign countries are attending colleges and universities. When students from a broad range of families and educational and social backgrounds meet in classes for instruction, in hostels for housing, in cafeterias and mess halls for eating, numerous problems crop up. Guidance and counselling facilities need to be provided to helping them tackle these diverse and complex problems.

To check migration: There is an unhealthy trend among the youth of migrating from rural to urban areas and from our own country to foreign countries. Unless migration is checked by proper guidance and counselling, cities will continue to swallow the rural talent and foreign countries the national talent and thus render both unproductive.

To make up for the deficiencies of home: A large number of students come to institutions of higher learning from homes which are not able to assist them adequately in dealing with their life problems. Because of various factors such as rapid industrialisation, political and social changes in the occupational structure of the country and the growing complexity of life there are greater pressures and strains in the family. The home is not able to provide the kind of support and help it did in earlier days. Also, there is a gap in the range of sympathetic adults who could be turned to in need, which formerly was filled by adults who could be turned to in need, which formerly was filled by adult brothers and sisters, friendly aunts and grand parents when communities and families were more intimate.

Also our homes are not equipped to be the source of information concerning the qualifications required for different kinds of courses or careers. Such information can come from agencies which make a full time job of supplying adequate and up-to-date materials. Similarly, home is not equipped for studying future labour shortages and the labour supply and demand situation. Besides, many parents are not trained for helping their grown up children to develop sound study techniques, and obtain reliable information in matters of sex, etc. Seth collected a sample of students at Allahabad University. The parents were indicated as the most usual source of help. Forty per cent of student respondents said that they could not discuss their problems with their parents. There is a strong evidence that professional help could be well-used.

4
Various Aspects

In today's complex life when a student faces difficulties while making wise curricular and co-curricular choices, acquire basic study skills for optimum achievement; adjust to the peers, teachers and parents; live with and share facilities with others in the institution; live in hostels with individuals from different social and economic backgrounds; secure adequate financial aid; adjust to hetero-sexual relations and spend leisure properly. Expert help is needed for optimum achievement and adequate adjustment in these varied life situations which can be grouped under seven major areas as follows.

Different Streams

1. *Education.* Educational problems head the list of student problems. Curricula today are fairly comprehensive. Work experience and vocations too form an important part of education. At the plus stage, a choice of stream has to be made. Co-curricular activities have increased manifold. Very wide differences exist among individuals. Some scientific guidance has to be provided to the students in making their choices and to enable them to make proper adjustment with school programme. They have to be provided opportunities to participate in educational planning. Education, therefore, is an important guidance area.

Students need to be guided for developing good study habits, and adequate preparation so that they develop confidence to sit in the examinations. Special guidance has to be provided at crisis points, for example, if students find difficulty in following certain subjects, they lack concentration, get poor grades and have to be guided to overcome these difficulties.

The students also need to be helped to explore educational possibilities beyond their present educational level like courses and careers, stipends and scholarships available, competitive and entrance examinations so that their journey ahead becomes smooth and profitable.

The students from all sections of society need the facility of guidance, particularly those from the backward social classes so that they progress smoothly. Special efforts have to be made to help first generation learners—students whose parents never went to school. Such students have special academic problems because of the deficiences in their own background and the inability of their parents to provide them guidance at home.

2. *Vocation.* All persons are not equally suitable for a vocation. Every vocation requires certain educational and professional qualifications and preparation and only those having them can succeed in it. Hence the need for guidance in a right vocation consistent with the assets and limitations of the individual. Students have to be helped in the selection of an occupation, preparation for it through the relevant courses and programmes, enter upon and progress in it. They have to be assisted in making decisions and choices involved in planning a future and building a career. They have also to be helped in developing an integrated and adequate picture of themselves and of their role in the rapidly changing occupational world. Fresh and new occupational outlets undreamt before are emerging. It, therefore, becomes essential that students are helped in acquiring a clearer perspective of the changes that are taking place.

3. *Avocation.* The student spends only five to six hours a day in classes. What he does during the rest of the time cannot be left to chance. Avocational pursuits in which the students engage themselves are important in giving a direction to their lives during the holidays—the autumn break, winter break, summer vacation and so many holidays in between. It is estimated that only about ten per cent of the number of students in our schools take part in

co-curricular activities. The rest are on-lookers. The participation of even a small number is just at a superficial level.

The filling up the vacant hours of the students is one of the important tasks of education if they are not to drift in a sea of confusion, doubt, anxiety, aimlessness in their most formative years. The students need to be properly guided in the selection of work experiences, hobbies, co-curricular activities, games, athletics, various emotional experiences and cultural programmes so that the out-of-classroom hours become a means of development, instead of being a drag. These activities have to be so arranged as to provide the students with an opportunity to shape their inter personal behaviour and widen their outlook outside the class.

4. *Social.* Students wish to be effective as individuals in society. They often have to sit with classmates they do not like or play with those for whom they have a positive aversion. These students need to be guided in social behaviour and relationships, making new friends, and becoming leaders in their own groups. Students in schools come from heterogeneous, linguistic and socio-economic backgrounds. There should be an arrangement to give adequate direction for their proper social adjustment.

5. *Moral.* Students face many awkward situations at home, in school, or with peer groups. They find difficulty to rise above them. They tell lies, try to dodge, and indulge in anti-social acts. Moral guidance has then to be provided to keep them on track and to lead noble lives.

6. *Health.* Society has a special stake in the health and physical well-being of its students. A sound mind can only be possible in a sound body for which the students have to be guided in the knowledge and practice of good food habits and ways of improving their physique and physiognomy. The total health of the students should be the goal for which the following preventive and restorative measures should be adopted:

(i) Supervision of sanitation in school hostels and canteens.

(ii) Specific protection through immunisation against diseases such as typhoid and cholera.

(iii) Health education through formal classes and informal propaganda.

For early diagnosis and treatment of illnesses, these measures may be taken up:

(i) An adequate physical examination of every student upon entrance to the school.

(ii) Follow-up treatment of detected disorders.

(iii) Referral of students to other medical resources, when necessary.

(iv) Maintenance of proper health records to keep track of mind and body's harmonious functioning.

Efforts have to be made for the rehabilitation of disabled students in collaboration with psychologists, teachers and social workers. Remedial measures also need to be taken into account with students suffering from speech and hearing defects.

7. *Personal.* Students have problems related to themselves, their parents and family, their friends and teachers. They often have memories related to home or family, which create feelings of disappointment in them. Their parents leave them with a feeling of incompetence and insecurity, when they fail to live up to their expectations. Often, parents nag their children and create an unfavourable atmosphere at home for studies. At times, the strained and unhappy relationships at home hamper progress in study. There may be jealousy among siblings, domination of elders, maltreatment of children, lack of a sense of being wanted, lack of a sense of belongingness which disturb the mental equilibrium of the young students, resulting in poor or low achievement. Expert guidance has to be provided to these students so that they face the situation boldly and with confidence.

Some students are obsessed with problems such as lack of friends, loneliness, failure, feelings of inadequacy, inferiority, and the like. They feel a sense of chaos and despair around which creates serious emotional conflicts among them. They need help while passing through these psychological situations.

Students also face difficulties on changing school due to transfer or for other reasons. The new entrants get involved in conflicting social situations and some feel demoralised as if alighting from a train at a station in a foreign country where nobody speaks their language. They need guidance for proper adjustment.

Students, at times, find difficulty in concentration, learning and recall; they feel tense, anxious and depressed. They need guidance and counselling to overcome these problems.

They also need information on sex for which parents are not well equipped. Educational programmes have to be so planned that the sex urge in the students finds healthy outlets

8. *Marital.* Students need guidance for the right choice of a life partner. Marital guidance needs to be provided when asked for.

Some students are hard-pressed for finances. They need to be guided regarding the freeships, fee concessions, scholarships, and stipends. They have to be guided about funds available in the institution and how and when to apply. The provision of financial assistance has to be ensured so that no meritorious student is denied education for lack of financial assistance.

Employment Potential

Here are some guidance programmes at different levels.

The National Level. The Union Ministry of Education in India established a Central Bureau of Educational and Vocational Guidance in 1954 for planning, organisation and coordination of vocational guidance in schools in the country. In 1961, the Bureau was transferred to the newly formed National Council of Educational Research and Training and was merged with the department of Psychological Foundations, National Institute of Education, NCERT at Delhi. In 1969, this Department was reorganised as the Department of Educational Psychology and Foundations of Education. Its main function in the area of guidance is to contribute to the improvement of education in India through fostering and giving leadership to a strong guidance movement.

Department of Educational Psychology and Foundations of Education

It has the following specific functions:

1. Training guidance personnel, particularly school counsellors and teacher counsellors;
2. Research in the field of educational and vocational guidance;
3. Extension work in the field of educational and vocational guidance;
4. Development of tests and aids for use in guidance work in schools and supply thereof;
5. Preparation of guidance literature for the use of school children, parents, teachers and guidance personnel;
6. Providing opportunities for discussion of ideas and dissemination of information to guidance personnel working in different parts of the country and helping to bring about coordination in the work of various institutions;
7. Providing technical consultation in setting up Educational and Vocational Guidance Bureaux in the States.

The consultative and field services of the Department are available to the Union Ministry of Education and Youth Service for planning the development of guidance service, as also to the State Departments of Education, private guidance agencies and teacher training colleges.

Now the Department has been bifurcated into two units. The Educational Psychology Unit is concerned with psychological tests, and the training of personnel in the administration of the tests. It also collects information regarding the tests standardised in our country. The other unit is concerned with the training of personnel.

This is another Central Government organisation concerned with guidance. Its headquarters are at the Directorate General of Employment and Training of the Ministry of Labour and

Rehabilitation, Government of India. This agency has been developing guidance services since 1957 when the first set of field units came into being. Over the years, their number has expanded through phased planning. The National Employment Service now has 561 units located in the different Employment Exchanges. It has completed three decades of its existence. From a limited placement agency, it has grown into a multifunctional manpower organisation concerned with the development and utilization of human resources.

Although this organisation is concerned primarily with the offering of vocational guidance to out-of-school youth and adults through the vocational guidance units existing in its network of employment exchanges all over the country, it also contributes to guidance programme in secondary schools. The vocational guidance officers of ths National Employment Service assist the state and private organisations in conducting training courses for career masters, They also give career talks and help in the organisation of conferences. The vocational guidance units of employment exchanges also help in the placement of school leavers in apprenticeships and vocational training.

The publication of occupational information literature and posters is one of the significant contributions of the National Employment Service to the guidance programme in the educational institutions. In fact, 'these publications are, today, the mainstay of occupational information libraries or corners maintained by the Guidance Bureaux and schools. The National Employment Service, apart from functioning as the agency for the placement of all categories of employment seekers, is also responsible for ths collection, compilation, analysis and interpretation of statistical data relating to employment and unemployment in India and for implementing programmes concerning vocational guidance and employment counselling, occupational research, surveys in the field of employment, unemployment and manpower planning and employment market information.

In most states, the service consists of a Regional/State Employment Exchange, a number of sub-Regional/Divisional Employment Exchanges and a District Employment Exchange at the headquarters of each revenue district, directly administered by the State Directorate of Employment, usually under the Labour Department of the State. There are also special exchanges/sections offering specialised services for the guidance and placement of physically handicapped persons and women. Besides, in some states, there are vocational rehabilitation centres for the evaluation and rehabilitation of the physically handicapped persons; coaching-cum-guidance centres for the benefit of Scheduled Caste/Tribe applicants; colliery exchanges for the placement of colliery labour; and project exchanges for handling the placement work in various river-valley and heavy industrial projects.

The DGE & T has also undertaken the development of a Guidance Battery of Aptitude Tests to be used at employment exchanges for counselling purposes. This battery purports to be used as a psychometric tool to give guidance and employment counselling to the guidance seekers. The work is underway to adapt General Aptitude Test Battery (GATB) of the United States Employment Service to suit Indian conditions. The DGE &. T has made Indian Versions of GATB by changing the verbal contents of the three tests of the eight paper and pencil tests which include verbal contents. These three tests have also been rendered into Hindi. The work on the development of Indian norms has already been taken up and some studies have been completed. More such studies are being taken up, so that occupational aptitude patterns based on the aptitudinal factors suitable to Indian conditions may be developed.

State guidance bureaux. Most of the State Departments of Education have set up organizations with different names for guidance at the state level. Some of them are administratively a part of the Directorate of Education, others are either a part of the State Council of Educational Research and Training as in Haryana and Andra Pradesh, or of the State Institutes of Education as in Kerala, or of a .training college or separate Institute of Guidance which are subordinate offices of the Directorate of Education as in Punjab. Some of the Union Territories have also made a beginning by way of setting up an organisation for guidance within the Directorate of Education or a part of training college. The functions performed by the State Guidance Bureaux vary depending upon the numerical strength of the Bureau.

The State Guidance Bureaux are responsible for the planning and coordination of educational and vocational guidance activities in the schools of the state concerned. Their chief functions are:

1. ***Collecting, compiling and disseminating educational and occupational information.*** The information is passed on to the schools in the form of bulletins, newsletters, leaflets or monographs. These are also made available to individual students or parents who either write to the bureaux or make personal visits.

2. ***Training of teachers.*** The training of teachers as parttime or full-time counsellors is an important function of the state bureaux. The training programme includes, besides the regular training courses, periodical conferences of guidance workers and refresher courses for staff members.

3. ***Organising seminars.*** Seminars of short duration are arranged by the bureaux for headmasters and principals, D.E.Os., C.E.Os, to acquaint them with their roles in the guidance programme.

4. ***Publication of suitable literature.*** This is an important function of the State Guidance Bureaux. The literature is published in the regional languages for the use of teachers and parents.

5. ***Testing and counselling services to local and mofussil schools.*** The state bureaux are well equipped with psychological tests. Most of them have trained psychologists and counsellors on the staff. Cases of maladjustment are also referred to the bureaux for psychological treatment.

6. ***Providing consultation service to the guidance units in the. schools.*** The educational institutions are encouraged to organise career/educational conferences where the staff of the bureaux serve as resource persons.

7. ***Arranging group guidance sessions.*** The bureaux arrange group guidance sessions for parents and senior members of the staff of the institutions, teachers and students.

8. ***Maintenance of state level educational and occupational information centre.*** The bureaux display occupational information material and other allied guidance material and also set up a library and reading room for the benefit of teachers and students.

9. ***Providing liaison between the activities of the state bureaux and the department of labour and employment.*** The bureaux collaborate with the Department of Labour and Employment in organising career planning fortnights, or weeks, career exhibitions, conducting courses, publication and circulation of literature, and publicising the guidance programme through the mass media like radio and television.

10. ***Conducting research.*** The members of the State bureaux conduct research of problems connected with guidance. They construct, standardise and develop psychological tools for evaluation. A number of bureaux have prepared norms on various tests. Some others have translated tests in regional languages for use among the local population. Still others have prepared adaptation of foreign tests.

Most of the bureaux perform, and are equipped to perform, these functions.

Official Level

The department serves the employers, the employment seekers and the parents/guardians through a network of employment exchanges spread all over the state. Below are listed special programmes of the department.

State occupational units. At the state headquarters in each state, there is an occupational information unit which functions under the supervision of the state vocational guidance officer. It undertakes the publication of guidance material such as occupational field reviews/monographs/career pamphlets, handbooks on educational and training facilities in the state for use by the vocational guidance officers, teacher counsellors and career masters. The unit also compiles and disseminates information on job opportunities, occupations, scholarships and competitive examinations.

Occupational information programme. The information gathered from different sources after it is identified, classified and codified provides a central source of occupational information for use in international migration, employment, placement and related manpower activities.

Employment market information programme. This aims at collection, compilation, analysis and interpretation of employment information in different industries, occupations and areas and is collected with a view to identify deficiencies and facilitate estimation of future requirements of manpower for formulating educational and training programmes to ensure a regular supply of the required manpower for the country's economic development.

Career study centres. A career study centre set up in the directorate of employment ensures that the literature concerned with the world of occupations and training facitities is kept up-to-date.

Foreign employment and training information bureau. Some governments, realising the need of young people desiring to go abroad for employment or further studies, have set up the foreign employment and training information bureaus for guidance and information on various aspects. The bureaus provide authentic information on foreign studies. They have the following functions:

1. ***Selection of courses and institutions.*** The bureau guides the students in the selection of educational and vocational courses and related foreign universities. Well known universities like Cambridge, Oxford and Harvard, Columbia receive thousands of requests for admission and scholarships from all over the world. They can accept only a very small percentage of those who apply, whereas there are many other universities which are equally good but not as well-known. In such universities, chances of admission and scholarships are comparatively better. The Bureau guides the students in the selection of such universities.

2. ***Admission matters.*** It guides the students on admission requirements, likely expenses required to meet the tuition and maintenance charges, proper time for applying for admission and admission procedures.

3. ***Scholarships, fellowships or assistantships.*** The bureau provides information about the availability of scholarships, fellowships, assistantship or apprenticeship facilities granted by foreign governments, universities, or agencies as well as by public or private organisations at home.

4. ***Passport and visa.*** The bureau provides information about the essential requirements needed for a passport and the related procedure for getting the same. It acquaints the aspirants about immigration regulations enforced by different foreign countries, basic requirements to be met and procedure to be followed for getting visa.

5. ***Foreign exchange.*** The bureau guides the applicants about the rules, particularly regarding academic achievement of students, under which foreign exchange is released by the Reserve Bank of India.

6. ***Employment prospects.*** The bureau gives information about employment prospects for various occupations overseas so as to enable them to try for employment.in suitable countries.

7. ***Part-time employment.*** Most of the foreign countries have their own policy on part-time employment of foreign students. The bureau gives information about the chances of part-time employment and the procedure required to be followed by them after reaching there.

8. ***Employment.*** Information regarding vacancies abroad including UNESCO postings, addresses of foreign firms and agencies, which generally employ or help in getting employment, are provided to persons so that they apply directly at their own level.

9. ***Living conditions.*** Persons who visit foreign lands find themselves in strange environment, where society has its own characteristics like dress, food, climate, manners, customs and language different from those prevalent in our country. The bureau enlightens them in advance about the conditions of living in foreign countries and the problems they are likely to face.

10. ***Free service in person or by post.*** The bureau renders free service to all who want information by post or in person.

Assistance in professional and executive employment. All postgraduate applicants and those with professional degrees or equivalent diplomas can get themselves registered with this employment office. Employment assistance to prospective employment seekers is also provided by this office on a centralised basis.

Special employment exchanges for the physically handicapped. These have been set up in all the states for placing a substantial number of physically handicapped persons in gainful employment and to help them become a useful part of the state economy.

Rural manpower units. These have been primarily established to provide occupational information, vocational guidance, and registration facilities to the employment seekers in the rural areas at their doorsteps.

Special cells for ex-servicemen. For the smooth absorption of ex-servicemen and disabled ex-servicemen in the economy of the state, special cells for ex-servicemen have been set up to help them get suitable civil jobs with reference to their educational/technical qualifications, age and seniority. Punjab was the first state to undertake this project and now some more states have established special cells. Ex-servicemen and disabled ex-servicemen living in any part of the state have the facility to get registered at the nearest employment exchanges which are under instructions to forward their records to the special cell immediately on registration.

Education, as a Subject

Among the state-level organisations, colleges of education, university departments of education and psychology offer courses in guidance in the programme for the degrees of B.Ed., M.Ed., and M.A. in psychology. These courses are useful and provide an orientation to the students. Besides, the extension services centres and inservice training institutions organise short-term courses in guidance for the teachers. Some of these courses have only an orientation value, while others are designed to train teachers to function as career masters.

Private Channels

A few private guidance agencies sponsored by charitable trusts, social welfare organisations and educational societies are also engaged in the guidance services. They offer individual guidance service to the students as well as to adults. Some of the important ones are the Vocational Guidance Society at Calcutta, Gujarat Research Society at Bombay, Y.M.C.A. of Calcutta, the Rotary Club of Bombay and the Lion's Club and the Junior Chamber of Baroda. They have made significant contribution to the development of guidance movement in India.

District counsellors. There are district counsellors appointed by the education department who look after the guidance programme in the districts under their jurisdiction. Generally, their office is attached to that of the district education officer and they are directly under the district education officer. The following are some of the functions of the district guidance counsellor:

1. maintaining an information centre at the district headquarters and also to make this information available to schools whenever required;
2. helping the schools in introducing cumulative record cards through school counsellors, career masters;
3. arranging career talks in schools through career masters/counsellors;
4. arranging career conferences in the higher secondary schools;
5. carrying out test administration in the schools; taking up simple individual cases from schools for counselling; and
6. organising guidance committees and establishing liaison between the agencies of guidance and employment at the district level.

Official Channels

The Training and Employment Services Organisation Committee set up in 1952 recommended that employment exchanges should provide special facilities for counselling of young men and women who come to them from schools or colleges with no previous experience and are unsure in their choice of employment. Advice in the choice of a career or an occupation should be made available to this population which represent the largest single addition to the country's manpower every year. Employment counselling is a means to an end, the ultimate end being suitable employment.

The main objective of the employment exchanges is to find one a job for which he is best suited. The attainment of this objective requires, on the part of the exchange, first, determination of a job or jobs which would take into account the employment seeker's interest and preference, his aptitude, his training and experience, and second, rendering of assistance in finding employment in the field so determined. It also requires on the part of the exchanges advising or counselling, to make a practical and satisfactory occupational choice for those who seek or are in need of such advice or counsel.

The scheme for vocational guidance and employment counselling has been introduced at the employment exchanges throughout the country. It guides the school and college leavers in the choice of careers in accordance with their interests, aptitudes and abilities taking into consideration the employment market. Students who desire to pursue further studies are assisted in the choice of educational and training courses which may lead to satisfying occupations. A close liaison is maintained with the high/higher secondary schools and colleges by the vocational guidance units with a view to disseminating occupational information to the students.

Individual and group guidance programmes are conducted at the vocational guidance units. An individual guidance programme consists of a discussion of employment problems of guidance seekers, taking into account their assets and liabilities. It also consists of providing occupational information regarding employment avenues, educational and training facilities, scholarships and self-employment opportunities, etc.

The group guidance programme consists of a group discussion in which information about employment opportunities and training facilities is rendered to homogeneous groups of applicants. This programme is further supplemented by career talks, by vocational guidance officers and outside experts in different fields of occupations. Career conferences, seminars, exhibitions and film shows are also organised from time to time by vocational guidance officers in collaboration with other agencies.

Another important part of this programme is career talks in schools. Though educational guidance at schools is primarily the responsibility of the State Departments of Education, the schools are also assisted by Vocational Guidance Officers in setting up career corners and in organising other guidance programmes.

For the benefit of special categories of applicants like the scheduled castes, tribes, ex-servicemen, physically handicapped etc., facilities for rendering guidance exist at these units.

Each unit maintains an Occupational Information Room, where information pertaining to various educational and training facilities, job opportunities, employment trends, etc., is displayed in the form of posters, charts, prospectuses, etc.

The school level. The guidance activities promoted and supervised in all schools by the state bureaux are finally the responsibility of the principal or headmaster of the school. The actual work is, however, undertaken by trained school counsellors, teacher counsellors, or career masters, depending on the pattern of school guidance services being followed in a particular state. The school counsellor is a wholetime guidance worker and the teacher counsellor or the career master is a teacher who is trained in guidance work and is allotted 6 to 12 periods a week for this work. The amount of relief depends on the work done by him. The school counsellor is primarily responsible for total guidance planning for which he uses the group guidance and individual counselling method. Through a series of guidance talks, he explains the importance of making an occupational choice, carries out the occupational orientation programme for pupils and shows them the way to self-appraisal and also how to understand the vocational and occupational significance of different subjects and courses of study offered by the school. He also maintains a contact with the employment exchange authorities from whom he obtains occupational information and details about the state of the employment market.

As it is difficult to afford a whole-time counsellor for every school, the provision of one visiting school counsellor for a group of several schools has been made in some states. They visit schools as often as possible or necessary and help the teacher counsellors or career masters in the guidance programme. This is an economical option for the schools.

5
Counselling for Students

Team work is a vary common concept now. Coaches and sportswriters consistently extol the virtues of the cooperative enterprise known as teamwork. Even though individual stars are clearly identifiable in most team sports, they are always quick to acknowledge the contributions of their team-mates to their stardom and the interdependence that each member of the team has on the others in the pursuit of their mutual goals. This harmonious working together to accomplish a mutual goal is also noticeable in such cooperative endeavours as musical groups, surgical team, army tank crews, and aircraft crews.

One could almost conclude that we have become a nation of "teams" as recent generations have seen the concept of teamwork expanded to encompass many organizations as well as institutional and agency settings. It is no longer uncommon, for example, to hear industrial leaders talk about the labour management team or the school principal to commend his or her educational team or a community agency to refer to its psychological team.

Regardless of the fact that the terminology may be overworked at times, we must accept the concept of teamwork as an important one if we are to efficiently and effectively bring all the potential resources of the psychological community to bear on behalf of its clients. In advocating a "team" concept we note the following:

1. Teams are composed of individuals who are bound together in the pursuit of a common goal. This pursuit is enhanced by their functioning together as a unit. Teams are most effective when members of the team learn

mutually complementary roles in order that duplication, overlapping, and competitive activities may be minimized.

2. Working together, sharing knowledge and teamwork, when feasible, permits each to use his or her unique talents while determining who will perform the shared talents

3. There is no single "best" team system or pattern of team organization; rather, many variations may be anticipated, since a team presumes the best available combination of personnel for the task at hand. For example, some teams may include both community and school personnel, faculty and student representatives, and/or professionals and paraprofessionals.

4. The counsellor, as well as other professional helpers, may have a variety of roles and may be a member of a variety of "teams" within a specific setting. We recognize that the number and variety of these roles will vary from setting to setting, as on some teams, for example, the counsellor will be expected to function as a leader, whereas on others, he or she will function as a follower. Like the skilled magician or juggler, she or he must be adept in "wearing the hat" most appropriate to the immediate activity in which she or he is engaged.

The school counselling program is an integral part—an important "team" in the total educational enterprise. Whereas this very fact is one of the potential strengths of the program, since by implication everyone is thus involved, it is also at the same time, a complicating factor. If, in fact, everyone is involved, then roles and relationships must be clarified to the point that each recognizes not only his or her own role and function but also that of colleagues in the total counselling and educational effort. Thus, whereas the team concept for schools has long suggested that the school counsellor, teacher, administrator, and other personnel specialists must work together to accomplish the objectives of the school counselling and guidance program, one of the perennial problems which countless studies have enumerated has been the failure to clearly define, in both theory and practice, roles and relationships in such programs.

Another contributing factor that must be taken into consideration is the continuous call for educational change and innovation which threatens to obliterate many of the traditional structures and roles within education. Thus, at a time when many counsellors are still trying to clearly identify their roles and relationships within the educational framework as viewed traditionally, change are taking place that may very well make this attempt to specify roles in terms of job descriptions, it is more appropriate to examine the special contribution each member of the "team" may be reasonably expected to make.

The central figure is the educational guidance team, for she or he is the specialist who brings unique knowledge and skills to the program without which it could not function. More specially, the counsellor is frequently the only professional in the school setting prepared to offer individual and group counselling to students, parents, and teacher. The counsellor also possesses special knowledge in the area of educational and career development and adjustment, future planning and placement needs.

In addition to these traditional skills and knowledge, school counsellors have, in recent years, played increasingly significant roles as consultants to other adults both within and without the educational setting who are also concerned with the pupil's well-being and development. Counsellors will recognize that on many occasions they will be more effective when working through and with other significant adults in the individual pupils' life, such as parents, other educators, ministers, and youth workers. This consultation involvement with parents, teachers, and other adults is receiving greater attention as "writers within the counselling profession indicate that all school counsellors must conceptualize pupils not as isolated individuals but as members of systems; i.e., family systems, learning systems, and community systems.

Several reasons can also be stated for the school counsellor's choosing to use the school setting for increased involvement and counselling with family systems. First, many personality theories support the idea that family environment and child-rearing ctices influence the developing individual. Second, there has ı increased acceptance of the school's becoming more involved with the home environment. Third, schools are established by society to maximize the potential effectiveness of its children and youth-and the counsellor, as a part of the school must accept this responsibility. Fourth, logic dictates that more information about the family can be obtained from first-hand observation of the family, rather than reports by the children. Fifth, efficient and proficient referrals of individuals and families by school counsellors to community agencies maximize the assistance available and enhance the professionalism of school counsellors. Finally, increased responsibilities of the school counsellor necessitate that all counselling strategies be the most effective possible.

In the "learning systems", counsellors should also more actively pursue their consulting roles with school administrators and classroom teachers in broad areas of student needs and concerns, such as course offerings, work-study programs, positive school and classroom environment, meaningful activities, and student representation in school affairs. In the broadening of their professional educational consultation responsibility.

Counsellors should also work closely together with curricular specialists to assist one another when curricular or guidance and counselling objectives are hindered or subverted by school structure and organization. Further, counsellors and curricular specialists should develop strategies and tactics in concern to overcome obstacles and rigidities in school structure and organization impeding legitimate outcomes for students. In so doing, counsellors and curricular specialists realize that structural and organizational improvements in schools may frequently bring about desired student behaviours just as validly as curricular or guidance measures.

In community systems school counsellors must frequently anticipate a role as career consultants. In this capacity the counsellor will plan for the integration of school and community career development resources to ensure their efficient and effective utilization. This suggests that counsellors assume a major role in the school's career education program. To this end, school counsellors will need to consider the following recommendations.

(a) Involve business, labour, community representative, and parents in the development of career education programs as teachers and resource people.

(b) Introduce occupational coping skills seminars to assist students in the transition from school to work, e.g., job seeking, interviewing, resume preparation, and self-analysis leading to self-improvement.

(c) Sponsor or teach career exploratory courses throughout the school year as a part of the total guidance program.

The effective school counsellor must also be able to assess social and psychological characteristics and relate these to educational developments and individual adjustments; be able to identify and recognize the influences of cultures and subcultures on their members: and be prepared to function as a human resources developer and agent of change in the educational-community setting. Podemski and Childers recommend that :

To establish more response by school, school counsellors, as a result of their professional training, experiences and organizational placement in schools, are in a position to harness forces that can stimulate the change process and thereby make school systems better learning environments. At a time when counsellors and other educators feel greater pressure for accountability than ever before, the counsellor is in a unique organizational position to serve as an institutional change agent. In the change agent role, the counsellor is concerned with organizational development as well as the shaping and reformulation of the school's curriculum, program, and the organization itself to meet more effectively the needs of students, parents, and the community.

As the counselling and guidance specialist on the guidance team, the school counsellor must also function as the guidance team leader. The development of the school guidance program, while involving other educational professionals, must, by virtue of the special knowledge and skills required, be directed by a trained, professional, and certified school counsellor.

Counsellors often have difficulty distinguishing themselves

from other helping professionals because their specialized skills and knowledge are not unique to counselling. As Pate notes :

'Our knowledge and skills are shared by psychologists, educators, social workers, and other helping professionals. While we cannot claim that counselling has a unique knowledge base, counsellor's interpretation of their knowledge and skills into service is an important aspect of our claim to professional status and suggests a place for counsellors in a psychological society'.

Pate goes on to suggest that :

(a) Counsellors must continue to emphasize the developmental nature of counselling. Our unique contributions are the assistance we give counsellees to realize their potential better and our interventions to remove institutional barriers to that realization.

(b) Counsellors should continue to recognize education as important to their profession, just as they so recognize the field of psychology. Much of what counsellors do for counsellees is education or reeducation. We teach counsellees to use their resources and to develop new resources.

(c) Certainly counsellors can take pride in the profession's historical ties with vocational counselling. Although we should not be content to equate counselling with career counselling, we should remind our pupils that we have a long record of commitment to career counselling.

Most comprehensive programs of pupil personnel services in schools will include other professionals whose training and anticipated role may share some similarities to that of the school counsellor. These include school psychologist, psychometrists, psychiatrists, and social workers, as well as the personnel whose training is more distinctive, such as the school nurse, physician, dentist, and dental hygienist. Each of these professional specialists also has unique contributions to make to the achievement of the school's objectives.

However, if each specialist is to make a meaningful

contribution, she or he must have some recognition of the roles and specialities of other pupil personnel workers, as well as a recognition of the expectancies normally assigned to him or her. We now briefly examine the special competencies of the more popular of these other pupil personnel workers.

School Level

The school psychologist is an important and integral member of the pupil personnel team. In most school settings, the traditional responsibility of the school psychologist is to diagnose and study individual children, who are usually experiencing problems in their educational or personal development. In this role, the school psychologist evaluates various aspects of a child's experiences and behaviour that are relevant to an understanding of the child's school difficulties and achievements. For this role the school psychologist is trained in the use of psychological tests and also is prepared to engage in individual or group therapy with disturbed children.

The psychologist may also aid teacher and parents in understanding the implications of child's behaviour. Although the school psychologist has often been thought of primarily as a problem diagnostician, there has been an increased effort in recent years to consider other options. For example, Granowsky and Davis suggested that the school psychologist has an option for three different roles: (1) the diagnostic approach. (2) the community-centered approach. and (3) the administration approach. Based on a rapidly changing society, the authors suggest that psychologists examine their role definitions and select the one that is most appropriate for their particular school. The traditional diagnostic role employs (1) diagnostic testing and reporting; (2) designing educational strategies for pupils and teachers; and (3) evaluating these strategies. Such an approach involves behavioural approaches and classroom intervention and service.

A second role model would be that of the community-based school psychologist. Such a person would operate from a mental health center, be administratively independent of the schools, and act as a consultant to the school staff. Granowsky and Davis state that this model allows (1) the school psychologist to place his or her allegiance with the child rather than the school; (2) direct and more intense contact with the parents; (3) expanded resources utilizing the total mental health center staff; and (4) dual therapy emphasizing educational remediation plus individual growth. The psychologist would, in addition, provide the school with traditional services.

The third role model views the school psychologist as a part of the central administration. The psychologist (1) facilitates the group process and interchange among the professional staff; (2) identifies high priority problems; and (3) organizes an effective team of psychological specialists. The author believe that the school psychologist in this role would be proactive rather than reactive.

Based on his or her skill in diagnosis, the school psychologist can assist the school counsellor and other pupil personnel workers in gaining a better understanding of individual students and their problems. The school psychologist can also serve as a resource person for case studies and as a source for referral for certain categories of disturbed pupils.

The school psychometrist is a pupil personnel worker whose training, background, and job functions are in many instances so similar to the school psychologist that little besides their job titles distinguishes them. However, the school psychometrist is often more limited in training and, as a result, is also more restricted in the kinds of activities in which she or he engages in the school.

The major emphasis in the training of psychometrists and on their job performances is usually in the area of psychological measurement. In some school settings, the major contribution of the psychometrist to the school pupil personnel and guidance program may be in the organization and administration of the school's standardized testing program.

The school social worker: The role and function of the school social worker, like those of the school counsellor, have evolved and broadened from its beginnings in the early 1900s, and have been influenced in heir development by compulsory education laws, new knowledge about individual differences among children, and a recognition of the impact of education and the school on school-aged youth. Today, the school social worker works so as to eliminate the social-emotional influences that handicap the students formal education.

To this end, the social worker actively works with the family, school, and community, and seeks the involvement and cooperation of parents in facilitating the development of their children. This may involve interpreting to the family their child's behaviour as the school views it and, in turn, receiving information regarding the child's behaviour at home. The end goals is to have the parents participate positively in the school-child-parent relationship.

The school social worker also functions in a liaison role between the school and community, and is particularly interested in eliminating the community causes of school problems rather than treating the results. In working with the family, school, and community, the social worker seeks to identify and eliminate the base cause of problems. Primary services of the social worker include case studies, group work, and consultation. In the school setting, the social worker is a valuable "Team" member who can make a significant contribution to the in-depth understanding of an individual student's problems through case studies and who also provides significant linkages between the school, home, and community.

Most school systems employ medical personnel on at least a part-time basis. These personnel consist typically of the school physician, school dentist, school nurse, school dental hygienist, and school psychiatrist. These personnel can contribute to achieving a better understanding of the pupils' physical or clinical problems. The school counsellor can, in turn, give to these personnel a better understanding of the causative factors of the students physical and mental well-being. Medical personnel can also contribute to increased counsellor understanding of pupil adjustment needs through in-service case studies and consultation.

The inter-relationships between school health services and school guidance services was noted in the publication *Suggested*

School Health Policies, prepared by the National Committee on School Health Policies of the National Education Association and the American Medical Association in 1966. This publication suggested four important aspects of the school health service: health appraisal, health counselling and interpretation, emergency care for injury and sudden illness, and communicable disease-prevention and control. Among the techniques suggested were; continuous observation, particularly by teachers, screening tests; psychological and social evaluation; and health records:

The publication also suggested the importance of interpreting pupil health needs to parents, pupils, and teachers. It was also recommended that health personnel be aware of the influence of the teacher and other educators on the emotional and social environment of the pupil. Thus, these commonly expressed concerns of both school counsellors and school medical personnel indicate their natural allegiance in the development of cooperative programs for the development and adjustment of the individual.

In addition to the previously described professionals who, by nature of their training and certification, are specially prepared for their contribution to pupil adjustment and development, others, by virtue of their assignment, are also often members of the pupil personnel team. These individuals most frequently have the titles of attendance worker, dean, director of student activities, and placement director.

The attendance worker is probably the oldest "traditional" pupil personnel worker. Although most schools no longer label this individual "truant officer', the basic responsibilities of this individual is still in pupil accounting. The emphasis in pupil accounting, however, has gradually changed from threats and punishment to encouragement and remediation. In this role, the attendance officer and the counsellor can each provide valuable information and consultation to each other. As an example, it is particularly important that the attendance officer and counsellor coordinate their efforts in seeking solutions to the perennial dropout problem, identifying its causes, consulting with parents of dropouts, and encouraging the re-entry of dropouts into school.

College Level

Whereas student deans have been more traditionally associated with college student personnel services, some high school and junior colleges often employ pupil personnel workers designated as deans of students, deans of boys and girls, or deans of men and women in addition to school counsellors. The function of these individuals has often appeared to be one of administering student facilities, activities, and regulations. As a result, they are frequently viewed more as administrators than personnel workers. Students deans have also been frequently cast in the role of the disciplinary agents for the school. In this role, their potential contribution to the school guidance program is discounted by many who contend that guidance and discipline are poor "mix". A number of programs utilize the title of "dean" for their counsellors, and traditional "deans" in other programs are trained counsellors.

The director of student activities, as the title implies, is primarily responsible for the administering of the student activity programs within the school. In this capacity she or he may regulate and coordinate student group activities, identify and plan for needed activities, and assess or evaluate the individual activities and the activity program in general. Through cooperation with the school counsellor, students may be assisted in participating in activities that will promote their growth and adjustment, serve their interests, and develop their special abilities. At the same time, coordination of guidance activities with other student and school activities can be facilitated.

Scope of Employment

Placement directors are most likely to be found in large secondary schools and institutions of higher education, where their role is primarily on part-time and/or full-time career placement. In addition, at the secondary school level, placement personnel will also be frequently concerned with the placement of students in post high school educational institutions. The increased emphasis of career guidance in the 1970s resulted in a corresponding emphasis on, and an increase in the number of, placement specialists in high schools.

Cooperation with the school counsellor and school psychologist will enable those responsible for pupil placement more effectively to coordinate pupil interest, abilities, and experiences with placement opportunities and needs. A few schools also have college counsellors or placement specialists whose major function is to facilitate the placement of interested and qualified students in a college of their choice.

Officials' Role

As indicated earlier in this chapter, the guidance team for schools consists not only of the professional counselling staff and other trained pupil personnel workers but also the school administrator. The school administrator, who may be a superintendent of schools, junior college president, or building principal, is justified in expecting the staff of the school counselling and guidance program to contribute to the achievement of the institutions' objectives. The administrator must also recognize that this contribution will be severely handicapped if she or he fails to realize his or her important responsibilities in the success of this program.

The school administrator represents the educational leadership both in the community and in the specific educational institution as well. In this capacity, it is the administrator's responsibility to give open and recognized support for the school counselling and guidance program. The administrator should also provide advice and direction on budget expectations, physical facilities, ancillary professional and service personnel, and policy guidelines.

The school administrator is also responsible for indicating to the school counselling and guidance activities which she or he views as mandatory or desirable in facilitating the goal attainment of the total educational program. In most setting, the administrator will have the primary responsibility for communicating program characteristics, achievements, and needs to school boards and others within the educational system and to the tax-supporting public.

The teacher-pupil relationship is the central, or key, activity in the educational endeavour. It is therefore obvious that other activities in the educational setting which are concerned with the pupils development, adjustment, and total growth must, of necessity, involve those who work closest with them and, as might be anticipated, usually know them best. This means that the classroom teacher is an indispensable member of the guidance team. The classroom teacher at every educational level has the opportunity to fulfill his or her important role in the school guidance program through functioning in the following ways.

Mary had been increasingly distracted from her schoolwork and in a rather absent-minded manner she had been inattentive in class for more than a week. This was unlike the vivacious, energetic, and capable student she was. Miss Jones decided that at the first opportunity she would examine Mary's record and consult with her school counsellor prior to initiation any discussions with Mary. Miss Jones is an example of a guidance oriented teacher who is alert to the needs of her students and aware of the valuable assistance that the school counsellor may be able to provide in helping her met these needs. Miss Jones and her fellow teachers at every educational level have countless opportunities to advise, consult, or just act as receptive adult listeners to students and their problems, concerns, decisions, achievements, and failures.

This, then, is a primary role and function of the classroom teacher. This role of a listener-adviser does not suggest that the classroom teacher is a counsellor in the professional sense (for counselling is a complex, special skill which requires specialized training), but does recognize that she or he is in the front line of the school counselling program.

If, in our previous situation, it became apparent that Mary's difficulties were too complex for Miss Jones to handle, a guidance-minded teacher like Miss Jones very likely would discuss with Mary the possibility and advantages of talking with Mr. Haseley. In this capacity, Miss Jones would illustrate the important function of the classroom teacher serving in a referral role in the school guidance program. It is obviously impossible for the school counsellor in his or her limited contacts with the total student population to be personally aware of all or even a small portion of students who may be in need of counselling assistance. Therefore, the alert classroom teacher in his or her role as a referral agent can ensure that students with significant problems will not go unnoticed and uncounselled.

Human Angle

When Johnny entered Miss Jone's class this morning, another pupil in the class spoke a cheery hello to which Johny replied, "Shut your damn mouth" Johny then proceeded to shove his way rudely through a group of girls who were standing near his desk. Coming to his desk, Johny noticed some books of another student on his seat. He kicked them on to the floor saying. "They aren't mine! What the hell are they doing here? The classroom provides an interesting platform. They have come to recognize the importance of the classroom setting for the development of human relationship skills in the individual student.

The classroom teacher then, as the normally recognized leader of the classroom group, has another important role-i.e., that of a human relationship facilitator and developer. This means, first of all, that the teacher reflects and demonstrates good human relationship before and with her or his students. It also means that the classroom teacher plans and directs group interactions which promise positive human relationship experiences for each individual participant. Further, many students will need individual tutoring in developing and mastering these skills, just as in any other type of learning. In the case just cited for example, the ever-alert Miss Jones might plan a strategy for improving his relationships with his fellow students, even though the teacher is the focus of human relationship development activities in the school, the school counsellor should be viewed and used as the human relationship consultant in the educational setting.

Another important role and function of the classroom teacher, which is emphasized by the national career education movement, is the planned contribution in every subject matter class for the pupil's overall career and related educational development.

In this role the teacher has the opportunity to provide a data base from which pupils will make their eventual career decisions and to understand the relationships between education and career planning. Indeed, at every educational level, the teacner has the opportunity to provide for career-oriented experiences that are appropriate to the levels of readiness of their students. The classroom teacher must also provide the student with an opportunity to examine and develop various career oriented skills and examine roles that may have career applications for him or her in the future. The school's program of career guidance must be centered in the classroom and integrated into the ongoing and total educational program of the institution. Since the total development of the individual is vital, the career aspects of this development cannot be separated from the whole.

For the classroom teacher's important role as a career and educational developer, the school counsellor can again function as an expert consultant. The counsellor can also assist the classroom teacher in securing appropriate educational and occupational development materials and can take responsibility for planning special activities that are related to the ongoing classroom experiences of the student.

Whereas the preceding paragraphs have described the overall role and function of the classroom teacher as a guidance -minded teacher of guidance team, the classroom of the guidance-minded teacher offers the most natural, consistent, and effective setting from providing pupils with developmental guidance. We, therefore, encourage teachers to seek preparation for their important role on the school guidance team.

In recent years education has witnessed an increase in the utilization of individuals who are not by training or experience classified as professional educators. These individuals, who have been labeled most commonly as paraprofessionals or educational aides, have served in a variety of capacities, such as providing clerical assistance to classroom teachers, supervisory assistance to study groups, tutorial assistance to younger and often "Slow" learners, and various service activities, i.e., cafeteria and transportation. Although the coming of the paraprofessional has not been without attending controversies, the economic and facilitative advantages appear to be slowly winning over the opposition that still exists to their employment.

The utilization and related controversies of the employment of paraprofessionals in school guidance and counselling programs has closely paralleled that of other areas of education. However, a study by Guidance Committee of the North Central Association of Colleges and Secondary Schools seems to indicate both acceptance and an increased utilization of paraprofessionals in school guidance programs.

In view of the increased acceptance of the paraprofessional in the school guidance program, four major principals relevant to the role and function of paraprofessionals are examined in the paragraphs that follow:

(a) Paraprofessionals are employed only : when their utilization enables the professionals in the program to function more effectively. Most practicing counsellors do not have to review the proliferation of articles in the professional journals to know that they are spending a disproportionate amount of their professional time and effort on clerical and other repetitive tasks which do not require their professional skills. The employment of paraprofessionals to relieve school counserlors of such routine chores, is a popular and appropriate paraprofessional role. However, when the paraprofessional is viewed as an alternate to the employment of additional professional personnel with the duties, the guidance program suffers both in image and function, as well as in potential service. This suggests that paraprofessionals should only be employed in those activities which are commensurate with their training and experience.

(b) Where employed, paraprofessionals should be provided with opportunities for both training and advancement. If the paraprofessional is an asset to school guidance and counselling programs, his or her contributions to; the program can be further enhanced by a planned training program that seeks to provide the paraprofessional; with additional appropriate knowledge and skills and to prepare him or her for increased program responsibility. The latter would also suggest the existence of career ladders that would enable the professional to anticipate and work toward advancement in school system. In some instances, it may be possible for the paraprofessional to complete a counsellor training program and thus move from the role of paraprofessional to professional.

Many community colleges around the country have developed human services training programs which focus on the preparation of paraprofessionals for work in psychological, social; welfare, and educational agencies and institutions. A few community colleges have also initiated programs that are tailored to a given paraprofessional specialty. Zimpfer notes that a community college program will typically lead to an associate degree, which provides a sense of status and achievement to the student.

The opportunities for job advancement are greater for this person than for the lesser-trained paraprofessional. Similarly, the opportunity for transfer into four-year and ultimately even into graduate training, if the student has the aptitude and the desire, is also afforded. Horizontal mobility is also an advantage of a community college program. Because of its breadth, the knowledge and skills acquired by the paraprofessional are often generalizable to a variety of settings.

(c) Individuals who are selected to work as paraprofessionals in school guidance programs should be carefully screened prior the their employment. As previously stated, school guidance program personnel should demonstrate positive human relationship techniques and understandings. This "modeling" cannot be limited to just the professional staff. Such nonprofessionals as the receptionist, student helpers, secretaries, and paraprofessionals will also be in contact with students and others served by the school guidance program. They, too, are important in the creation of models and perceptions by which others make judgments.

(d) Paraprofessionals should function within the ethical guidelines of the professionals they are assisting. Those

> paraprofessionals who are associated with the school guidance program should be informed of, and expected to function within, those ethical guidelines prescribed for their professional colleagues. This initially means that they must be informed of their guidelines and the resultant expectancies, and that adequate supervision must be provided to ensure their conformity to the guidelines, the objectives of the school guidance program could be thwarted if, for example, paraprofessinals inadvertently broke rules of confidentiality or good human relationship practices.

The Community Mental Health Centers Act of 1963 and its subsequent amendments stimulated a nationwide development of community-based agencies that provided services for the prevention and treatment of mental health disorders. The act originally provided for five essential services: inpatient care, outpatient care, emergency services, partial hospitalization, and counsultion and education. Later, additional services, prepare and aftercare services, training, research, and evaluation. These services are available in mental health centers to all individuals who reside in the geographical area designated as the center's responsibility. The inability of individuals to pay for these services need not prevent them from being utilized. No minimum period of residence in the service area is required for treatment. Self-referral or referrals by the family of clients is the most popular approach to the services of community mental health centers. Next in popularity are referrals from family physicians, the legal system, schools, and other community agencies.

The professional team for community mental health centers may include psychiatrists, psychologists, social workers, and other mental health personnel, including counsellors and psychiatric nurses. In addition to the professional team, administrators and support personnel and even volunteer workers also work in many centers. The responsibilities of the professional staff is dictated by their professional training and background.

In Service of Society

Small Community-Based Social Service Agencies: During the

past fifteen years, thousands of small, nonprofit, community-based social service agencies have been established. Community-based social-service agencies are those whose scope of operation is focused on the immediate community or on specific needs within a community and whose principal function is to meet a specific social or human-service need. These grass roots organizations are usually effective, because they are able to take risks, adjust to societal changes, and provide opportunities for people willing to engage in one-to-one relationships with clients.

The staffs of these agencies usually consist of a director, an assistant director or project coordinator, a secretary (usually part-time), and a volunteer support system. Volunteers perform highly specialized functions that require experience and skills as well as odd jobs that require no formal training.

The services provided by these small community-based agencies may emphasize or include referral assistance; educational activities such as consumer skills, remedial education, and training for the handicapped; job placement and job training related to placement; and advocacy and outreach functions. The small social service agencies provide assistance to a wide range of individuals; elderly people who have limited financial resources, teenagers "on the run", veterans involved with drug abuse, family members coping with divorce, recently widowed individuals struggling to deal with their loss, and countless others.

The team for these small agencies may consist of only one or two full-time professionals, frequently psychologists or sociologists, "backed up" by a variety of volunteers, and, in some settings, by part-time employees as well.

The "graying of America" has led to increased interest in and services for the aged.

The largest network of agencies to serve out aging population are those agencies that were established under the 1973 amendments to the Older Americans Act. Approximately 600 agencies nationwide are operative under this Act. Each agency is responsible for determining the needs of the elderly in its area and planning a strategy to meet these needs. Roles and activities for which counsellors may be particularly well qualified are providing retirement counselling, assisting in adjustments to the deaths of spouses, and providing a vocational and recreational guidance.

Aging agency "teams" are typically headed by the agency program administrator whose staff may include social workers, psychologists, counsellors, nurses and nurses aides, and nonprofessional assistants, who are often volunteers.

Rehabilitation counsellors work with disabled clients to assist them kin overcoming defects in their skills. In these efforts the counsellor is seeking to bring physically, mentally, or emotionally disabled adults, this includes entry into an appropriate career. The rehabilitation counsellor's role is a complex one and may include providing for a broad range of psychological and career-oriented services,. coordinated with other community agencies and consultation with families and employers or types of clients such as the deaf, blind, the mentally ill, or the physically handicapped. The majority of rehabilitation counsellors work for government agencies or nonprofit organizations. In these settings, they often work in close cooperation with physicians and/or psychiatrists.

Practically all pupil services specialists may become involved in counselling SLD pupils. Counselling has proven effective with this subpopulation. Due to the fact that behavioural and adjustment problems often overlap cognitive deficits, there is a need for the counsellor to deal with coping and self-control skills. In dealing with these strategies, the helper may choose to use either a counselling or consultation model.

In addition to the student, the counsellor will work with the teacher(s) and parent(s). Students with long standing SLD problems will demonstrate a variety of behavioural symptoms, chief among them will be low self-esteem, anxiety, anger and frustration. Counselling strategies which apply particularly to the adolescent, should:

1. Offer a chance for success, no matter how small.
2. Build an inclination to try by structuring small segments of assigned tasks.

3. Minimize situations where threats, punishment, and strong reactions of adults are prevalent.

4. Keep the student to a reasonable time schedule once he begins to make progress.

5. Ally deep-seated fears that he is somehow mentally subnormal.

Counsellors who deal with students who have ambivalence over intelligence may find it useful to use Lloyd Thompson's book entitled *Language Disabilities in men of Eminence.* In this provocative piece, Thompson uses a psychohistorical approach to illustrate that some great men in history probably had SLD. Among the people described are Thomas Edison, Harvey Cushing, Auguste Rodin, George Pattern, Woodrow Wilson, Paul Ehrlich, Albert Einstein and George Washington, Adolescents can identify with these eminent people and realize that all is not necessarily lost because one had a learning problem in school.

Counselling techniques will differ on the basis of specific problem behaviour. However, Edge, Brown, and Brown suggest some that may be generally applicable.

1. For inadequacy, try "strength bombardment" in a group setting.

2. For anxiety, try relaxation training.

3. For anger, try a cognitive approach, perhaps rational-emotive counselling, or "I messages."

4. For frustration or inappropriate interactions try "time out".

There is also need for parent and family counselling. Stress and sibling rivalry are commonly found in families of learning-disabled students "parents feel ambivalence, guilt, fear...but... must always subside to the reality that theirs is still a handicapped child who seems normal, but doesn't appear to learn and/or behave normally. This is the essence of the parental frustration, namely, trying to understand how a child who is normal in most ways can fail to learn in school, even with massive amounts of tutoring and family support.

As is true with most mildly handicapped adolescents, the youth who make up this subpopulation will most likely enter the competitive work force after graduation from high school. Of course, some will advance to higher education but it is apparent that an academically delimiting handicap like SLD will dictate circumscribed horizons. Too little attention has been paid heretofore to the postsecondary future of the SLD pupil. Part of the problem is related to the difference between career and vocational education/development. Vocational development has a narrower focus and in terms of special education populations has tended to emphasize a limited clientele.

Vocational education programs, albeit sorely limited in some parts of the country, have been targeted primarily at those pupils categorized as educable mentally retarded. This targeting developed, in part, from the belief that the mildly retarded had very few choices. The learning-disabled, however, comprise a heterogeneous group with much broader options. Accordingly, the concepts of career preparation and development are highly applicable. If a career is the totality of work or activities over a life time, then a more comprehensive approach is necessary with SLD pupils. However, before strategies are instituted there must be a realization that the SLD pupil required career development assistance.

Due to the fact that the SLD pupil has the given "normal" intelligence it is often assumed that he or she can move through the secondary school situation in lockstep with non handicapped pupils. The implication is that SLD pupils will somehow absorb incidental career information that will be self-utilized upon graduation. While this rationale is difficult, at best, for even the non-handicapped pupil, it is disastrous for the SLD pupil. A SLD pupil is typically exerting every ounce of energy to survive the academic demands of the secondary school.

If one accepts this restraint it is easy to see why little attention will be given to incidental types of learning that are part of the repertoire of informal career preparation and development. Bingham has observed that boys with SLD are less mature in their responses on the Carrier Maturity Index and require planned experience to develop vocational maturity. Kendall found that subjects enrolled in vocational-training classes were superior in social maturity and career attitudes.

Another hurdle for school counsellors who are concerned with career development is the often unreasonable expectations of the parents. This "hidden handicap" will sometimes lead parents astray and arouse expectations of educational and occupational choices that are far beyond the proven capabilities of the SLD pupil. This can be a particular problem for youth who come from college-educated or professional families.

Although some youth have internalized these parental expectations, most will feel relieved to be guided toward more realistic choices. An additional variable is the actual range of possibilities that may be available. It has been pointed out previously that some colleges are now opening their doors to the identified learning-disabled motivated, successfully-coping pupil. However, the range of possibilities between vocation and college education is much less appealing. Technical schools and related occupations have yet to feel the need to adapt to the needs of the learning-disabled.

The pupil services administrator and staff must be alert to the need for career preparation and development for the SLD adolescent at these times. If quantity and quality of academic programming were the issues of the seventies then post-secondary career issues will be the frontier of the eighties. It should be reiterated that P.L. 93-112, the Rehabilitation Act of 1973, does recognize specific learning disabilities as an adult disorder. The SLD person is entitled to the same considerations as others with more visible handicaps. The pupil services staff must forge a linkage with rehabilitation counsellors and employers. This is a task that will fall to school counsellors, school psychologists, and school social workers.

Development Issues

There are a number of issues conforming the pupil service administrator within the domains of both development and management. The problems may differ depending on the maturity of the department, but the problem areas have similarities. An initial development problem centres around the instructional delivery system that is best for the district and the student configuration. For example, is it better to go with a tutoring program as opposed to the resources room concept? Once a procedure has been initiated, it is difficult, but not impossible, to change. The pupil services administrator must examine the nature of the SLD staff/parental expectations and financial resources and act accordingly.

A development or redevelopment should utilize the needs-assessment technique so all parties are in agreement. Another development issue to be faced in the 1980s is when expansion should cease. During the 1970s the objective was to increase services so as to meet the needs of an unserved population. The time will come when not only will it be appropriate to limit expansion but also to reduce services. At a time when general school enrollments are decreasing and regular class teachers are being dismissed, can one in good conscience continue SLD services at the same level? This issue must be resolved through analysis of caseloads and the generation of "hard data" for justification.

Specific management problems may revolve around the maintenance of identification standards, standardization of caseloads, interstaff relationships, least restrictive environment, and evaluation/accountability.

As, the nationwide concern for specific learning disabilities has increased, it was inevitable that more mild conditions would be included. There are many pupils in school with learning problems and some may have some of the characteristics associated with definitions of SLD. The issue for a pupil services administrator is whether such pupils are eligible for special education. Gearheart recognizes this issue but believes that preventive efforts may be one of the most effective ways to deliver learning disabilities programming. Others would agree that prevention is the best way to approach any emerging disability but might quarrel with the designation of the delivery system. The instruction of mild cases, which may not meet formal identification criteria, might properly belong in the domains of remedial or compensatory education.

A pragmatic view would hold that the pupil should receive service wherever it is available, with the recognition that the budget climate of the eighties is not conducive to either the establishment or maintenance of non-special education programming. The team, whether by school or district, will decide who is eligible for services and the pupil services administrator must exercise leadership in developing a philosophical point of view as to what constitutes a specific learning disability which, in turn, will influence standards. The problem for the pupil services administrator is not an easy one, for it involves a number of variables differing from district to district. Some of the questions that can be posed are:

1. Will the dilution of standards eventually do more harm than good by resulting in reduction for funding brought on by greater numbers?
2. If some kind of service is provided, even if not condoned by the regulations, will it eventually reduce the prevalence of SLD?
3. Should the broad range of learning problems be served, from whatever source, for the greater good of society?

A building-oriented approach to specific learning disabilities is becoming standard in many parts of the country due both to the ubiquitous nature of SLD and to the fact that it is often the preferred choice of most general administrators and parents. That there is no threat or stigma to having an SLD center in a given school contributes to its desirability and popularity. As this development occurs, SLD teacher who are completely building-based become increasingly under the jurisdiction of building principals.

There is nothing wrong with this traditional supervisory model if it presents a problem to the pupil services administrator because principals tend to view services from a different perspective. As building managers, principals are under pressures different from those of central office administrators. Principals, unlike most pupil services administrators, have a constituency that is composed of the parents and/or pupils of the entire school.

Accordingly, the principal is to meet the demands of the constituency in terms of services. If remedial services in the school are limited or non-existent, he/she may be inclined to request services from the SLD center even though a pupil may not have yet cleared a team meeting or, at best, is marginally eligible. The motivation in such requests is usually commendable and eminently pupil-centered so the principal cannot be faulted on help-giving grounds. Naturally, such requests are difficult if not impossible to deny for a building-based special education teacher. As a result caseloads in individual schools may vary widely, sometimes from 15-30 pupils per teacher. When such a discrepancy is revealed it causes a furor among special education teachers and parents. It is the responsibility of the pupil services administrator to insure that standard caseloads are observed both for quality of service and staff morale.

To his extent, it is advisable to have an approved policy statement on record to indicate minimum and maximum pupil limits. Once these and similar questions are addressed the pupil services administrator may determine if the standards are set, it is certain that they will not be popular with all segments of the administrator's constituency, whether other administrators, teachers, pupil services staff, or parents. Therefore, in trying to modify or maintain standards, the administrator will have to use all the managerial skills at his/her command.

Atmosphere in Premises

Relationships among SLD teachers, psychologists, speech-language pathologists, and social workers often need improvement. Specifically, the different specialities sometimes are at variance with regard to the identification and instructional needs of those pupils who are described as learning-disabled. This kind of intergroup conflict seems to occur with the SLD population more than with other exceptionalities. It is due, in part, to the nebulous quality of the handicap but, in addition, it reflects the compelling need of all specialists to get involved in program planning.

All have a take in the IEP whether by virtue of professional identity, administrative requirements, or parental expectations.

Due to "turf" issues interstaff relationships often deteriorate and assume conflicting proportions. For a host of reasons, among them being popularity and acceptance, most staff members want to participate in SLD program planning and development. It is probably crucial that IEP meetings be attended by representatives of all the disciplines.

This is a good strategy because no one specialty will feel slighted or left out. The essence here is participation and not necessarily decision making. Another potent device is to involve all disciplines in policy-making decisions that affect the SLD subpopulation. Non-involvement can lead to feelings or rejection, frustration, and hostility.

Another technique is to involve all specialities in any efforts at parent education. With regard to SLD it is expedient to allow each specialty to become identified with SLD in the parents' minds. The parental lobby in specific learning disabilities has been a powerful one and this has not been lost on pupil services staff. The hidden agenda here is that if programs are expanded, usually at the behest of parents, then all specialities should have an opportunity to partake of the largesse.

Nowhere is the debate about the least restrictive environment more intense than in the arena of specific learning disabilities. Support and arguments run the gamut from advocates of total normalization to the need for private school placement. It is possible to make a case for this range of placements as it is for no other exceptionality. Normalization or mainstreaming is not always successful because it is often administratively inspired and a "competency-based assessment" has been suggested. P.L. 94-142 leans a variety of ways. An activist parent of a severely learning-disabled adolescent will often see least restriction being offered in a residential private school.

Sometimes, representatives of the "us,"—namely, school personnel—become advocates for the parent posture which presents an interesting loyalty dilemma. The pupil services administrator must deal with this explosive issue, which represents one of the persistent Guidance and Counselling challenges. First, the pupil services administrator must campaign actively for a true continuum of environments within the school district so that parents can perceive that they have a variety of options. Second, the pupil services administrator may convey to all that he or she is a fair person who can see the merits in an opposite point of view when a case is well made and laced with facts. Third, there must be a staff development of team participants so that case materials are reviewed objectively and recommendations made on personal conscience and not because of administrative fiat.

6

Counselling on Education

Educational Guidance is the methodical process of helping the individual through education and interpretative procedures to exploit his own characteristics and potentialities in an effective manner and to relate himself more satisfactorily to social requirements and opportunities in accordance with social and moral values. Traxler considers guidance as a help which enables "each individual to understand his abilities and interests, to develop them as well as possible and to relate them to life-goals, and finally to reach a state of complete and mature self-guidance as a desirable member of the social order." According to Jones, "Guidance involves personal help given by someone; it is designed to assist a person to decide where he wants to go, what he wants to do or how he can best accomplish his purpose; it assists him to solve problems that arise in his life."

The Procedure

It helps every individual to help himself, to recognise and use his inner resources, to set goals, to make plans, to work out his own problems of development. It is needed right from early childhood, adolescence, adulthood and even in old age. Choice and problem points are the distinctive concerns of guidance as here the individual's unique world of perceptions interacts with the external order of events in his life context. It is assistance to the individual in the process of development rather than a direction of that development: The aim is to develop the capacity for self-direction, self-guidance and self-improvement through an increased understanding of his problems and his resources as well as limitations to solve the problem.

The Practice

It is a regular service which is required at every stage for every student, not only for awkward situations and abnormal students. It is a positive programme geared to meet the needs of all students. It is both generalised and a specialised service. It is a generalised service because everyone—teachers, tutors, advisers, deans, parents-play a part in the programme. It is a specialised service because specially qualified personnel as counsellors, psychiartists, psychologists join hands to help the individual to get out of his problem. Very few terms have been more loosely or inter changeably used than the terms 'guidance' and 'counselling'.

According to Tolbert, "Guidance is the total programme or all the activities and services engaged in by an educational institution that are primarily aimed at assisting an individual to make and carry out adequate plans and to achieve satisfactory adjustment in all aspects of his daily life.

Guidance is not teaching but it may be done by teachers. It is not separate from education but is an essential part of the total educational programme. Guidance is a term which is broader than counselling and which includes counselling as one of its services," Bulter makes a logical separation of the counselling process discerned as having two phases called 'adjustive' and 'distributive'. In the adjustive phase, the emphasis is on the social personal and emotional problems of the individual; in the distributive phase the focus is upon his educational, vocational and occupational problems.

Teachers in technical institutions develop instructional plans, implement them and evaluate the effectiveness of their instruction for the main purpose of enabling their students to acquire the knowledge and skill prescribed in the courses of study.

Students often encounter difficulties in understanding what is taught in the classrooms, laboratories and workshops. They will be found wanting in achieving the explicitly spelt out instructional objectives, failures in examinations and tests, poor standards or assignments, unsatisfactory involvement in the academic work by students are some of the often-noticed problems. These result in improper utilisation of institutional facilities and resources, unsatisfactory benefits of the efforts of instruction and frustration to students. Efforts must be made to ensure that problems of the above types are solved to the maximum extent.

Aims and Motives

- To monitor the academic progress of students studying in the institution
- To acquaint the students with the prescribed curriculum
- To identify the academically gifted, backward, creative and other category of special learners
- To cater to the educational needs of special learners
- To assist students in getting information about further education
- To diagnose the learning difficulties of students and help them overcome the same
- To assist the students to maximise their scholastic achievement
- To help students to review and reflect on their performance on the course, and where appropriate to identify ways of seeking changes in work habits or behaviour.
- To help students face the consequence of acceptance of their role and to respond to the demands legitimately made on them.

The following are some of the principles on which educational guidance must be based

- Must be objective-oriented
- Every student is capable of achieving the best of his ability
- Individual differences in academic achievement of students must be recognised
- Strategy must be student-oriented

- The strategies must take into consideration the resources and facilities available to the students
- It is not for a few students only; it needs to be provided for all.

A class in which all students have more or less the same abilities for coping with instruction is ideal for teaching-learning. Teachers may employ the same instructional strategy for an entire group of students whose entry behaviour characteristics, learning ability, interest motivation, attitude to learning are the same. In such situations they do not encounter much difficulty in guiding students for optimal learning.

In reality, classes are never homogeneous and teachers have the challenging task of coping with a variety of students' characteristics. Students in any class can be ordinarily classified into three categories viz., the average, below average and above average on the basis of their academic performance.

The below average students are those whose performance is below the average performance of the class. Those whose performance is above the average of the class are categorised as above average. In this category, we may notice creative and gifted students as well. There are other types of students called slow learners, who have the ability to perform satisfactorily but are only slow in doing so. Their slowness may be attributed to a combination of a variety of causes. There may be some students, whose performance in comparison to that of the class may be satisfactory. Yet, their own performance may not be commensurate with their ability.

Problems in learning are most common in all categories of students. An above average student is likely to have as much of learning difficulties as a below average one. By providing educational guidance, efforts must be made to ensure that students maintain their level of academic performance. In all other cases, the efforts should be towards enabling the students to overcome their educational difficulties. In doing so it is important to identify those students who have problems and find solutions to their actual problems.

Identification of students is possible by continuous and careful observation of the 'academic behaviour' by teachers. The aspects of behaviour that may be observed include the interaction of students with the teacher during instruction, the types of questions put by them, interest shown for involvement in the teaching-learning activity, keenness exhibited for learning, alertness in grasping whatever is taught in the class, performance in tests and assignments, perusal of assignments and other assigned work.

Teachers can easily observe their students in the classes. However, care must be exercised in drawing conclusions based only on observation. For, a student who may be shy to answer questions or ask questions should not be identified as a weak student.

It is important to spot out those students who require educational guidance not only on the basis of observation, but also on the basis of discussion with other faculty.

Achievement tests are used to find out what has been learned i.e. what habit and skills have been developed in students as a result of instruction. They are valuable as a means of determining to what extent the student has attained a certain degree of progress towards a desirable goal, whether he is ready to undertake the next step and how his attainment compares with that of other members of his group. These tests, based on the prescribed syllabus enable these teacher to find out the strengths and weaknesses of the student.

It is possible to find out the improvement on achievement. Diagnosis which forms one of the basic steps in providing guidance is possible through achievement testing.

Achievement tests serve a variety of purposes for use in educational guidance programmes. These are useful to survey students in order to find out those with educational problems, diagnose the actual difficulties and for prognosis.

The survey type of achievement tests comprise items that include the content covered in a subject area in order to find to what extent students meet the accepted norms and standards of academic performance. Diagnostic tests serve the purpose of finding out the actual weaknesses of students. Prognostic tests are to determine a student's readiness for learning.

Aptitude of a person is latent trait accounting for the probability of his success in a field related to the traits on giving necessary training. Aptitude is a combination of inborn capacities and developed abilities, skills etc., that make the person what he is at any given time and predicts what he may become. Aptitude tests are expected to measure the potential for specific abilities and skills such as music, graphic arts, medicine, law, engineering, teaching etc. They tell us how well the individual is equipped to excel in a specific skill.

Intelligence tests are used to determine an individuals' learning capacity. The results of intelligence tests may be used to organise learners into relatively homogeneous teaching learning groups. It is important to note that a fairly high degree of mental alertness is required in pursuing various courses of study. Learners who have low intelligence level experience learning difficulties, if they choose certain types of courses. It has also been found that success in certain vocational areas is dependent upon a high degree of intellectual ability.

Interest inventories indicate that success in any course of study or vocation depends to a considerable extent upon the interest the individual takes in it. Interests are closely related to aptitude. In certain cases interests are intrinsic. In most cases, interests are to be created externally. This provides a constant incentive to continue until the goal is reached. It must be noted that worthwhile activities are better supported by intrinsic interest, because the pleasure continues even if the goal is not reached. Finding out the interest (or appraisal) is difficult. However, the methods used are to ask the individual about their interests, to analyse the various activities in which the individual is involved, and measuring interest using interest inventories.

The first two methods have obvious limitations. While in the first case, the individual's oral explanation cannot be relied upon very much in the latter case, individual may be involved in work because of necessity. It would be difficult to find out whether the activity involved is freely chosen or chosen out of compulsion.

Information or data about an individual's personality achievement, interest, aptitude etc., are very vital for any guidance activity. The data obtained must be valid and reliable which, therefore, implies that the tools used for collecting such data must have high validity and reliability. Certain points are to be kept in mind about the information collected. Wherever a test has to be administered to an individual, it should be clone in a relaxed and friendly atmosphere. The test should never be thrust upon him. He should never be allowed to take it when he is under stress or strain. Readiness to take the test is in important aspect. Test scores should not be disclosed to any other person than the student himself without the explicit knowledge and permission of the client. Strict confidentiality has to be maintained whenever the data needs to be used for research purposes, special care is to be taken to see that the identity of the student is not at all revealed. Any information provided by him either as responses to test items or interviews should be treated confidentially.

Guidance is a time-consuming process and several sessions will be required to provide adequate guidance. Each session may result in some new facts emerging which can provide some nearer insights into the problems of the individual concerned. The information so emerging should be very carefully recorded. Obtaining information alone is not important but storing the same is equally important. The work involved in recording and filing is tedious and uninteresting, yet most important.

The record should be cumulative and, in addition to up-to-date identifying data, should include important items concerning a student from the time he enters the institution until he leaves it. Such information about a student can be stored in a guidance folder. This is designed to cover a period of years. Suggested items for guidance folder are: Identifying data, home background, economic condition, health record, academic record, out-of-class activities, character and personality traits, special or peculiar incidents (details), special interests and achievement, educational plans, vocational plans, experiences, details or outcome of each guidance/ counselling session. Particular care must be taken in maintaining the folder. The entries must be made as accurately as possible. Where tests are administered, the date, time and conditions under which the tests were administered have to be correctly recorded. When interpretation of information is recorded, it has to be done under specific headings.

Guidance folders should be made available to the concerned teacher as well, since the learner's aims, interest, potentialities, degree of accomplishment, application to work represent valuable data to teachers in evaluating classroom work and in guiding learning. There is one exception to this general procedure, confidential information about an individual that is of value only to the counsellor should either be removed from the folder before the latter is made available for general use or be kept in a separate file. The information collected about students must be properly recorded. It is suggested that a master register may be developed for the purpose. The register may contain information about the different aspects of all students such as their place of education, medium of instruction at the school, study habits, level of motivation, performance in tests and assignments. Great care must be exercised in filling up the record sheet for each student. This sort of a register can be used for maintaining information about all students of a class.

Teachers must build educational guidance as an integral part of their everyday instruction. Every teacher consciously or otherwise, deliberately or not deliberately attempts to provide, guidance to their students in learning. Sometimes it may be given in a formal way and at. other times in an informal manner.

The guidance may range from suggesting/ advising students to be systematic in their studies, to planning and implementing individualised instructional strategies. Educational guidance strategies to be used by teachers depend upon the nature of the problems, and the extent of their effect and the purposes of providing for such guidance. These strategies should be situation-oriented and student-oriented. The strategies employed must help in enabling students to achieve to the best of their abilities in scholastic areas. Guidance and counselling strategies can be classified into two categories viz., group approach and individual approach.

Every student must have the freedom (and be helped) to choose the courses of study considering his educational ability, interest, future needs etc. The purposes of this type of guidance are:

- Encourage students to utilise their abilities in specific areas
- Assist students in understanding and appreciating the instructional obligations which they are required to complete. This may include information regarding the assignments, tests, project work they are required to complete as part of the course work
- Provide information to students regarding further education programmes
- Give general orientation to students regarding the facilities and resources available such as library, laboratories, workshops, scholarships etc.
- Provide opportunities for group thinking in regard to common problems and experience

Group guidance approach for educational purposes must be organised for disseminating educational information of a general nature to students. Care must be exercised in organising group guidance.

Group guidance may be in the form of group discussion and talks to enable students to plan their educational activities. This is possible by giving them information about the courses of study, curriculum requirements, scheme of evaluation etc. by teachers.

It is advisable to organise group guidance sessions for students who have common problems by identifying students. Poor achievers, students whose level of motivation is low, those whose study skills are not satisfactory may be provided guidance through a group approach. Besides the general group guidance programmes, teachers may have to design and implement group guidance in their own class for the purpose of general improvement in academic performance. Such guidance must form an integral part of instruction. In these programmes, teachers may have to often focus on the progress of the students, common problems faced by them and suggestions for overcoming them, common mistakes, committed in tests and assignments and suggestions for improving their performance. For effective organisation of group guidance it may be necessary to have a team of faculty for planning, implementing and evaluating these programmes. The team members have to be properly identified with one of them, preferably a Head of Department as the coordinator of the programme. The task of the team would be:

- to identify the areas and scope of guidance for students
- to plan a schedule of guidance programmes spread throughout the year
- to decide the strategy such as lecture, conference, seminar, etc. appropriate for the spelt-out objectives
- to conduct the guidance programmes as per the schedule drawn
- to evaluate the effectiveness of the programmes organised to get feedback for purposes of improvement
- to plan and monitor the follow-up.

Several problems of students in the area of learning be attributed to a lack of knowledge of what the institution can offer and how it can do so. This calls for a knowledge of the facilities and resources available in the institution. These facilities may be laboratories, workshops, library, recreation, co-curricular, hostel etc. Each of these are meant for specific purposes, work, under a set of rules and regulations, have certain expectations from students.

It is important to have an understanding of the rules and regulations of the academic administration of the institution. Certain areas under which such information is required are attendance requirements, scholarship and stipend awards (conditions for award, criteria and mode) academic and extra curricular activities, guidance services rendered by the institution. It is not that such information is not provided by institutions. Some institutions give these as part of their prospectus which is supplied with the application form for admission.

Most often students do not go through the rules. It is taken as a routine information. Even when the same is read, it is read rather casually. Thus, the purpose of giving the information in the prospectus gets defeated. The practice that should be followed in institutions is to hand over a copy of the rules and regulations and get the students committed to these. It is only then that they try to adhere to the same. Institutional induction is an activity which is intended to 'introduce' the institution in its totality to the students.

It is during such an activity that students come to know of the objectives of the institution, its development, traditions, resources, faculty etc. This activity enables the students to know the environment in which they are required to work/study. It lays the foundation for their continuous interactions at the institution. It enables them to accept the institution as a place where their needs would be met, their aspirations and goals fulfilled. Students will be able to see themselves in the context of the institutional environment.

The objectives spelt in the above paragraph can be realised if induction programmes are efficiently organised. The main intention of such programmes should be a mutual understanding involving the students, staff and the administration of the institution.

The beginning of the academic programme would be the most ideal period for the organisation of induction programmes. In fact, all the academic activities planned by the institute should follow this programme. Care should be taken to cover all aspects of the life of students during their stay in the institution.

It is also advantageous to introduce all members of the faculty and office of the institution to the students during these programmes. A visit to the different departments and laboratories including the library will be very useful. A well drawn time table for the induction programme goes a long way in its effective implementation. It is useful to involve all members of the faculty in the organisation of such a programme.

Special learners are those who stand out as a distinct set from other students in a class and therefore require special attention. Educationally, they deviate from the average students in their academic achievement. These learners require special attention by teachers. They do not profit much from learning in average group situations. Special learners in institutions may be classified as :

Talented Ones

Gifted students are those who show consistently remarkable performance in educational endeavours. They possess a superior intellectual potential and functional ability to achieve academically in the top 15 to 20 per cent of the students in the institution, and/ or talent of a high order. Creative students are those who exhibit creativity.

Creativity is the process of sensing gaps missing elements; forming ideas or hypothesies and testing the same. It is the ability to change one's approach to a problem, to cope with ideas that are both relevant and unusual to go beyond the immediate situation to redefine the problem.

The Backbenchers

Slow learners are those students who require more time for learning than the normal/average students in a class. Hence, they show marked educational deficiency. They learn at a slower rate than others. In order to provide guidance to the above category of learners, it is important to identify them. For these learners, individual guidance will have to be arranged. Identification of the special learners will have to be carried out systematically. It may be based on teachers' observation, academic records and performance in mental ability traits.

System at Work

Educational guidance helps us determine what a student is good for and what type of education will reveal his inborn capacities and help him to develop them. It is a process concerned with bringing about a favourable setting for the individual's education and includes the assistance in the choice of subjects, use of libraries, laboratories, workshops, development of effective study habits, evaluation techniques and adjustment of school life with other activities. Educational guidance is a conscious effort to assist in the intellectual growth of an individual by self-direction.

It helps the children in choosing the courses of study; planning for their future on the completion of their secondary/higher secondary schooling; and helps in arresting backwardness while promoting proper adjustment.

Major Objectives

Educational guidance is intended to achieve the following purposes:

(*i*) To provide pupils with scientific assistance in their choice and adjustment in relation to subjects of study and co-curricular activities and with school life to effect maximum intellectual, emotional and physical development.

(*ii*) To help the pupil with specific problems like lack of relationship between ability and achievement, deficiency in one or several school subjects, faulty study habits, defective methods of learning and poor motivation.

(*iii*) To help the pupil choose the educational course best suited to him.

(*iv*) To help the pupil relate the course chosen to prospective jobs.

(*v*) To help the pupil to make educational plans consistent with his abilities, interests and goals to select appropriate curricula and courses.

(*vi*) To help the pupil succeed in his educational programme.

(*vii*) To enable the faculty members to know the modifications required in the curriculum and in the administrative arrangements of the school to meet the needs of the students.

Various Levels

Elementary stage: Educational guidance has the following specific functions at the elementary stage.

(i) *Assisting pupils to make a proper beginning:* The pupils should be helped and guided to make a good beginning in their educational career. The possibilities that a good and complete education can open before them should be explained so that they are motivated to stay.

(ii) ***Assisting pupils to plan intelligently:*** The pupils should be made familiar with the different types of courses and activities available. They should be given the basic information regarding occupational divisions and occupational families, special skills they require, and the relationship of school achievement to employment.

(iii) ***Assisting pupils to get the best out of their education:*** During the process of education, pupils experience many learning difficulties. Handicaps have to be detected to ensure progress. Pupils need to be helped according to their abilities and interests.

(iv) ***Preparing pupils to enter the secondary stage:*** Since guidance is a continuum, it is one of its functions at the elementary stage to assist the student to recognise the direction in which he is going and to map out in general the highways that have the greatest promise of leading to his goals. That means one of the important functions of educational guidance here will be- to prepare the pupils for entry into the secondary stage of schooling.

Higher Secondary stage: As the child enters the secondary school stage, he develops certain peculiar characteristics:

(i) He develops new ways of thinking, new associations and new spheres of concern.

(ii) He forms certain attitudes towards the school, the teachers, and education.

(iii) He develops certain likes and dislikes; some of his interests mature.

(iv) By this time, intelligence and abilities grow almost to the maximal point and those that remained underdeveloped have limited possibilities to grow now.

(v) Personality traits also become somewhat stabilised.

All these characteristics determine the child's unique relationship with his educational environment and affect his intellectual behaviour. Moreover, the secondary school student is no longer a member of a single class under a single teacher. He now comes in contact with a number of subject teachers and the rather complex learning situation makes new demands upon him. He must make decisions; he has to be made capable enough to adjust himself to his studies and activities by making a wise choice; he has to develop healthier habits of thought and work for proper adjustment. The guidance programme at this stage will have the following functions:

(i) *Assisting pupils to orient themselves to the new purposes of education:* Through talks, each pupil needs to be helped to look at secondary schooling as fulfilment of liberal education for all, education for employment for many and education for leadership for the few. They should be made to realise the role education can play to enable them to live a happier and a prosperous individual and social life.

(ii) *Assisting pupils to select courses and activities:* The pupils have to be helped in choosing courses and activities which are of interest and value to them at this stage of development. They also need to be assisted to qualify for advanced work in courses for admission to higher secondary schools, junior colleges, vocational institutions, or for employment, and for future social and cultural development.

(iii) Assisting pupils to make an appraisal of their abilities, aptitudes, skills and interests, and to relate them to the curriculaum courses.

(iv) *Assisting pupils to make progress in their education by removal of subject difficulties and development of good study skills:* Pupils may face difficulties in learning some subjects. Guidance procedures should help in solving these difficulties.

(v) *Assisting pupils to build proper motivation for study:* Motivation is a significant component in the process of learning. Each school has to find its own ways of motivating children for better learning.

Higher secondary stage: At this stage, educational guidance has the following functions:

(i) Assisting pupils in the selection of courses/vocations in line with their abilities and interests,

(ii) Assisting pupils in understanding the objectives of higher education so that they decide the line of action for themselves.

The Schemes

In the new pattern, a great deal of stress has been laid on relating curriculum, which has been made comprehensive, to the needs and aspirations of the nation. It includes social sciences, life sciences, mathematics, socially useful productive work, languages, arts, music and other aesthetic activities. The number of subjects is twelve. The multiplicity of subjects and the making of mathematics and sciences compulsory can give rise to a number of problems. It has been observed that neither are all the students interested in all the subjects, nor do they possess the ability to grasp them. This is particularly true in the case of science and mathematics where the standard expected is high. The children, particularly from the lower socio-economic background, can experience difficulty in these subjects. The failure to learn can cause emotional disturbance in terms of the damage it does to the child's self-image. Often, inner emotional turmoil and mental confusion make attentiveness and perseverance impossible. The lack of self-confidence can lead to failures and a number of adjustment problems. The guidance work has to do something here—to enable the children to learn the new subjects, ensure satisfactory progress, and success.

Socially useful productive work and vocationalization of education are other important features of the new pattern of education. It is envisaged that they will solve certain ills of the society. But there is a fear that these may give rise to new adjustment problems for the students who have to be helped to plan realistically and prepared to select a specific stream in view of their abilities, aptitudes and interests.

As the people today are not well attuned to vocational courses, special efforts will have to be made by the guidance worker. Drastic changes are called for in the attitude of students, as well as the parents, so that they do not consider it below their dignity to follow the vocational courses. Since emphasis has been laid on co-curricular activities which should be varied enough to cater to individual needs and aptitudes, the school counsellor should help plan and select such activities keeping in view the special needs of the students.

Similarly, many factors of learning—importance of experience, motivation and reinforcement for learning, have been emphasised. The teacher at his level, with proper training and orientation, can effectively handle them and facilitate the learning on the part of the students. This requires urgent attention especially with children whose parents are uneducated. The teacher's attitude and general behaviour towards these children is important for the adjustment of such first generation learners in the school. It is all the more necessary at the elementary level where children face adjustment problems because of the transition from home to school.

During the middle stage, more social demands and responsibilities create further difficulties for the children leading to conflicts and tensions. The guidance personnel has to help them resolve these and find the best solutions. Special attention has to be paid to the talented, the creative, the under-achiever, the educationally backward and the physically handicapped because of their special needs, and personality characteristics. Arrangements for diagnostic testing and remedial instruction need to be made for such children.

At the end of class X, students have three options:

(i) They can enter the world of work;

(ii) They can take up vocational courses;

(iii) They can take up higher level academic courses of study to prepare for first level degree courses in a college or university.

The guidance worker can help the students in three ways:

(i) For the first category, he can create awareness among 'the pupils regarding the development of knowledge and skills, effective work habits, attitudes and character which can be helpful in their personal and vocational development.

(ii) For the second category, he can help in the choice of occupational courses and socially useful productive work in the light of their future career plan.

(iii) For the third category, he can help in the choice of academic courses in the light of their future career plan.

In the +2 stage, the guidance worker should enable the pupils to choose a stream on the basis of their abilities, aptitues, interests and achievement. He should also enable them to develop realistic understanding about the work and obtain valuable information about the educational and vocational opportunities and institutions.

At this stage, special efforts need to be made for organising information, counselling and placement services. It is also important that students are provided information regarding community resources, jobs and socially useful productive work. Guidance service also needs to be provided to those students who want to change academic and vocational courses.

All educational activities in an institution of learning are, in a way, guidance activities. Besides these, the following activities should also be introduced:

(i) Systematic collection of comprehensive scientific information about pupils and their maintenenance in cumulative record cards.

(ii) Systematic development of interests in pupils according to scientific methods.

(iii) Systematic development of desirable personality traits in pupils according to scientific methods.

(iv) Systematic development of proper vocational motives in pupils.

(v) Taking remedial measures for helping pupils suffering from backwardness and problem behaviour.

(vi) Counselling pupils individually whenever they face special problems.

7

Counselling for Groups

Group counselling is something different. It is not simply individual counselling applied to groups, nor is it merely an economical use of counsellor time. Many of the features of group counselling are quite unique and it would be wrong to think of it as 'individual' counselling in the mass. Because of the differences in the two processes, a counsellor trained in the skills of individual counselling might find herself in difficulty if she attempts group counselling without having some training in group interaction. It is essential that a counsellor wishing to work with individuals and groups should have a thorough theoretical and practical grounding in individual counselling theory and practice together with some experience of principles and practices of group dynamics.

The term multiple counselling is sometimes used to describe counselling carried out in groups. This seems a misleading term since it is not clear whether it is the counsellors or the students who are 'multiple'. It is used in this book to denote a situation in which there are two counsellors working either with one student, as in the chapter on training, or with a group. The term group counselling is used here to describe a situation in which there is one counsellor working with a group of students.

Group counselling is a relatively new way of working to help people and although it has a unique contribution to make to our range of helping skills, it is not the complete answer for all psychological ills or needs.

Carkhuff has written quite strongly that Group processes are the preferred mode of working with difficulties in interpersonal functioning. We can do anything in group treatment that we can do in individual treatment and more. Since groups are inherently interpersonal, they offer the helpee the means not only to relate to the helper and himself with the helper's guidance but also to relate to other members of the group and to the group as a whole. Group processes offer the prospect for the greatest amount of learning for the greatest number of people at one time.

Carkhuffs unqualified approval as inappropriate and potentially damaging as attempting to gather peaches with a combined harvester. Certainly group counselling is sometimes successful with students who have not responded well to individual counselling, and there are several combinations of group and individual counselling in use. The two extremes are to use either group counselling or individual counselling only as a main technique. Some counsellors feel that it is unwise to make the two methods available to the same students at the same time because students may not bring out their deepest problems in the group, reserving them for the individual counselling sessions, which could inhibit the work of the group. Other counsellors feel that individual counselling offered concurrently with group counselling gives opportunity for a student to discuss more deeply and extensively personal problem areas which they have been unable to bring out in the group, either because of their own inability or because of a lack of opportunity and a need to share the time of the group with other members.

Group counselling overlaps with group guidance in its partial cognitive and factual content and with group therapy in its emphasis on feelings and emotion, and it has some similarities to the individual counselling situation, with the addition of the interaction of other members of the group and the sharing of counsellor. The effectiveness of group counselling may be partly attributable to the fact that, theoretically, it makes available the services of a number of potential helpers in the form of other group members, one or several of whom may be able to offer more help to a particular person at a particular point than is the counsellor herself.

Group counselling is a particularly useful way of helping adolescents for whom peer group values are important. The interaction which takes place in a counselling group offers the students a means of gaining insight and understanding into his own problems through listening to other students discussing their difficulties. Ideas and values which a student has previously found unacceptable may become more understandable and sometimes more acceptable. The counselling group not only helps the individual student to change, but also often encourages both his desire an his ability to help social situation, for any group is more than the sum of its members: it is also the sum of its interactions.

The physical arrangements which are desirable for a counselling group are similar to those which pertain to the individual counselling situation namely, a warm, sound-proof room with fairly comfortable chairs. It is difficult, though not impossible, to conduct a counselling group in the average classroom, and even more difficult to conduct it in a cupboard. It is helpful if the same room can be used each time the group meets, because of the effect of a changed environment on the functioning of the group if their meeting place is not a familiar setting.

The time factor in the group counselling situation is related to the purpose of the group. If it is intended that most of the 'work' of the individual members is to take place in the actual group counselling session, it is necessary for the group to meet more often than it would if the counsellor and the group members feel that the students need time between meetings to absorb and test some of the experiences learned. IT is usual for the counselling groups used in education to meet once, or perhaps twice a week. If the group meets too often, for example more than three times a week, there is the possibility that the frequency of sessions will restrict the group members' external social contacts and limit their opportunities for social reality testing outside the group. The length of each group meeting will be related to the age of the people involved, and the frequency with which the group meets, but sixty to ninety minutes is probably a reasonable time span for college students, thirty to sixty minutes for secondary school pupils and no more than thirty minutes for junior school children.

The composition of a counselling group is another practical consideration which is related to the purpose of the group. Sometimes it is felt that a homogeneous group consisting of students of the same age or sex, or students who seem to have similar problems is the most helpful, whilst other counsellors find that the wider talents of a heterogeneous group make for a better counselling situation. It is necessary to look carefully at the desired outcomes for the group, and to try to ensure that the purposes of the counsellor and those of the students are the same. It is important to recognize that groups can be homogeneous only in certain limited respects. A group chosen for homogeneity in sex or age is likely to be heterogeneous in other factors such as socio-economic background, maturity, activation and, of course, temperament. It has been suggested that it is unwise to include in a counselling or therapy group people who are excessively aggressive or hostile because they are likely to destroy the atmosphere of an acceptance in the group; people who are psychologically sophisticated or those who are not sufficiently in contact with reality have also been seen as undesirable group members, but it is ilficult for the school or college counsellor to exclude students on these grounds unless they know them personally. A preliminary interview can help, though this may be more appropriate as screening for therapy groups than as a means of choosing members for a counselling group in an educational setting.

The size of a counselling group, like that of any guidance group, is related to the methodology used. A directive counsellor or one who prefers task oriented discussion may choose to work with a larger section. A group of six to eight students is probably the best size for maximum group interaction.

The term group counselling has become very popular and practices under this name have been introduced in a variety of settings. There is still variation in what it means to different individuals.

Professionals working in counselling and related fields have been asked to reach a consensus as to why; a group is beyond the definition that a group consists of three or more members who influence each other and are influenced by others. Such a group of individuals who meet and interact with one another in a face-to-face setting tend to believe that they belong to a particular group for the purpose of achieving objective or goal.

Most professionals would agree that individuals meet to satisfy personal needs and to develop an interdependence upon one another. As will be shown in later chapters, these individuals establish roles and norms as a result of sharing common attitudes, feelings, and times. In addition, these groups go through stages that can be observed and described by those who study such group behaviour. Before looking at some specific definitions of group counselling, it may be valuable to look at distinctions between three major types of group activities. Gazda says that group guidance is "organized to prevent the development of problems".

Gazda suggests three major differences between group guidance and group counselling, while acknowledging that they share a great deal of similarity. First, he points out that group guidance is recommended for all individuals on a regular basis, while group counselling is generally recommended only for those who are experiencing some coping difficulties in their lives. Second, he points out that group guidance makes an indirect attempt to change attitudes and behaviours, while group counselling makes a direct attempt to modify attitudes and behaviours. Third, Gazda says that group guidance can be done with large classroom-size groups; whereas group counselling is most effective in small and intimate groups.

A third type of group activity is that of group psychotherapy. Used primarily as part of in-patient treatment for individuals who are suffering from severe emotional distress, group psychotherapy is most often seen to be remediative-adjustive-therapeutic, while counselling is thought of as developmental-educative-preventive. While most professionals in the field believe that there is a difference between group counselling and group psychotherapy, most also agree that there is a great deal of overlap between them. The distinctions between group counselling and group therapy are difficult to define, although it is generally accepted that such differences exist. George and Cristiani suggest that a clear distinction between the two can best be made by giving counselling and psychotherapy as points on a continuum in regard to various elements: goals, clients, settings, practitioners, and methods.

Overall, differences may be best understood in terms of the kind of goals that are seen for each. Whereas counselling is most often described as being educational, supportive, vocational, problem- solving, conscious awareness, and short-term in nature; psychotherapy is most often perceived as being reconstructive, analytical, and long term, with an emphasis on severe emotional problems. The confusion resulting from a lack of agreement concerning a definition of group counselling can be seen by looking at various definitions that have already been offered.

Most individuals work as a part of a group, most individuals interact with social acquaintances as part of a group, and most individuals spend much of their leisure time as part of a group. Since the realities of community existence require community interaction, people are highly concerned with the nature of their relationships with family, friends, and colleagues. These relationships produce and/or reduce stress, feelings of loneliness, low self-esteem, a sense of failure, or a desire to improve their lives. In a sense, the counselling group provides an opportunity for the individual to participate in a small microcosm of society the individual experiences daily. As such, the group process reflects the world beyond and adds an ingredient of realism to a setting and interaction which can often be seen as artificial.

New Trends

Group counselling can make factors such as peer group pressure, social influence, and conformity come into play as part of the therapeutic process, just as they influence and affect the individual's attitude and behaviour change outside the group.

Corey points out that "the group process provides a sample of reality. The struggles and conflicts that people experience in the group situation are no different from those they experience outside of it". In such a setting, participants have the opportunity to explore their styles of relating with others and to learn more effective behaviours in those relationships.

The group setting becomes an opportunity to receive feedback and support from others concerning their perceptions of one another of how each is experienced in the group. As such, the individuals often learn to take risks regarding new attitudes such as trusting, caring, and helping, as well as new behaviours. Group members have the opportunity to get to know others at a relatively intimate level, if they wish, as a result of experiencing one another in a highly safe environment. Thus, a group setting provides a good setting for the individual to learn and practice new skills. In a group setting, the peer pressure that is involved often brings about a greater push to action both within the group and outside the group. Thus, members of the group are urged toward activity involved in facing and acting on the real issues and concerns in their lives. Likewise, the possibility of learning new behaviours is increased by the opportunity to observe other members of the group who may be seen as role models in terms of the specific behaviours which the individual wishes to change. Group discussion can strengthen discrimination learning as members come to compare effective behaviour with behaviour that does not achieve desired goals. Most important in this process, group members develop a sense of belonging, and the kind of closeness that develops provides a caring, but challenging environment for personal growth and development. Part of this results from individuals becoming aware of similarities between their problems and the problems of other group members, which leads to decreased feelings of isolation and peculiarity and a sense of commonality with others. The economic advantages to a group format may be overstated.

Many professionals agree that it is generally less expensive when the counsellor/leader is able to meet with a number of individuals simultaneously. This is particularly true when the purpose of the group is such that there is material to be learned and common skills to be developed. It is important to point out that group approaches are not the answer to limited members of professional personnel or to the limited financial resources of individuals seeking help. Although group settings enable counsellors to see more individuals in the same amount of time than would be possible in individual therapy, group experiences are generally less efficient than individual approaches because they cannot be tailored to meet the individual needs of the patient.

The goals of a particular counselling group should be established by the members and leaders of those groups themselves. There is some agreement in terms of general goals to be accomplished via group settings.

Frank suggested general treatment goals as being

(a) to facilitate the constructive release of feelings,

(b) to strengthen patients' self-esteem,

(c) to encourage patients to face and resolve their problems,

(d) to improve their skills in recognizing and resolving both interpersonal and intrapersonal conflicts, and

(e) to fortify them to consolidate and to maintain their therapeutic gains.

Kelman continued the focus on clients' means for improving interpersonal skills by establishing the following goals: (a) to overcome feelings of isolation, (b) to enhance self-esteem and increase acceptance of self, (c) to develop hope for improved adjustment, (d) to help each client learn to be himself and to express his feelings, (e) to accept responsibility for himself and for solving his problems, (f) to develop, practice, and maintain new relationship skills, and (g) to enhance his commitment to change his attitudes and behaviours, and to generalize his insight and skills by implementing them in daily life.

The Objectives

General goals have to do with establishing a psychological environment within which individuals can work toward achieving their personal goals. Process goals have to do with clients learning appropriate self-disclosures, being willing to share feelings with other members of the group, being willing to talk about themselves in a personal way, being willing to talk about current feelings, providing feedback to others within the group, learning how to confront with care and respect, and expressing reactions to what is going on in the group. Perhaps the best list of general goals shared by most counselling groups is one proposed by Corey.

The term therapeutic group is used as a general term for any of a wide variety of groups. By therapeutic, it is not meant that the group is used for the treatment of severe emotional and psychological disorders, but rather that the group's overall purpose is to have a positive, healing effect on whatever issues the members of the group may bring to it. These issues may have to do with individuals' wanting to learn more about themselves by increasing their awareness of their feelings, values, and beliefs. Other therapeutic experiences might also include providing information to individuals that will enable them to make more appropriate decisions about the course of their lives, as well as giving them tools necessary to make the kind of changes they would like.

As a result, the term therapeutic group may be utilized for such diverse counselling groups as growth and development groups, T-groups, encounter groups, awareness groups, sensitivity training groups, consciousness- raising groups, therapy groups, and task-oriented groups, as well as groups where the focus is on specific behaviour change and/or the learning of specific new skills. Before looking at some of the various types of groups that exist, it is important to note that one major difference among the various kinds of groups has to do with the degree of structure of the various group activities. Most growth and development groups utilize minimal structuring in which the direction and progress of the group is generally left to the input and expressed needs of the group members.

Only general goals related to the growth and development of those group members are verbalized. Behaviour-change groups often provide greater structuring to the group process. Leaders of these groups often convey precisely what they expect of group members, what group members can expect of the leader, how previous group members have been helped through these experiences, and a relatively formalized outline of planned activities.

Perhaps the greatest emphasis in counselling groups during the past few decades has been in group experiences that focus on the personal growth of the individual. Such groups are not specifically designed for the rehabilitation of individuals suffering from specific psychological or emotional difficulties, but are intended for relatively normal people who are hoping to enhance their personal living skills particularly as these skills involve relating to others. Such growth-centered groups tend to focus on helping individuals gain specific skills; develop insights into their own sets of values, beliefs, and attitudes; enhance their socialisation abilities; and learn how to become more aware of the feelings that they are experiencing. Groups for such growth purposes have been identified by several names depending on the areas of growth which are emphasized.

T-groups, or laboratory training groups, tend to emphasize the development of human relations skills which enable the individual to be more effective in a business organization, focusing more on group process than on personal growth per se. T-groups emphasize education through experience in an environment in which experimentation can occur while receiving support and feedback from the other members of the group. Individuals are encouraged to try out new behaviours, and those behaviours are analysed so that the individual learns how his or her behaviour is seen by others in the group. T-group members usually increase their sensitivity to the feelings and behaviours of other group members, as well as increase their understanding of group behaviour dynamics. Thus, in a sense, the T-group provides an opportunity for group members to learn how to learn by discovering that the only real answers in terms of becoming more effective as a leader are answers that are provided by their own experiences and not answers that come from some authority figure. Likewise, T-group members are encouraged to focus on the "here and now" as a means of becoming more aware of what is happening to them at the moment and how they feel about it. Encounter groups, which are the type of groups most often known as personal growth groups, generally offer an intense group experience in which the emphasis upon personal growth through expanding awareness and the release of dysfunctional inhibitions is utilized as a means of helping relatively healthy individuals gain more effective, valid contact with themselves and others. While such groups are diverse in their methods, in the experiences of their members, and in the styles of leadership involved, their common goal is to teach individuals how to deal with themselves and others in a more open, honest manner.

The emphasis is on eliciting emotions and on expressing these emotions fully. Frequent confrontations within the group are often encouraged so that the members of the group learn that such confrontation is not only acceptable but also effective in improving relationships with other people.

Thus, encounter groups usually encourage intimacy and sharing, openness, honesty, and intense interpersonal relating, with an emphasis on the spontaneous expression of one's feelings, especially risk-taking expressions and living in the present.

In addition to the verbal interaction that occurs in an encounter group, nonverbal techniques are often utilized to foster interaction. These may include touching, the use of fantasy, massage, dance, art, meditation, centering, and various encounter games.

Various types of interpersonal communication exercises are frequently used to hasten members' awareness of themselves, to promote contact with the feelings of those members, and to promote increased group participation.

In particular, marathon groups focus on individuals' learning more about the mask they wear in daily life, the social facades they present to others, the genuine aspects of themselves that are often hidden by those masks and facades, and how to give up some of these pretenses as they reenter their normal living activities. Other types of growth and development groups have included sensitivity training, awareness groups, Gestalt groups, and transactional analysis groups. Sensitivity groups generally refer to the kind of experiences provided by both T-groups and encounter groups, but with a particular focus on individuals' becoming more sensitive to their own emotional experiencing as well as to the impact of their behaviour on other individuals. Awareness groups, on the other hand, tend to emphasize awareness and expression of one's physical body through movement, spontaneous dance, and other physical activities. Gestalt groups focus on a concept of awareness, in which an expert therapist focuses on one individual at a time, while utilizing other members of the group to provide additional input that will enable the individual on the "hot seat" to become more aware of the total experiencing that he or she is going through. Likewise, transactional analysis (TA) groups provides a framework based on a TA therapeutic model in which members of the group become more aware of their behaviour in terms of the ego state they utilize in various interactions with others as well as the kind of interactional patterns they prefer. This is done in such a way that group members examine their pasts, their current ego states, scripts, games, and so forth.

Systematic human relations training is closely related to T-groups, but differs in placing much greater emphasis on specific skill development. It is largely based on the work of Carkhuff, who, expanding on Rogers's work regarding the conditions for therapeutic success, developed a systematic model for training people in various interpersonal skills. Gazda and Egan have translated the Carkhuff model to the group experience in such a way that group members are able through experiential learning to develop these skills. Some of the same psychological conditions that exist in the T-group—a small group, feedback the encouragement of experimentation, psychological safety, and here-and-now focus—are provided so that individuals develop the kind of skills which will enable them to be more effective in their interaction with other persons and thus develop a more satisfying life experience for themselves.

Task-centered groups are those which focus on the successful development of a performance or product through collaborative efforts of the group members, while little effort is used in changing the various group members as individuals. Examples of such task groups would include committees, industrial work groups, conflict resolution groups, community interest groups, and various task forces. These groups are important, not because of the counselling experiences that are provided, but because the successful working of these groups depends on the kind of group dynamics that occur.

Behaviour-change groups are distinguished from other group approaches in that they specify desirable changes in the behaviour of each group member that are to occur as a result of the group experience. Generally, individuals who become part of such a group know in advance what the focus of the group will be and therefore why they are there.

While the focus is on the successful change in behaviour of the various members of the group, a major aspect of dynamic is support from other group members. Alcoholics Anonymous, Overeaters Anonymous, and Smoke Enders are examples of support groups which exist. Other groups may focus on the development of such specific behaviours as study habits, social interaction skills, and parenting skills.

Learning groups are those in which the focus is on the acquisition of specific information and knowledge, especially in terms of vocational and academic information. Such groups are typically more structured, with carefully defined goals and more explicit, generally accepted expectations of the group members. Although the focus is on learning specific information, the process involves a great deal of group interaction, with members of the group sharing feelings, attitudes, and values.

A group that is focused on developing job-seeking skills, in which participants learn how to find job leads, prepare a resume, prepare for an interview, and present themselves to the employer, will also focus on individuals discussing the kind of fears they have about the total experience. In addition, the members will be continually discussing the kind of internal forces that affect the type of jobs in which they are interested as well as the kind of jobs they will actually seek.

Other learning groups might include mid-life career change groups, career exploration groups, work adjustment groups, and various kinds of child-raising groups. One structured group that has received a great deal of attention is parent - effectiveness training, in which parents meet to learn better ways of relating to and managing their children. Group members learn definable skills, while participating in a process that includes group interaction and support.

Psychotherapy groups are usually made up of psychiatric patients who are hospitalized as a result of their difficulties and outpatients who have more severe emotional or psychological problems. Generally, therapy groups are aimed at reconstructing the personality, although many people who participate in group therapy do so in an attempt to alleviate specific symptoms or problems, such as depression, anxiety, psychosomatic disorders, eating disorders, chemical dependency, and sexual problems. In such groups, the focus is on identifying and correcting the emotional or psychological difficulties that impede the individual's functioning. Thus the goal may be a minor or a major change in the personality structure both depending on the nature of the difficulty of the individual and the specific theoretical orientation of the therapist. Psychotherapy groups tend to be of longer duration than the other kinds of groups that have been discussed.

By re-experiencing these situations and the accompanying feelings, the individuals are given the opportunity to resolve "unfinished business" and to express the kinds of intense feelings that have stayed below the surface for a long period of time.

As members become aware of and gain insight into their past, they are able to reconstruct a more healthy emotional attitude about themselves and those experiences and to eliminate the emotional blocking that has interfered with the group members' current functioning.

Many psychotherapy groups utilize psychoanalytic concepts and procedures, such as working with dreams, focusing on the earliest memories of the individual, trying to uncover the unconscious, and symbolically reliving, thus reconstructing, unhappy significant relationships. Other groups may utilize cognitive techniques, behavioural techniques, and other psychotherapeutic modalities to bring about therapeutic change. Many psychotherapy groups are made up of individuals who are relatively healthy and are not experiencing severe emotional or psychological problems.

These individuals participate in group therapy for many of the same reasons that others participate in growth and development groups; that is, to be part of an experience in which a safe climate is provided so that they can become healthier, more effective individuals who live more satisfying lives.

Guidance is concerned with presenting information in a way which will enable each individual student to find some personal meaning in what he has read, seen or heard.

It is not sufficient to present information to students, and to assume that they have all heard and understood the same thing, for each one reads personal meanings in what may be considered 'objective' facts. If we exclude group counselling, then group guidance becomes a set of activities used with a group of students to help each in his individual learning.

It is mainly a cognitive process with little attention given to feelings or emotions and is concerned with helping people to discuss the meaning of various kinds of information. The focus is on ideas, explanations, and verbal expression as an aid to a personal understanding of information or to the completion of a set task.

There are certain problems which are common to adolescents as part of the developmental processes of this age group, there are also certain kinds of educational, vocational and social information which can be of help to young people as they grow up. These may be presented in a group situation and discussed with the realization that their difficulties are not peculiar to them as individuals, as they often think, but are shared by fellow students.

There are essentially two types of information needed for intelligent decision-making: information regarding oneself as a person with assets and liabilities, talents and limitations; and information regarding the particular situation about which a decision is to be made, or to which the self is related. When a person has this information, he needs some way of dealing with it. There are various models of choice or decision-making used by people in making vocational or other choices, which vary according to the individual concerned and his circumstances.

The trait and factor model is based on the idea that any individual possesses a variety of traits and any occupation demands certain requirements of those who enter it.

The individual can match his traits with the occupational or educational requirements and determine which job or course he is best fitted for. This model is often used in vocational guidance in our schools and its main disadvantage is that it is too static and does not take into account the changing and developing nature of neither the student or the environment to which he must relate.

An individual using the economic model chooses an occupation or a college which will maximize his gain, minimize his loss; for example, going to college might be a means of achieving greater status and mobility. The gains achieved are not necessarily economic or financial but may consist of anything which is of value to the person concerned.

The individual using a social structure model of choice is restricted in the decisions he can make because his knowledge of the various opportunities available is limited by family, social and economic circumstances.

This is particularly so as disadvantaged students for whom narrowness of cultural or social class horizons places restrictions on their educational or vocational selection had often led to the equally narrow perspective of immediate gratification as the basis for choice.

A person may be forced into using the information processing model of choice when the facts necessary for him to make a decision are so overwhelming that he is pressured into a premature decision. Some students chose a particular college or job because their friends have done so, or because they are vaguely aware that a college has a particular college or job because their friends have done so, or because they are vaguely aware that a college has a particular reputation. This type of choice supports the individual's rationalization and reduces his anxiety.

The need reduction model is a comprehensive one which subsumes certain elements of the other models. It assumes that an individual has a self-concept and that he implements this picture of himself in his choice of course or occupation, by gravitating towards a career, or a course of study which he sees as compatible with his needs and interests. This may be a result of unconscious motivation, or a relatively rational conscious choice. This provides for change in the person's behaviour, environment and expectations between the individual and his environment. It suggests that making decisions about important areas of one's life is a complex and on-going process forming part of a developmental sequence extending from childhood through adulthood and not an isolated event at a particular point in time.

It is no good giving information to students who see no need for it. So motivation should precede instruction in group guidance. The presentation of information is only part of the process and must be followed by some feedback to ensure that it reached each student accurately

Whilst large groups offer an economical way of disseminating information, large group audiences tend to be passive listeners, or merely passive. We need to supplement this type of presentation by work in smaller groups and with individuals in which there is more opportunity for interaction and feedback.

Unless tutors in school have one period each day with their students the tutorial group is not an effective way of providing information on which to base choices, or of providing help in other areas. Tutors also need training in group work, and the support of a carefully planned, effectively led guidance programme.

Orientation usually takes the form of large group information giving, plus smaller orientation groups which continue throughout the year and are aimed at helping the students to develop independence. This applied at all levels of education not just at the school level. American studies indicated that three out of the four college students had difficulties with the "transition from the orderly, fairly directive secondary school to the non-directive environment of college. Some of the reasons given for these difficulties were irrealistic expectations of college, social and education life; an inability to organize their time; going to college without a strong desire to attend; and financial difficulties. Closed circuit television can be a medium for orientation purposes.

Guidance groups are concerned with effective knowledge

about the impact, of information and also about problems arising from some personal problems and difficulties. Affective discussion are always useful in this area, as they form a link between the purely intellectual discussion group and the counselling group with its emphasis on empathy. They need planning ad structuring, and some of the techniques for initiating affective discussion are role-playing, case-studies, role-models, literature and audio-visual media. Although the two concepts of group guidance and group counselling overlap to some extent in the area of affective discussion, group guidance tends to be more cognitively oriented and is usually used in an attempt to personalise information, whereas group counselling is used in an attempt to meet emotional needs and is often closer to group therapy and to group guidance.

There are two basic assumptions upon which a counsellor may choose to build her role. One is that it is the task of the counsellor to work with the group to encourage the students to be more self-sufficient and self-directed, so that the counsellor herself may then become another group member and the interaction of the group itself will provide any help which members need. An alternative assumption is that the counsellor works towards the development of the students' self-sufficiency, but because she considered that the group members are not always able to help each other she does not abdicate her special helping role.

There are six phases which are involved in group counselling:

1. rapport.
2. acceptance.
3. listening and observing.
4. promoting group and individual understanding.
5. problem solving skill development.
6. closing evaluation and procedures.

Whilst the counsellor's acceptance of all the group members and their problems is assumed in the nature of the role of the counsellor, as is the acceptance of the student in individual counselling, the creation of rapport and acceptance within and amongst the group members themselves, and between them and the counsellor, is a unique experience which differs from the one-to-one counselling relationship in its patterns of development.

Rapport involves the gradual building of an association of mutual respects and trust and it can be introduced by initial discussion of the group, whether the group should be 'open', so that members may leave when they wish or new members may be brought into the group as it proceeds, or whether it could be 'closed'[1], retaining its initial membership for a specified period of time.

Questions directed at the counsellor can be referred to the group for discussion and decision by means of a counsellor response such as 'What does the group feel about this?' If multiple counselling is being done, the role and function of the co-counsellor may be discussed. The structuring of the group by the counsellor in the early stages may also help in the growth of rapport. Structuring should be brief and should focus attention on the particular goals of the group, which may be self appraisal, to encourage the free expression of feelings by group members to each other and to the counsellor, and the avoidance of purely intellectual discussion. The limits of the group may be expressed, for example, in terms of the permitting of verbal but not physical expression of hostile feelings. The emphasis of the observance by all group members and the counsellor of confidentiality about the proceedings of the group is also a part of structuring which can help to bring about trust.

Initial resistance is a natural phenomenon of groups and the creation of an accepting climate is a gradual process which the counsellor tries to encourage by her own acceptance of each student's feelings and his expression of them. From the counsellor, the students learn to accept and help one another.

Listening and observing actively and intensely are two of the essential skills of the counsellor, and a group situation gives an added complexity to the use of these in order to promote both group and individual understanding. The counsellor's task is more complicated in group counselling. He not only has to understand the speaker's feelings and help him become aware of them, but he must also observe how the speaker's comments influence the group members.

The counsellor must not only be aware of the discussion, he must be perceptive of the interplay of relationships among the members. The counselling group can make little significant progress in developing the skills for solving problems until the initial stages of rapport, acceptance, understanding and insight have been established. It may be that the process of group counselling itself will uncover more problems that it actually solves, but if it is effective it also helps to bring about the attitudes and draws out the resources which will enable students to work at these problems themselves once they have been brought to conscious awareness. Alternatively, it may lead them to seek individual counselling help for these.

Different Groups

There are a number of group models appropriate for a wide variety of situations.

Guidance/psycho-educational groups. These groups are preventive and educational. Their purpose is to teach group participants how to deal with a potential threat (such as AIDS), a developmental life event (such as growing older), or an immediate life crisis (such as the death of a loved one). These types of groups are often found in educational settings. One of the most important parts of the process in such groups revolves around group discussions of how members will personalize the information presented in the group context. In school settings, instructional materials such as unfinished stories, puppet plays, films, audio interviews, and guest speakers are employed in guidance/ psycho-educational groups. In adult settings, other age-appropriate means are used.

Counselling/interpersonal problem-solving groups. These groups "seek to help group participants to resolve the usual, yet often difficult, problems of living through interpersonal support and problem solving. An additional goal is to help participants to develop their existing interpersonal problem-solving competencies so they may be better able to handle future problems. Non-severe career, educational, personal, social, and developmental concerns are frequently addressed".

Gazda distinguishes group counselling from group guidance in the following ways:

- Group counselling is recommended for individuals who are having temporary or continuing problems, whereas group guidance is recommended on a regular basis as a personal educational measure.
- Group counselling is more direct than group guidance in attempting to modify attitudes and behaviours. For instance, group counselling stresses the affective involvement of participants, whereas group guidance concentrates more on the cognitive understanding of its members.
- Group counselling is conducted in a small, intimate setting, whereas group guidance is more applicable to classroom-size environments.

These groups are set up to help individual group members remediate in-depth psychological problems. "Because the depth and extent of the psychological disturbance is significant, the goal is to aid each individual to reconstruct major personality dimensions". Group psychotherapy often takes place in inpatient facilities, such as hospitals or mental health facilities, because greater control may be necessary for the people involved. Certain types of individuals are poor candidates for outpatient, intensive group psychotherapy. Among them are depressives, incessant talkers, paranoids, schizoid and sociopathic personalities, suicidals, and extreme narcissists.

It may be easier to identify group psychotherapy candidates who should be excluded than choose those who should be included. Regardless, group psychotherapy is an American form of treatment and has provided much of the rationale for group counselling. The relationships among group guidance, group counselling, and group psychotherapy.

Groups at Work

Task/work groups help members apply the principles and processes of group dynamics to improve practices and accomplish identified work goals.

The task/work group specialist is able to assist groups such as task forces, committees, planning groups, community organizations, discussion groups, study circles, learning groups, and other similar groups to correct or develop their functions.

Several traditional and historical groups belong in one of the four categories of speciality groups just described. Some of these groups, however, do not fit into any category well. Furthermore, all these types of groups developed before groups were classified as they are today. T-groups and encounter groups are seldom conducted in their original forms any more but are important because of their contributions to the field of group work. Psychodrama, group marathons, and support/self-help groups continue to be used in their traditional ways and are important therapeutically

T-groups. The first T-group (the T stands for training) was conducted at the National Training Laboratories (NTL) in Bethel, Maine, in 1947. These groups appeared at a time when neither group counselling nor group psychotherapy was popular. Kurt Lewin's ideas about group dynamics formed the basis for the original groups. Since that time, T-groups have evolved from a focus on task accomplishment to a primary emphasis on interpersonal relationships.

It is difficult to classify T-groups in just one way. Members of such groups are likely to leam from the experience how one's behaviour in a group influences others' behaviour and vice versa. In this respect, T-groups are similar to forms of family counselling in which the emphasis is on both how the system operates and how an individual within the system functions.

Encounter groups. According to Lynn and Frauman, encounter groups emerged from T-groups in an attempt to focus on the growth of individual group members rather than the group itself. Encounter groups are intended for "normally functioning" people who want to "grow, change, and develop". These groups took many forms in their heyday, from the minimally structured groups of Carl Rogers to the highly structured, open-ended groups of William Schutz.

Group marathon. A group marathon is an extended, one-session group experience that breaks down defensive barriers that individuals may otherwise use. The concept was pioneered by Frederick Stoller and George Bach in the 1960s. Group marathons have-been used successfully in working with substance abusers in rehabilitation programs and normally functioning individuals in group counselling settings.

Self-help/support groups. Since the 1970s, self-help and support groups has counsellors grown in prominence. A self-help group usually develops spontaneously, centers on a single topic, and is led by a layperson with little formal group training but with experience in the stressful event that brought the group together. For example, residents in a neighbourhood may meet to help each other make repairs and clean up after a natural disaster, or they may assemble to focus government attention on an issue, such as toxic waste, that directly affects the quality of their lives.

Self-help groups can be either short or long-term, but they basically work to help their members gain greater control of their lives. Yalom reports that over 10 million people were involved in approximately 500,000 such groups in 1980 and the number continues to increase. A support group is similar to a self-help group in its focus on a particular concern or problem, but it is organized by an established professional helping organisation or individual. Some support groups charge fees; others do not. The involvement of lay people as group leaders varies. Like self-help groups, support groups center around topics that are physical, emotional, or social.

Self-help and support groups partly fill the needs of populations that can best be served in group formats and that might otherwise not receive services. They meet in churches, recreation centers, schools, and other community buildings as well as in mental health facilities.

Theoretical approaches to counselling in groups vary as much as individual counselling approaches. In many cases, the theories are the same. For instance, within group work, there are approaches based on psycho-analytic, Gestalt, person-centered, rational-emotive, transactional analysis, and behavioural theories. Because the basic positions of these theories are examined elsewhere in this text, they will not be reviewed here. In an evaluation of seven major theoretical approaches to groups, Ward analyses the degree to which each approach pays attention to the individual, interpersonal, and group levels of the process. For instance, the psychoanalytic, Gestalt, and behavioural approaches are strong in focusing on the individual but weak on the other two components of the group process. On the other hand, the Rogerian approach is strong on the individual level and medium on the interpersonal and group level. Ward points out the limiting aspects of each approach and the importance of considering other factors, such as the group task and membership maturity, in conducting comprehensive group assignments.

Group leaders and potential group members must know how theories differ in order to make wise choices. Overall, multiple theoretical models provide richness and diversity for conducting groups. Three factors, in addition to the ones already mentioned, are useful for group leaders to consider when deciding on what approach to take:

1. Do you need a theoretical base for conducting the group?
2. What uses will the theory best serve?
3. What criteria will be employed in the selection process?

A theory is a lot like a map. In a group, it provides direction and guidance in examining basic assumptions about human beings. It is also useful in determining goals for the group, clarifying one's role and functions as a leader, and explaining the group interactions.

Finally, a theory can help in evaluating the outcomes of the group. Trying to lead a group without an explicit theoretical rationale is similar to attempting to fly an aeroplane without a map and knowledge of instruments. Either procedure is foolish, dangerous, and likely to lead to injury. A good theory also serves practical functions. For example, it gives meaning to and a framework for experiences and facts that occur within a setting. Good theory helps make logical sense out of what is happening and leads to productive research. With so many theories from which to choose, the potential group leader is wise to be careful in selecting an approach.

Groups, like other living systems, go through stages. If an individual or group leader is not aware of these stages, the changes that occur within the group may appear confusing rather than meaningful and the benefits may be few. Leaders can maximize learning by either setting up conditions that facilitate the development of the group or "using developmentally based interventions, at both individual and group levels". In either case, group members and leaders benefit.

There is debate in the professional literature about what and when groups go through stages. Developmental stages have been identified in various types of groups, such as learning groups and training groups, yet much of the debate about stages centers around group counselling. Group counselling is most often broken into four or five stages, but there are models for as few as three stages and as many as six. Tuckman's stage model is considered mainstream. Tuckman was one of the first theorists to design a stage process for group counselling. He believed there were four stages of group development: forming, storming, norming, and performing. This concept was later expanded to include a fifth stage: adjourning mourning/morning.

In each stage certain tasks are performed. For example, in the forming stage, the foundation is usually laid down for what is to come and who will be considered in or out of group deliberations. In this stage, members express anxiety and dependency and talk about nonproblematic issues. One way to ease the transition into the group at this stage is to structure it so that members arc relaxed and sure of what is expected of them. For example, before the first meeting, members may be told they will be expected to spend three minutes telling others who they are. In the second stage, storming, there is usually considerable turmoil and conflict, as in adolescence. Group members seek to establish themselves in the hierarchy of the group and deal successfully with issues concerning anxiety, power, and future expectations. Sometimes the group leader is attacked at this stage.

The third stage, norming, is similar to young adulthood, where "having survived the storm the group often generates enthusiasm and cohesion. Goals and ways of working together are decided on". This stage is sometimes combined with the storming stage and leads to performing, which parallels adulthood in a developmental sense.

At this stage, the group members become involved with each other and with their individual and collective goals. This is the time when the group, if it works well; is productive. Finally, in the adjourning or mourning/morning stage, the group comes to an end, and members say good-bye to one another and the group experience. In this death stage, members feel either fulfilled or bitter. There is often a celebration experience at this point of the group or at least a closure ceremony. One of the easiest ways to conceptualise groups, regardless of the type being led, is through the four-stage group model: forming, norming, working, and terminating.

Overall, the developmental stages of a group are not readily differentiated, group does not necessarily move step by step through life stages, but may move backward and forward as a part of its general development". It is necessary that a group have at least a beginning, a middle, and a closing. After that, the question of what stage a group and where it is heading can best be answered through retrospection or insightful perception.

There are a number of issues involved in conducting successful groups. Some deal with producers for running groups; others deal with training and ethics.

Screening and preparation are essential for conducting a successful group. Some individuals who wish to be members of groups are not appropriates for them. If such persons are allowed to join a group, they may end up being difficult group members and cause the group leader considerable trouble. Or they may join with others who are at an equally low level of functioning and contribute to the regression of the group. When this happens, members become psychologically damaged, and the group is unable to accomplish its goals.

There are distinguishing qualities of effective and ineffective group leaders, instance, group leaders who are authoritarian, aggressive, confrontational, or emotionally removed from the group are ineffective and produce group casualties. On the other hand, four leadership qualities have a positive effect on the outcome of groups, if they are not used excessively:

Caring the more, the better

- Meaning attribution: Includes clarifying, explaining, and providing a cognitive framework for change
- Emotional stimulation: Includes activity, challenging, risk taking, self-disclosure
- Executive function: Includes developing norms, structuring, and suggesting procedures

It is vital that group leaders find a position between the two extremes of emotional stimulation and executive function for the well-being of the group. Leaders should not allow members to experience so much emotion that they are unable to process the material being discovered in the group nor structure the situation so rigidly that no emotion is expressed.

Effective leaders understand the forces operating within a group, recognize whether these forces are therapeutic, and, if they are not, take steps to better manage the group with the assistance of its members. His assessment of leadership complements that of Yalom's and Osborne's, who believe that good group leaders behave with intentionality because they are able to anticipate where the group process is moving and recognize group needs. An example of this phenomenon is the ability of group leaders to treat the group homogeneously when there is a need to manage group tensions and protect members and to emphasize heterogeneous qualities when the group has become too comfortable and is not working.

Effective group leaders are committed "to the never-ending struggle" to become effective as human beings. He lists a number of personal qualities that are "vitally related to effective group leadership". Among them are presence, personal power, courage, willingness to confront oneself, sincerity, authenticity, enthusiasm, sense of identity, and inventiveness/ creativity.

A group approach to counselling individuals is a well-established mode of treatment. At the same time, the question of what it is about the group approach that makes group counselling effective is poorly understood. One part of the difficulty in answering the question results from the fact that any kind of therapeutic change is an enormously complex process and occurs through a multiple interplay of various experiences. Since this process is as complex as it is, efforts have been made to identify the crucial aspects of the group experience which are most important in promoting therapeutic change. One of the difficulties, however, in studying the literature related to group counselling results from a wide assortment of theories seeking to explain the therapeutic process. Likewise, empirical research sometimes tends to complicate the picture even further, since the research findings are often inconsistent and the quality of the research varies considerably.

One approach to the problem involves the overall concept of therapeutic elements. Researchers such as Frank, Truax and Carkhuff, and Berenson have sought to identify and validate that certain elements are consistently related to effective individual counselling. However, there have been only limited efforts made to discover those same kinds of consistent, basic elements in group counselling that constitute the therapeutic process, no matter what theoretical model is being applied. Such research would not only provide a more solid scientific footing for group counselling, but would also enable the group leader to integrate into his or her counselling process those factors that have been shown to be most important in therapeutic change.

It is reasonable to believe that the more skillful the group leader is in utilizing therapeutic elements, the more effective the therapy process will be. The focus, in this chapter is on those therapeutic elements, which have been tentatively identified. These elements were originally proposed as the result of the group experiences that various individuals encountered. In some cases, such elements are included because the observations made were done in a systematic, although not empirical, manner. Where empirical research is available to demonstrate the relationship of a particular therapeutic element to outcome, such research will be briefly summarized. Part of the difficulty in identifying those therapeutic elements results from a tendency among group theorists to use different language and different ideologies to describe the same phenomenon. Successful group leaders frequently attribute their success to the use of certain techniques or strategies. While these techniques and strategies may be extremely important in facilitating the group movement, an analysis of therapeutic elements must go beyond these specific strategies and look at the broader concept of what is happening within the group when such strategies are utilized. The concept of a therapeutic element is based on the assumption that the group process involves a specific set of elements that can be differentiated from one another as to their exerting specific effects on members of the group, thus facilitating change. These elements, while inherently therapeutic, may be misused by the group leader either because the leader lacks appropriate skill or because a group member is unable to accept that kind of therapeutic factor.

With this in mind, a definition of therapeutic element can be proposed. The definition that we are using is that proposed by Bloch. Bloch defines a therapeutic factor as "an element occurring in group therapy that contributes to improvement in a patient's condition and is a function of the actions of the group therapist, the patient, or fellow group members". This definition takes into account the fact that the means by which therapeutic elements are important varies considerably. The definition also helps to distinguish between therapeutic elements and two other aspects of the group process which are closely related: conditions for change, and techniques. Conditions for change are important in the operation of therapeutic elements, but do not in themselves have therapeutic force. For instance, self-disclosure requires listeners, and the actual presence of several individuals to hear that self-disclosure increases its therapeutic effect. Similarly, a technique does not have direct therapeutic effect but is simply a strategy available to the group leader to increase the effectiveness of a therapeutic element. While therapeutic elements, conditions for change, and techniques can be isolated, they often overlap and are interdependent with one another.

Corsini and Rosenberg published the first major effort to produce a unifying classification of those therapeutic elements shared by group counsellors of various theoretical persuasions. Basically, Corsini and Rosenberg conducted a "factor analysis" ' abstracting the therapeutic factors identified in 300 pre-1955 gro , counselling articles from which they identified 220 statements reflecting therapeutic factors. They then reduced those to 166 by combining identical statements and then, through a set of hypotheses suggested by a study of those statements, clustered them into nine major categories. Those nine categories formed a classification system for identifying therapeutic factors in grou counselling. These categories are:

1. *Acceptance:* A sense of belonging
2. *Altruism:* A sense of being helpful to others
3. *Universalization:* The realization that one is not unique in one's problems
4. *Intellectualization:* The process of acquiring knowled about oneself
5. *Reality Testing:* The recognition of the reality of such issues as defenses and family conflicts
6. *Transference:* A strong attachment either to therapist or to co-members
7. *Interaction:* Relating within the group that brings benef
8. *Spectator Therapy:* Gaining from the observation ar imitation of fellow patients
9. *Ventilation:* The release of feelings and expression previously repressed ideas

Hill attempted to take the classification further; he interviewed nineteen group therapists and proposed six therapeutic factors: catharsis, feelings of belongingness, spectator therapy, insight, peer agency (universality), and socialization. The next classification, produced by Berzon, Piovs, and Parson used group members rather than leaders as the source of information for determining the essential therapeutic elements. Berzon studied eighteen members of two outpatient, time-limited therapy groups which met for fifteen sessions. After each meeting the patients filled out a questionnaire in which they described that incident which was most important to them. As a result, 279 incidents were obtained. Judges then sorted those incidents into nine categories in order of frequency. The resulting nine categories closely resembled those of Corsini and Rosenberg and included:

1. Increased awareness of emotional dynamics
2. Recognizing similarity to others
3. Feeling positive regard, acceptance, sympathy for others
4. Seeing self as seen by others
5. Expressing self congruently, articulately, or assertively in the group
6. Witnessing honesty, courage, openness, or expressions of emotionality in others
7. Feeling responded to by others
8. Feeling warmth and closeness generally in the group
9. Ventilating emotions

The main therapeutic mechanisms were reported to result from the interaction among group members with few of the reports involving the group leader. To a large extent, the major focus was on the interpersonal feedback which group members received, enabling them to modify their self-image and to validate the universality of problems. Ohlsen proposed a somewhat different set of therapeutic forces which were based on a series of research conclusions that he summarized.

Yalom proposed his landmark classification of curative factors. Based primarily on a series of research studies which Yalom and his colleagues performed, Yalom emphasized an interactional dimension to the group process and, in particular, highlighted the interaction taking place among the group members themselves. He proposed the term "interpersonal learning" as a major curative factor which had two components: input, chiefly through feedback; and output, an actual process whereby the group member attempts to develop more effective modes of relating to others.

Yalom also included three new therapeutic factors that had not been earlier proposed: the installation of hope (the member feels optimistic about change as a result of observing progress in others); guidance (the member receives advice from the group leader or from fellow group members); and an existential factor (the member becomes aware that one alone is responsible for the way one lives one's life). Yalom's list of curative factors then included:

1. Installation of hope
2. Universality
3. Imparting of information altruism
4. The corrective recapitalization of the primary family group
5. Development of socializing techniques
6. Imitative behaviour
7. Interpersonal learning
8. Group cohesiveness
9. Catharsis
10. Existential factors

Bloch, Reibstein, and Crouch have sought to exploit the assets of the aforementioned classifications while avoiding the limitations they believed to exist. Their ten-factor classification resembled Yalom's classification but with certain modifications. For instance, they omitted Yalom's existential factor because they believed it did not correspond to their definition of a therapeutic factor; that is, it was not an element of the group process that exerts a beneficial effect. They suggested that the existential factor instead calls for the group member to think about life in a specific way along lines laid down by a particular theory and is therefore better conceptualized as a therapeutic goal. They also omitted family reenactment, since they felt this assumes that the group member should identify a specific cause of his or her difficulties—unresolved family conflict.

At the same time, they proposed a new factor of self-understanding which was all-embracing in quality in the sense that it was based on the members learning about some important aspect of the self. They also made a distinction between two forms of expression: self-disclosure, the members revelation of highly personal information reflecting honesty and openness; and catharsis, the members release of intense feelings, bringing about a sense of relief. Their final difference from Yalom's was one of emphasis and concerned interaction. Bloch and his colleagues saw interaction as an attempt by the member "to relate constructively and adaptively within the group either by initiating a pattern of behaviour or by responding to other group members".

In an attempt to build on the work of those individual, whose work we have just summarized, as well as others who have made significant contributions to our understanding of group counselling, we propose a somewhat simpler model for identifying those therapeutic elements which are necessary and sufficient for effective group counselling. Like some of the others who have preceded us, we are basing our ideas concerning therapeutic effectiveness elements on the research that we have reviewed, the conceptual ideas that others have presented, and our own experience in leading various kinds of groups. From our viewpoint, then, the essential elements that contribute to therapeutic effectiveness in group counselling include the following:

1. Installation of hope
2. Sense of safety and support
3. Cohesiveness
4. Universality

5. Vicarious learning
6. Interpersonal learning

Installation of hope is a therapeutic element through which the group member gains a sense of optimism about his or her progress or potential for progress through actual counselling experience. Although the concept has been emphasized by a number of theoreticians over the years, it has been virtually neglected by those individuals doing empirical research in group counselling. As Frank, Hoehn-Saric, and Imber have suggested – that hope may act as a placebo factor in psychotherapy generally – it is possible that the installation of hope in a group setting is even more of a placebo effect than in individual therapy since the potential sources of a group member's hope includes all of his or her peers.

If future research can somehow prove this placebo effect to be true, the installation of hope will still be an important element since, whether placebo or not, group leaders are only concerned about what it is that helps to bring about therapeutic change among the group members. Certainly, the installation and maintenance of hope is crucial, since hope is required to keep the member in the group so that other therapeutic factors can take effect. When the individual remains within the group, other "hope-installing" factors can take place. For instance, other members of the group will have often suffered from some of the same concerns as the individual group member.

Such individuals who have had similar problems and have coped with those problems effectively provide hope for others that their own concerns and problems can be resolved. Effective group leaders frequently exploit this factor by calling attention to the improvement that group members have made. Likewise, if the group members are to possess a sense of hope about the group counselling experience, it is important that the group leader believe in himself and in the efficacy of the group. The belief that the group leader is able to help every member who commits himself to counselling and remains with the group for an appropriate period of time is important for the group leader; sharing this belief with each group member can be an important part of increasing that member's optimism about his group experience.

One of the great strengths of such support groups as Alcoholics Anonymous, Overeaters Anonymous, and Synanon is the fact that the leaders are almost always individuals who have suffered from the same disorders as the current members. These leaders then become living inspirations to the new members, who are able to believe that because the leader was able to overcome his or her problems they will be able to do so also.

A major part of the meetings of these groups is dedicated to testimonials from not only the group leader but from the various members of the group. These testimonials are of major importance in the effectiveness of these groups. Corey and Corey point out that hope is a belief that change is possible, that "one is not a victim of the past and that new decisions can be made". Such hope comes not only from a sense of identification with other individuals who have solved similar problems, but also emerges from the recognition that one has untapped reserves of spontaneity, creativity, courage, and strength. As individuals recognize and accept that they have the internal resources necessary to direct the course of their lives, their sense of hope greatly increases.

Because individuals enter group counselling with the hope that it will be helpful to them, it is important that the group leader build on that hope so it will block or destroy concurrent feelings of these group members that "maybe nothing can help." One way of maintaining this hope is to develop clear-cut expectations of what will be expected from each member. The more members understand and adopt those expectations—to discuss their problems openly, to work toward specific behaviour change, and, when necessary, to confront other group members toward implementing new behaviours—the more those group members will increase their feelings of power and optimism about changing their own lives.

The need to feel reasonably secure within the counselling group—where individuals can be themselves, give up their facades, discuss their problems openly, accept other persons' frank reactions to them, and express considerately their own genuine feelings toward others—is a need that is clearly essential to a therapeutic experience within group counselling. Part of this sense of safety and security results from a feeling of genuine acceptance by other group members. This group acceptance not only enhances self-esteem, but provides quality support for various changes in behaviour which the individual wishes to attempt. Such acceptance ordinarily involves the affirmation of the individual's right to have his or her own feelings and values and to express them. It also comes from demonstrated caring. This caring is sensed when individuals believe that others are listening to them and have an involvement with their concerns. When group members are able to sense that their concerns are important to others and that they are valued as persons, they are more likely to risk the kinds of changes in their lives that will be therapeutic in the long run. Risking involves opening oneself to others and actively doing those things in the group experience that are necessary for change. As such, this kind of riskiness results in the person's feeling vulnerable to rejection. Perhaps the key word is trust. A sense of safety and support within the group can come only after the individual feels a large level of trust in the group. As Johnson and Johnson have pointed out, trust is a necessary condition for effective communication. They go on to add, "the higher the trust, the more stable the cooperation and the more effective the communication. A group member will more openly express his thoughts, feelings, reactions, opinions, information, and ideas when the trust level is high".

When group members trust the group and feel this sense of safety and support, two particularly important behaviours or effects are likely to occur: self-disclosure and catharsis.

A number of studies indicate that successful group members self-disclose. Self-disclosure has two major effects: (a) a member is able to receive understanding and acceptance from the other group members that will let that member know that he is okay as a person and (b) group members discover that their fellow members whom they may admire have problems as difficult as their own and that they are not giving up. The effect of universality, which will be discussed later, can begin to take effect.

Catharsis—the release of strong feelings, bringing relief—can be therapeutic in that energy is released that has been tied up in withholding certain threatening feelings. Catharsis often permits an individual to realize that negative and positive feelings toward another person or situation may coexist. The relief that results from the individual's knowledge that other people now know about these intense feelings and the situations that brought them about is a major step in that individual's feeling understood and accepted. Although catharsis has been emphasized by a number of individuals, it has received little attention by those who do empirical research on group counselling variables. One reason for this may be the intrinsic nature of catharsis and the difficulty of measuring its impact. Another reason may be a feeling that catharsis by itself has little value; only when catharsis is complemented by subsequent cognitive reflection does it result in individual growth.

The Lieberman, Yalom, and Miles study is the major study which has attempted to clarify the value of catharsis per se. These researchers asked 210 Members of a thirty-hour encounter group to describe the most significant incident that occurred during the course of the group.

While experiencing and expressing feelings was frequently selected, this critical incident was not related to positive outcome. Incidents of catharsis were as likely to be selected by group members who showed little change as by those who showed good. They point out that "catharsis was not unrelated to income; it was necessary but, in itself, not sufficient". They believed that their study showed that individuals who had profited most from their group experience showed a profile of catharsis plus some form of cognitive learning. Thus, the open expression of feelings is without question, vital to the group therapeutic process. In its absence, the group would flounder in a sterile nonmeaningful exercise. Rather, catharsis is intricately related to cohesiveness and provides the kind of bonding that enables the group to work honestly in the therapeutic change of its members.

Although Corsini and Rosenberg, as well as each of the other theorists summarized in this chapter, included the concept of cohesiveness in their classification of therapeutic elements, its precise definition remains elusive. Although acceptance is an element of the sense of safety and support, described earlier, we are including it in this section as part of an individual's feeling that he or she belongs and is part of a particular therapeutic group. This sense of togetherness, which we have labelled group cohesiveness, involves many aspects, including allegiance, agreement with the group's objectives, and attraction to the group leader as well as to peers.

Corey and Corey point out that a group is characterized by a high degree of togetherness, at times, providing an environment in which "participants feel free to share problems, try new behaviours, and in other ways reveal the many dimensions of themselves". From a practical standpoint, cohesiveness is important because it has an impact on the attendance of individuals at group sessions as well as their involvement. Thus, when a group feels a sense of cohesiveness, they are more likely to take those actions which result in therapeutic change. A number of research studies have been performed which support the idea that cohesiveness is an important element within group counselling. Dickoff and Lakin, for instance, in a study of former group psychotherapy patients, found that the patients believed that group cohesiveness was of major therapeutic value. They found that over half of those former patients indicated that the primary help they had received in group therapy was the result of mutual support.

Also, those patients who perceived their group as cohesive attended more sessions, experienced more social contact with other members, and judged their group as having been therapeutic. Likewise, a positive association was found by Kapp, Glaser, in their study of long-term members of discussion and therapy groups. In this study, members rated their own level of change as well as the degree of cohesiveness they perceived in the group. Kapp and his colleagues concluded that cohesiveness may be important in bringing about change.

However, a study by Yalom, Houts, and Zimerberg indicating that patients perceived cohesiveness as positively relating to self-ratings of change, also showed that there was no relationship between the degree of cohesiveness perceived by patients and independent judgments of therapeutic outcome. In 1977, Jones studied 130 patients who responded to questionnaires at a student mental-health service. These patients had attended one of tinny therapy groups offered at the service, consisting of twenty two-hour sessions over a five-month period. The respondents stated that the most positive aspects of their group experience was the feeling of security and acceptance they had experienced in the group.

Jones concluded that the amount of cohesiveness was positively related to the degree of self-reported improvement; that is, that those groups that received high cohesion scores from its members were more likely to have a higher number of patients who improved during the course of therapy.

Yalom summarized a large segment of the research that has been done in laboratory, related to group cohesiveness. He concluded that the overall evidence from this research demonstrates that the members of a cohesive group, in contrast to the members of a noncohesive group, will:

1. Try harder to influence other group members;
2. Be more open to influence by the other members;
3. Be more willing to listen to others and more accepting of others;
4. Experience greater security and relief from tension in the group;
5. Participate more readily in meetings;
6. Self-disclose more;
7. Protect the group norms and, for example, exert more pressure on individuals deviating from the norms;
8. Be less susceptible to disruption as a group when a member terminates membership.

Two factors that may contribute to the importance of cohesiveness as part of the therapeutic process are intimacy and empathy. As people experience closeness in a group, an intimacy develops creating a stronger sense of trust in others. Individuals may become aware, as a result of this new sense of closeness to others, of the barriers in their outside lives that have prevented intimacy. Empathy may also be a part of cohesiveness, since a true sense of empathy involves a deep understanding of the struggles of another individual. In the group setting, commonalities among the individuals emerge that unite them, forming a cohesive bond. The feeling that one is alone lessens with the realization that certain problems—such as fear of rejection, fear of intimacy, loneliness, or fear of getting hurt resulting from previous experiences—are universal. We have also chosen to include, under the umbrella of cohesiveness, the concept of altruism, which various theorists have proposed as a separate therapeutic factor. In a cohesive group, the individual is more likely to become part of the therapeutic process of offering help to other group members.

As a result, the individual is more likely to engage in those activities that will enable him or her to benefit from the realization that he or she can be of value to his or her peers. This results in the realization that, in counselling groups, members receive through giving, not only as part of the reciprocal giving-receiving sequence, but also from the very intrinsic act of giving. Such giving undermines the sense of being demoralized and of having nothing of value to offer others. Thus for the group member, it is a refreshing, self-esteem-boosting experience to find that they can be of importance to others. Even more important, group members are enormously helpful to one another in the group process itself. By offering support, reassurance, suggestions, insight, and understanding, they provide spontaneous, truthful reactions and feedback, permitting other members to gain insight into how they relate to others.

Carkhuff pointed out this importance of altruism in the therapeutic process in his comments regarding training as a preferred mode of treatment. His basic concept was that by training individuals to help others, those individuals would receive the greatest degree of help themselves. Perhaps the major reason why this occurs was pointed out by Frank when he suggested that it is only when we as individuals have transcended ourselves, when we have forgotten ourselves in an absorption in someone or something outside of ourselves, that we obtain self-actualization and meaning in life.

Another key element in the therapeutic process of group counselling is that of universality, the sense that one is not unique in one's problems—that others share these problems. Since many clients enter a group setting with some reluctance because they believe that their problems are unique to themselves and have little relationship to the kinds of problems that other people experience the positive impact that occurs whenever those individuals learn that others do have concerns similar to their own is enormous.

A sense of relief often results as these clients hear the self-disclosure of other group members, and a growing insight into the nature of their own problems results. Yalom reports that clients often indicate that they feel more in touch with the world and see this process of commonality with other group members as one of a "welcome to the human race" experience. As trainers of counsellors, we have often had our counsellors in training practice an empathy exercise in which each member of the training group would write a secret that he or she would be highly unlikely to share with the rest of the group,

After the secrets have been written, they are collected and redistributed, with each member receiving a secret other than his or her own to share with the group. The individual then reads someone else's secret and tries to describe the way he or she believes the other person feels with a secret such as that. Over the years, we have learned that one of more positive outcomes has been that those who had shared the secrets in the first place discover that their secrets were not devastating to the other group members, but were accepted. In addition, the pattern over the years of those secrets seems to indicate that the kinds of issues which create the major problems for most of us have a great deal in common. Yalom reports having utilized a similar technique and finding that the most common secret revealed was that of basic inadequacy, followed by a sense of interpersonal alienation. Thus, as members of the group learn the kinds of feelings, thoughts, and concerns which have disturbed them and made them feel as if they were somehow less than other individuals, they begin to feel a sense of commonality with other people and to lose the sense that something is wrong with them.

Like several other of the therapeutic elements, universality has had little research that demonstrated its importance to group counselling. There has been a growing theoretical interest in it as a concept, especially in the study of self-help groups. Lieberman suggests that universality is a major feature of the self-help group in providing a supportive effect on the group's members. At about the same time, Robinson highlighted another dimension: The value of universality as a means of reducing a sense of stigma, so commonly associated with emotional, mental problems.

Vicarious learning has been called different things by different theorists. From the very beginning, it has been recognized as an important element of group counselling. Corsini and Rosenberg spoke of spectator therapy, " which they described as gaining from the observation and imitation of fellow patients.

George and Cristiani point out that while clients in groups are focusing on resolving their own interpersonal or intrapersonal difficulties, they are also exposed to interpersonal relationship skills being modelled by both the group leader and the other group members. In a previous work, we reviewed some of the research that had been done on the effects of imitative learning as part of the group process. Modelling can be deliberately used in group counselling sessions as a means of demonstrating desirable behaviour before group members try out the new behaviour with the group providing feedback. Bandura, Ross, and Ross have been leaders in the emphasis on social learning as a major therapeutic technique. They demonstrated the power of imitation by successfully treating a large number of individuals with snake phobias by asking them to observe their therapist handle a snake.

Jeske has conducted one of the most important studies of vicarious learning in group counselling. Jeske had each group member who was participating in short-term counselling press a button whenever that individual found himself or herself identifying with another group member. Those patients who showed the greatest improvement recorded twice the number of such identifications as did those who did not improve at all. Jeske concluded that the group leader should promote such intermember identification as a means of facilitating the therapeutic progress.

Although listed last in this set of therapeutic elements in group counselling, there is little doubt that interpersonal learning plays a major role in the course of group counselling. Several research projects have asked group members to evaluate those factors that have been most helpful to them during the group process. In eight major studies, six of them ranked interpersonal learning among the top three. Interpersonal learning was ranked among the top five in the other two studies. In personal growth groups, interpersonal learning is even more highly valued, ordinarily being ranked first by the members of the group.

Bloch points out that interpersonal learning has two components: input, chiefly through feedback; and output, an actual process whereby the group member attempts to develop more effective modes of relating to others. Certainly the attempt to relate constructively and adaptively within the group becomes an important aspect to many group counselling members as they attempt to develop new ways of interacting in a more satisfying manner with those around them. As gregarious persons who live our lives in a social setting, we are only able to develop self-esteem, a sense of satisfaction, and security from those social contacts that we make. Thus, as a group develops, individuals within the group begin to interact with one another in the same way they interact with others in their lives. Thus, the group becomes a laboratory in which is revealed maladaptive interpersonal behaviour and attitudes—arrogance, grandiosity, nonassertiveness, sexualization and overcompliance.

As individual group members receive feedback from the other members of the group, the individual learns the effects of his or her behaviour on others. When feedback is given honestly and with care, group members are able to understand more clearly the impact they have on others and to learn how often they create the kinds of reactions that they receive from other individuals. As a result, each group member can then decide what to do with this feedback. As group members become fully aware of the impact of their behaviour upon (a) the feelings of others, (b) the opinions that others have of them, and (c) the opinion they have of themselves, they become more aware of their own responsibility for what happens in their interpersonal worlds. Likewise, as each individual fully accepts personal responsibility for that interpersonal world, he or she can begin to struggle with the resulting implication that he or she is the only one thus able to alter that world.

In facilitating the interpersonal learning element of group counselling, the group leader must focus on the present the here-and-now of the group interaction. If each group member is to learn as much as possible about the effects of his or her interactions with the group leader and with the other members, the group focus must be upon the immediacy of the interactions occurring in the group.

In doing so, the group de-emphasizes the past as well as de-emphasizes the current outside life of each of the members. This does not mean that group counselling undermines the importance either of the past or of the current life situation. Rather, it places a focus on the power and efficiency of the interpersonal interactions that are occurring right now. Such an immediate experience involves both an affective and a cognitive component. That is, group members not only share important emotional experiences, but they also step outside of that emotional experience and examine, understand, and integrate the meaning of that experience they have just undergone. Thus, the most effective here-and-now focus consists of a rotating sequence of affect followed by cognition. To facilitate both components of the here-and-now requires that the group leader has two different sets of techniques. For the first stage—the stage of emotional experiencing—the leader needs a set of techniques that will plunge the individual, and the group, into an intense awareness of what each experiencing. This involves the use of the same kinds of techniques that counsellors use in individual therapy for helping clients get in touch with their current experiencing.

The group leader must be active and continually work toward the shifting of material from the outside to the inside, from the abstract to the specific, from the generic to the personal. In addition, the therapist is often able to encourage a focus on the here-and-now by genuine self-disclosure of his own experiencing. The second component of the here-and-now—the understanding and clarification of the emotional experience—requires a set of techniques that enables the group to transcend itself in order to examine, explain and interpret its own experience.

This demands reflection, explanation, and interpretation. This phase of group work is called "group process." It refers to what the content of a group discussion or of an individual's comments reveals about the nature of the relationship of the individuals involved in the discussion. In facilitating this cognitive stage of the here-and-now, the group leader must focus on process, listening to the group discussion with an ear toward examining how the words exchanged shed light on the relationships among the participating individuals.

To understand this process, the group leader needs to register all of the available data, both verbal and nonverbal. This includes such simple issues as choice of seats, attendance patterns, being on time, eye contact when talking, and socializing patterns after the group session. However, the most likely productive source of information concerning the group process comes from the group leader's own feelings. If, for example, the group leader feels impatient or discouraged or bored or frustrated, he or she must recognize this as important data about the working of the group and utilize this information to the group's advantage.

Catharsis, which involves the group member's release of intense feelings bringing about a sense of relief, can be an important process factor within several of the therapeutic elements. Even Yalom, who earlier had defined catharsis as a curative factor in group therapy, points out that catharsis is "intricately interwoven with other therapeutic factors". Certainly, strong expression of emotion is an important aspect of group counselling. It enhances the development of cohesiveness, by binding together members who express strong feelings toward one another. It often results in a sense of relief when the individual learns that his or her expression of intense feelings does not result in rejection by the other group members.

Likewise, we have not included as a therapeutic element what Yalom called 'imparting of information.' Again we believe that while imparting of information is important as part of the group experience, its function is to be part of various of the therapeutic elements. This aspect of group counselling can include information that is rather specific in its nature, for instance, information about various career issues that might be important to a career counselling group.

One other therapeutic element that occurs across the others and is, therefore, identified individually involves the use of humour in the group counselling process. Although humour can be a negative factor in group situations, especially when it consists of a pseudo-humour which is exercised at the expense of some person or subgroup, humour can become an important healing aspect of the group. There are some truly humorous dimensions of the human condition. When group leaders possess the ability to laugh at themselves and to see the humour in their own human frailties, the group becomes more likely to do so also. This humour is certainly not sarcasm, ridicule, or cynicism. Rather, spontaneous and natural laughter with one or more of the group members which can help establish an additional bond of genuine caring for each other and confidence in the helping nature of human rapport.

The use of humour may allow the group leader to deal with the group member's irrational ideas by taking those ideas to ridiculous extremes or reducing them to absurdity. When this is done, the members are able to see the ridicule of their own ideas, not a ridicule of themselves. Such humour, as long as it is not used to derail an important immediate dynamic to express anger or to conceal an individual's deep feelings, has curative value all by itself.

Ideas and Thoughts

As a means of understanding the results of counselling, we can examine what outcomes of successful group counselling have been hypothesised by proponents of selected theories. The selected theories are Gestalt, Adlerian, Personal Growth, and Cognitive-Behavioural. Each section is divided into goals of the individual member, interactional goals between members of the group, and overall group goals or group process goals.

Various Groups

Although Frederick Perls was not himself a group therapist, many students may have the impression that Perls was conducting group counselling sessions. Instead, Perl's workshops had only one purpose: to demonstrate his Gestalt techniques. Nevertheless, by examining the writings of other Gestalt writers, it is possible to piece together an approximation of what a Gestalt group counsellor might include as a list of expectations for a successful group.

Individual Goals. The major goal for a Gestalt group leader is to increase the self-awareness of each individual. This increased self-awareness is itself curative, according to Gestalt concepts. For the most part, all the goals which follow are either process goals to help increase the self-awareness or they are specific examples of increased awareness.

Additional transparency for each individual is a major goal. Melnick has described how individuals come to recognize and accept more and more aspects of themselves and how these individuals also become more willing to communicate formerly hidden or self-disguised aspects of themselves. An increase in responsibility for one's self is another goal. This frequently comes about through interactions with the group leader and with other group members and can be seen through an increase in their statements. An increased integration of individual conflicts and greater self-reliance are additional goals for the Gestalt approach. Within each individual, inherent conflicts become split into polarities. These polarities are extreme tendencies that individuals hold simultaneously. For example, as one wishes to be loved by a person, there is a tendency to wish to dominate the same person. The top dog-underdog polarity is a commonly used example of such conflict. Increased integration has been called "the overriding objective of Gestalt counselling". The split in self-image concepts is gradually reduced as individuals come to accept the divergent, often contradictory, aspects of these images of self. Gradually, roles are reduced or eliminated as the person incorporates the other goals listed above. This results in increased integration of the self.

Interpersonal goals. Members will perform more and more self-disclosure in a Gestalt group as it develops. Increased communication which is focused on the immediate is a goal of a Gestalt group. As individuals become more aware about self, they will increasingly give here-and-now reactions to the group leader and to other group members as well as communicate about themselves in a here-and-now fashion.

As individuals interact within a Gestalt group, they will invariably act out sibling rivalries and familial patterns. The interactions and the communications of conflict between group members will increase the self-understanding of each group member. Another goal of Gestalt counselling is to stimulate the investigation and exploration of polarities for each individual, mentioned earlier. Much of this exploration occurs as individuals compare and contrast themselves with other group members.

Group Process. Group process goals are centered on the climate which is most conducive to individual exploration and growth. A Gestalt group counsellor would be likely to stimulate group exploration of the group's structure and the group's process. As the group facilitator stimulates each member's self-exploration, the counselling group will also be involved in exploration and examination of the group itself. Just as the growth for individual members occurs through discovery, a group process goal is for the group to make discoveries about its own functioning.

Much of the writing in Adlerian group counselling currently specializes in groups for elementary-aged children as well as groups for parents. Nevertheless, there are certain general goals which would be hypothesized for any Adlerian group, including groups for younger children.

Individual goals. An Adlerian group counsellor helps the client see the beliefs and feelings as well as the motives and goals that determine the individual's life-style. Clients develop insights into their mistaken goals and self-defeating behaviours. They are then helped to develop appropriate life goals. Group counsellors also try to maximize the responsible freedom and personal effectiveness of each individual group member, develop feelings of personal worth in each individual group member, and help each individual consider alternative life-styles and make a commitment towards change.

Interpersonal goals. As each group member is encouraged to explore his or her feelings and reactions to other group members, self-understanding is furthered. This goal could be described as providing opportunities for group members to learn about their own style of coping through exploring their interactions with other group members. In addition, self-understanding is increased by helping each individual member learn how he/she decided to belong to the group. To develop and to further social interest in group members through their encouraging others and becoming involved with other members' specific life changes is another Adlerian goal.

Group Process. Although not emphasized as much as in Gestalt groups, process goals for Adlerian group counselling would include developing an empathic relationship between the group leader and each individual member, encouraging empathy and acceptance by the entire group for each individual member, developing the social interest of individuals through the group climate and the development of an encouraging group, providing a climate of encouragement for individual group members so that they will risk making a commitment to change their behaviours and their life-style, and developing a cooperative climate and norms within the group.

Several types of groups -- including human potential, T-groups. and some types of encounter groups -- are considered under the general heading of personal growth. Diversity of goals among groups of this type may very well be as large as the diversity of goals for the entire range of counselling theories. Nevertheless, a collection of selected goals representative of personal growth group follows.

Individual goals. As members are given time in the group to relate personal information, self-understanding is an important goal, much as it is for individual client-centered counselling. Furthermore, as individual members are encouraged to explore the meaning of their interactions with other members, self-understanding is said to be increased. Several specific goals are usually included in personal growth groups. One of these is to increase self-awareness and the awareness of the individual's potential. A second is to increase individual self-exploration and thereby heighten the ability of the individual to achieve greater self-awareness and communicate this awareness. A third goal is to increase individual acceptance of self. As the individual member experiences acceptance from other members of the group and from the leader, self-acceptance then leads to increased self-understanding.

Interpersonal goals. Interactions between group members are a means to increasing individual self-understanding. Interactions are explored and examined so that all group members are able to consider their own reactions and to incorporate individual learning. The goal of self-acceptance is furthered as the leader models an accepting individual, even within conflict situations. Individual members are encouraged to be less judgmental and more accepting of each group member. Encouraging the individual's reliance on self as a source of evaluation rather than the reliance on others' appraisal is a major goal as is increasing the frequency of spontaneous reactions and expressions of feelings to other group members.

Group process. For some proponents of personal growth groups, the totality of the group's interactions, including changes in group interactions over time, are an important focus. The mutuality of goals for individual members, namely, to foster and to spur individual growth and change, provides an emphasis on certain climate or group process goals. Another important group goal is to develop a climate of intermember support. The feeling of support from other members encourages individuals to explore and to communicate about themselves. To explore, examine, and increase individual awareness of the interdependence of members is still another goal. As individuals are encouraged to learn about themselves, many will offer help to other members and also learn to receive help. An important group process goal is to create an accepting atmosphere.

The reduced fear and self-consciousness in individual members that results is believed to increase self-disclosure and thereby to further individual self-understanding. Another goal mentioned frequently with growth groups is to increase the group leadership. Increasing self-direction by the group rather than relying heavily on group leaders for direction is seen as a process goal.

Although there has been some confusion as to the distinction between groups where interaction among members is encouraged and those where the only interaction is from leader to individuals, this focus on cognitive-behavioural groups is limited to groups in which members have clearly identified changes which they would like to make in their lives outside the group.

The central goal of a cognitive-behavioral group is to help individual members make changes in their lives or ways of their choosing. The emphasis is on change outside the group. Such changes would include the decrease of behaviours regarded by the individual as maladaptive and an increase in adaptive behaviours. To help an individual practice and receive reinforcement and encouragement would be a major goal so that the individual will succeed with the new behaviour outside the group. Another goal is to help the individual learn techniques to influence his or her environment. Such techniques might help the individual to set up certain stimuli or change certain stimuli preceding crucial behaviours; to perform designated behaviours; to alter his or her own thinking, and to seek out or otherwise to provide reinforcement for targeted behaviours. To help individuals examine and carry out changes by interacting with other group members having similar problems is another goal.

To provide appropriate models for other group members is a behavioral goal. Use of multiple models could be encouraged so that an individual member could benefit from seeing more than one group member perform designated behaviours. Increasing the support for individual members through encouragement and social reinforcement is a goal. Interpersonal goals might also include members agreeing to check up with a member, to prompt another member, or to reinforce a member. The opportunity for rehearsal and practice is an important goal of behavioral groups. Members can be especially helpful by being willing to participate in role plays. An advantage of group counselling lies in the potential for feedback from other individuals. At times, this goal will be directly influenced by the group leader's providing training for members in the skill of behavioral feedback.

Although it is often difficult to determine whether group behavioral counselling actually includes group interaction variables such as discussion, sharing feelings, and providing feedback, behavioral group counselling as defined in this section would focus on the group climate. Especially important would be a group climate which would encourage individual exploration and risk-taking which would further the specific goals of the particular group. At times, group members would be trained in certain techniques such as providing feedback, providing social reinforcement, or providing encouragement. It is desirable that the group provide a climate which seems safe enough for members to share personal concerns and to take risks as they attempt to practice new, and sometimes difficult behaviours. The group process should be work-oriented. This requires commitment from andividual members to stay on a task as well as to offer support and social reinforcement to other members of the group.

Reviewers of research in group counselling have puzzled over the poorly-defined terms and concepts. They have lamented the lack of effective research methodology. Yet, the professional literature reflects a rich interest in this area with long lists of studies and many reviews in many settings. What follows is a "me!" look at recent studies in the effectiveness of group counselling and psycho-therapy. Because of the infrequent use of comparative studies, the theoretical sections used earlier in this chapter are not used to organize the selected studies here. Instead the categories of goals used for each of the theories provide the organizing headings found later in the review individual change, interpersonal change, and group process. Although a rich and extensive literature exists in the group counselling area, reviewers have consistently complained about the quality of this research. What makes research in group counselling so difficult? A few of the factors are line inability of writers in group counselling to agree upon definitions of terms; the difficulty in comparing theory to theory, complaints that group studies performed in a laboratory or for one 20-minute session are not transferable to real groups; and finally, the extreme amount of effort and persistence needed to compare comparable counselling groups in a counselling setting.

When one writer uses a term such as insight in a specific way, other writers may very well invent or use their own special meaning for the term insight. When writers from varying theories of group counselling use similar terms, all too often the definitions do not agree. It has been pointed out that many widely used terms in the group area such as self-disclosure and cohesiveness have never had operational definitions which were agreed upon. This lack of operational, agreed-upon definitions, of course, makes comparing results from one study to another virtually impossible. In addition, there has been a tendency in the literature for writers to use group in the title or in their introductory paragraph but to never specify exactly what the group consisted of, or what the experience and style of the leader was, what specific interventions were used in the sessions, and whether the same members existed at the end of the group as in the beginning. In many areas of counselling, great strides in research have been gained by looking in the laboratory at very narrow, specific aspects of complicated processes. For example, a study which looked at role taking or, even better, at varying aspects of role taking, might very well result in a hypothesis that could be tested by group leaders in the field or by researchers with the capability to conduct group counselling research in a help-giving setting. However, a lot of the practitioners, and several of the writers in the area of group counselling, have complained violently about the lack of practicality of laboratory studies for the group counselling practitioner.

The significant outcome studies of counselling and psychotherapy have compared counselling of three to five different theoretical backgrounds with one another at the end of counselling. To find on-going, comparable groups at the same time and then to compare results, has been an exceedingly difficult task for group studies. This task has been made even more complicated by the finding that theoretical labels have not differentiated between interventions and techniques used by group leaders. In his thorough review of therapeutic factors in group psychotherapy over a 25-year period, Bloch confirmed how little definitive research has been done which indicates the effectiveness of various therapeutic factors within groups.

The studies which were included here, selected because they seemed like clear examples of the three headings, namely, individual change, interpersonal change, and group process; or because they were especially effective studies taken from agency or educational settings. Studies were not included which focused on family counselling and psychotherapy, on in patient groups, or which featured special populations. Studies were included which had been published since 1977. In the event that a study does feature an in-patient client group or does focus upon special population, the text will make note of this.

One recent study has been selected as an example which indicates the difficulties of conducting research in group counselling while at the same time providing an effective, exemplary sample. Shadish conducted an experiment using 49 undergraduates who had volunteered for the study. These subjects re randomly assigned to six groups. Shadish assigned his six groups as follows: 10 subjects to a pretested control group, 8 subjects to an unpretested control group, eight subjects to a pretested verbal group (his treatment), eight subjects to an unpretested verbal group, seven subjects to a pretested nonverbal group, and eight subjects to an unpretested nonverbal group.

One of the troubling questions in successful research is that of a control group. This study met this by providing three controls- a pretested control group, an unpretested control group plus the two groups, one in each treatment, which had been pretested along with the other two groups which had not been pretested. This type of design allows the researcher to determine what effect the pretest may have had on the subsequent results of the findings. However in Shadish's study groups of unequal size were used.

All too often, studies do not indicate the experience level of the group leaders. In this study, four pairs of group leaders were made up of clinical psychology graduate students. These pairs were counterbalanced by sex and experience. In addition, all eight group leaders went through an 18-hour educational experience which consisted of didactic and experiential training. In addition, this experiment used a follow-up. The follow-up in this study was of 3 weeks, not very long, but in our opinion better than no follow-up at all.

One difficulty in conducting research in counselling and psychotherapy is the ability to determine whether the treatment groups, as well as the control groups, actually did contain a treatment or in the case of the control group, no treatment at all. In this study, Shadish had two senior psychology students observe meetings of the six groups. The two senior students were able to identify correctly whether they were viewing a control group, a nonverbal group, or a verbal group. The treatment consisted of three brief sessions plus a marathon weekend session. Although no description was given of the control groups or the treatment groups, a sample nonverbal and verbal exercise is described.

Several measures were used in this study. A difficulty of comparing group outcomes is the tendency for researchers to use their own, home made of change. Shadish used standardized iniments. For example, the Personal Orientation (PO1) resulted in no differences before the , after the treatment or after the follow up.

Sciizbacher, Wong, McKeen, Clock, and MacDonald used the POI as an outcome-measure as well as a self-concept instrument. The treatment was a 3-month intensive resident human growth program with 33 participants. Thirteen members of the participants' a milies served as the control group. The instruments were administered before the group program, at its conclusion, and at a 1-year follow-up. Highly significant increases were found in self-analyzation and self-concept for the participants. These increases were maintained at the end of 1 year. No changes were found at the end of the three months in members of the control group.

Shapiro, Sank, Shaffer, and Donovan studied crises in group member depression, state anxiety, anxiety and assertiveness. Forty-four enrollees in a maintenance organization were used as vects. Of these, 35 completed all assessment processes. The subjects were described as mildly behaviour. Participants were randomly assigned three treatment groups: cognitive behaviour therapy traditional inter-personal process group, and actual cognitive behaviour therapy. The cognitive behaviour group was given relaxation training and cognitive restructuring practice. The traditional interpersonal group used an unstructured treatment which included elements of insight development, interpersonal feedback, and focus on group process. All three treatments, including the individual treatment, met for 10 weekly sessions (1½ hours for group treatment and 1 hour for individual treatment).

All three treatments resulted in reduced depression, less state anxiety, less trait anxiety, and a significant increase in assertiveness. In a 6-month follow-up, the experimenters found maintenance of several changes in the individual participants. Follow-up data was completed on 29 of the original 35 participants. The changes in anxiety and assertiveness were maintained. However, depression had returned towards but did not reach pretreatment levels.

Barrera also studied the effects of group therapy on depression. This study used a subscale of the same measure as Shapiro et al. The Minnesota Multiphasic Personality Inventory (MMPI) and a personal screening interview were used to diagnose participants as depressed. Twenty subjects were assigned to an immediate treatment group and 20 others to a delayed treatment group. Leaders for both groups were a male and female co-leader.

At the end of four weeks, when the immediate treatment group was completed, and at the end of 8 weeks, when both groups had received treatment, there were no differences between the two groups. At the end of one month, the delayed-treatment group was described as much improved on the depression scale. The authors were unable to explain the lack of treatment effect in the immediate treatment group.

In a one year follow-up to a study comparing I and group cognitive behavioral counselling, MacDonald reported significant changes in a study conducted in a school. Teacher ratings of group participants indicated significant behavioural change in the group and at a one year follow-up from treatment ratings. In addition, group and Mfcndual participants in the study were no longer otirwvd as different from other students by the Barbers. However, teacher ratings indicated that the oniiinnol subjects in the study continued to be rated as Mem from the majority of the students. The actual treatment and the group treatment were as equally successful in this study.

Olson, Ganley, Devine, and Dorsey described a follow-up study with 137 participants in a which compared behavioral versus insight therapy. One hundred thirteen subjects were available out of 137. The control group received the standard treatment for 1 month. Treatment group 1 two or three lectures a day plus "traditional tip therapy" that focused on feelings. Treatment group 2 received Transactional Analysis (TA) sessions 5 times a week. Treatment group three received behavioural treatment conducted by two therapists. Treatment group three received Transactional Analysis combined with behavioral under the same leaders. In addition, all groups received bibliotherapy and attended Alcoholics Anonymous meetings, individual consultations each week, recreational and a weekly family group counselling. The follow-ups were conducted on them with a second interviewer listening on a telephone. The reliability of the two interviewers was described as 0.86 and 0.94. No group differences were found 4 years after the treatment, although there was a nonsignificant trend for the TA group to do poorly.

Although interaction and interpersonal communication among group members is commonly described as a reason for group counselling, relatively few research studies in group counselling have focused on interpersonal change. Morran, Robison, and Stockton described a study which focused on feedback among counselling group members. "Interpersonal feedback occurs when one group member shares his or her perceptions of and reactions to another's behaviour with that other person". Earlier studies indicated that effective definitions of feedback must include informational aspects as well as motivational aspects. In addition, group members have been found to accept positive feedback more readily than negative; to respond to positive and negative feedback differently at different stages of group development; and to value behavioral rather than emotional feedback.

This study interrupted the group process in order to devote one session to gathering feedback at either the second, fourth, or sixth group session. Three groups participated in feedback at each of the three sessions (nine treatment groups). Sixty-three subjects participated in 6-week "personal growth groups," meeting 2 hours each week. The nine groups were co-led by male-female or female-female advanced doctoral students who were interns in a counselling agency. The study was interested in who provided feedback-the members or the leaders; the timing of the feedback -- which session it was given in; and positive versus negative feedback.

During the special session, group members and the leader completed a form to give feedback to each member. After writing the feedback, each person in the group read his or her feedback to each member. Positive and negative feedback were separated with the order being randomly assigned. Recipients immediately rated the feedback. Results showed that the sex of feedback givers and receivers was not a tactor. Recipients rated positive feedback as more accurate than negative.

In addition, feedback in Session four was rated as more helpful than feedback in Session two. Member and leader feedback was rated equally, feedback from members was more specific when positive, while leader feedback specificity was the same for positive and negative. Negative feedback was less directive in the later session in which it was lathered.

A second example of studies regarding interpersonal change can be found in member activenesess for the group (cohesion). Falloon used behavioral group therapy with 76 out-patients described as neurotically depressed or with inadequate personalities who reported having difficulties with their social skills. These results, rather than shedding light on differential group treatments causing different outcomes, can better be seen as an example of an outcome study for a treatment setting. Six role rehearsal groups and three discussion (control) groups were formed. Each group met for 10 weekly 75-minute sessions. The control groups used the same topics, handouts, and homework as the treatment groups. Leaders praised "constructive discussion and rational help." The treatment groups were also enquired about weekly topics. Patients exchanged ration about homework but also participated in deep muscle relaxation, listening to MUSIC and other tension relieving activities. Leaders modelled effective behaviour each week followed by member rehearsal. Group attractiveness was greater for the behavioral groups than for control groups. The authors suggest that cohesiveness can be improved by role rehearsal activities. No differences were found among the behavioral groups.

The final area of organization for expected goals of theories is group process. Only a few theories focused their expectations on specific group process goals. Likewise, the research on group counselling has tended to slight this aspect of groups, an aspect that is unique to group counselling. Once again, Defiritions pose a problem in this area. Topics such as member interaction and cohesiveness, treated under interpersonal change above, could be viewed as elements of group process. While some authors focused on "group dynamic processes" or "group climate" little research exists on group process changes in the literature. Interpersonal learning is viewed as an important therapeutic factor by many group writers. However, this concept is usually measured in any research by obtaining individual group members' self-estimates. In some studies, these measures may be averaged, with the resulting mean seen as an indication of group process change. Such a procedure is not really a group process measure, however. As summarized by Bloch et al. "... there is no evidence of how interpersonal learning occurs or its effect on outcome.... ". Coche and Dies point out the overemphasis on group research on the individual. Research in group counselling has exhibited several difficulties including a lack of studies which compare outcomes of groups using different theories, lack of studies which focus on expected outcomes for any theory, lack of agreed-upon definitions or measures, and difficulty in establishing comparable control groups. Nevertheless, a sample study was shown which illustrated the type of research which is lacking. In addition, research was described according to the categories used earlier for expected group theory outcomes; namely, individual change, interpersonal changes, and group process.

It is not sufficient to present information to students, and to assume that they have all heard and understood the same thing, for each one reads personal meanings in what may be considered 'objective' facts. If we exclude group counselling, then group guidance becomes a set of activities used with a group of students to help each in his individual learning. It is mainly a cognitive process with little attention given to feelings or emotions and is concerned with helping people to discuss the meaning of various kinds of information. The focus is on ideas, explanations, and verbal expression as an aid to a personal understanding of information or to the completion of a set task.

The following purposes particularly emphasize group guidance in the secondary school setting.

1. To assist in the identification of common problems.
2. To provide information useful in the solution of adjustment problems.
3. To provide opportunities for group thinking in regard to various problems and experiences.
4. To provide opportunities for experiences that promote self understanding.
5. To lay the foundations for individual counselling.

There are certain problems which are common to adolescents as part of the developmental processes of this age group, there are also certain kinds of educational, vocational and social information which can be of help to young people as they grow up. These may be presented in a group situation and discussed with the realization that their difficulties are not peculiar to them as individuals, as they often think, but are shared by fellow students.

Deciding Factors

There are essentially two types of information needed for intelligent decision-making: information regarding oneself as a person with assets and liabilities, talents and limitations; and information regarding the particular situation about which a decision is to be made, or to which the self is related. When a person has this information he needs some way of dealing with it.

There are various models of choice or decision-making used by people in making vocational or other choices, which vary according to the individual concerned and his circumstances.

Trait and Factor Model. The trait and factor model is based on the idea that any individual possesses a variety of traits and any occupation demands certain requirements of those who enter it. The individual can match his traits with the occupational or educational requirements and determine which job or course he is best fitted for. This model is often used in vocational guidance in our schools and its main disadvantage is that it is too static and does not take into account the changing and developing nature of neither the student or the environment to which he must relate.

Economic Model. An individual using the economic model chooses an occupation or a college which will maximize his gain and minimize his loss; for example, going to college might be a means of achieving greater status and mobility. The gains achieved are not necessarily economic or financial but may consist of anything which is of value to the person concerned.

Social Structure Model. The individual using a social structure model of choice is restricted in the decisions he can make because his knowledge of the various opportunities available is limited by family, social and economic circumstances. This is particularly so as disadvantaged students for whom narrowness of cultural or social class horizons places restrictions on their educational or vocational selection and often leads to the equally narrow perspective of immediate gratification as the basis for choice.

Information Processing Model. A person may be forced into using the information processing model of choice when the facts necessary for him to make a decision are so overwhelming that he is pressured into a premature decision. Some students chose a particular college or job because their friends have done so, or because they are vaguely aware that a college has a particular college or job because their friends have done so, or because they are vaguely aware that a college has a particular reputation. This type of choice supports the individual's rationalization and reduces his anxiety.

Need Reduction Model. The need reduction model is a comprehensive one which subsumes certain elements of the other models. It assumes that an individual has a self-concept and that he implements this picture of himself in his choice of course or occupation, by gravitating towards a career, or a course of study which he sees as compatible with his needs and interests. This may be a result of unconscious motivation, or a relatively rational conscious choice. The advantage is that this provides for change in the person's behaviour, environment and expectations between the individual and his environment. It suggests that making decisions about important areas of one's life is a complex and on-going process forming part of a developmental sequence extending from childhood through adulthood and not an isolated event at a particular point in time.

It is no good giving information to students who see no need for it, so motivation should precede instruction in group guidance. The presentation of information is only part of the process and must be followed by some feedback to ensure that it reached each student accurately.

Large Groups or Assemblies. Whilst large groups offer an economical way of disseminating information, large group audiences tend to be passive listeners, or merely passive. We need to supplement this type of presentation by work in smaller groups and with individuals in which there is more opportunity for interaction and feedback.

Tutorial Groups. Unless tutors in school have one period each day with their students, the tutorial group is not an effective way of providing information on which to base choices, or of providing help in other areas. Tutors also need training in group work, and the support of a carefully planned, effectively led guidance programme.

Orientation Groups. Orientation usually takes the form of large group information giving, plus smaller orientation groups which continue throughout the year and are aimed at helping the students to develop independence. This applied at all levels of education, not just at the school level. American studies indicated that three out of the four college students had difficulties with the transition from the orderly, fairly directive secondary school to the non-directive environment of college. Some of the reasons given for these difficulties were unrealistic expectations of college social and education life; an inability to organize their time; going to college without a strong desire to attend; and financial difficulties. Closed circuit television can be a useful medium for orientation purposes.

Discussion Groups. Guidance groups are concerned with effective discussion about the impact of information and also about problems arising from some personal adjustment and difficulties. Affective discussion groups can be useful in this area, as they form a bridge between the purely intellectual discussion group and the counselling group with its emphasis on empathy. They need planning and structuring, and some of the techniques for initiating affective discussion are role-playing, case-studies, role-models, literature and audio-visual media.

Anne Jones offers a useful description of their use in a secondary school in School Counselling in Practice.

Although the two concepts of group guidance and group counselling overlap to some extent in the area of affective discussion, group guidance tends to be more cognitively oriented and is usually used in an attempt to personalise information, whereas group counselling is used in an attempt to meet emotional needs and is often closer to group therapy as compared to group guidance.

Group counselling is not simply individual counselling applied to groups, nor is it merely an economical use of counsellor time. Many of the features of group counselling are quite unique and it would be wrong to think of it as 'individual' counselling in the mass. Because of the differences in the two processes, a counsellor trained in the skills of individual counselling might find her/himself in difficulty if he/she attempted group counselling without having some training in group interaction. It is essential that a counsellor wishing to work with individuals and groups should have a thorough theoretical and practical grounding in individual counselling theory and practice together with some experience of principles and practices of group dynamics.

The term multiple counselling is sometimes used to describe counselling carried out in groups. This seems a misleading term since it is not clear whether it is the counsellors or the students who are 'multiple'. It is used in this book to denote a situation in which there are two counsellors working either with one student, as in the chapter on training, or with a group. The term group counselling is used here to describe a situation in which there is one counsellor working with a group of students.

Group counselling is a relatively new way of working to help people and although it has a unique contribution to make to our range of helping skills, it is not the complete answer for all psychological ills or needs.

Carkhuff has written quite strongly that Group processes are the preferred mode of working with difficulties in interpersonal functioning.

We can do anything in group treatment that we can do in individual treatment-and more. Since groups are inherently interpersonal, they offer the helpee the means not only to relate to the helper and himself with the helper's guidance but also to relate to other members of the group and to the group as a whole. Group processes offer the prospect for the greatest amount of learning for the greatest number of people at one time.

I find Carkhuff s unqualified approval as inappropriate and potentially damaging as 'attempting to gather peaches with a combine harvester'. Certainly group counselling is sometimes successful with students who have not responded well to individual counselling, and there are several combinations of group and individual counselling in use. The two extremes are to use either group counselling or individual counselling only as a main technique. Some counsellors feel that it is unwise to make the two methods available to the same students at the same time because students may not bring out their deepest problems in the group, reserving them for the individual counselling sessions, which could inhibit the work of the group. Other counsellors feel that individual counselling offered concurrently with group counselling gives opportunity for a student to discuss more deeply and extensively personal problem areas which they have been unable to bring out in the group, either because of their own inability or because of a lack of opportunity and a need to share the time of the group with other members.

Group counselling overlaps with group guidance in its partial cognitive and factual content and with group therapy in its emphasis on feelings and emotion, and it has some similarities to the individual counselling situation, with the addition of the interaction of other members of the group and the sharing of counsellor. The effectiveness of group counselling may be partly attributable to the fact that, theoretically, it makes available the services of a number of potential helpers in the form of other group members, one or several of whom may be able to offer more help to a particular person at a particular point than is the counsellor herself.

Group counselling is a particularly useful, way of helping adolescents for whom peer group values are important. The interaction which takes place in a counselling group offers the students a means of gaining insight and understanding into his own problems through listening to other students discussing their difficulties. Ideas and values which a student has previously found unacceptable may become more understandable and sometimes more acceptable. The counselling group not only helps the individual student to change, but also often encourages both his desire and his ability to help social situation, for any group is more than the sum of its members: it is also the sum of its interactions.

Practical Aspects

The physical arrangements which are desirable for a counselling group are similar to those which pertain to the individual counselling situation namely, a warm, soundproofed room with fairly comfortable chairs. It is difficult, though not impossible, to conduct a counselling group in the average classroom, and even more difficult to conduct it in a cupboard. It is helpful if the same room can be used each time the group meets, because of the effect of a changed environment on the functioning of the group if their meeting place is not a familiar setting.

The time factor in the group counselling situation is related to the purpose of the group. If it is intended that most of the 'work' of the individual members is to take place in the actual group counselling session, it is necessary for the group to meet more often than it would if the counsellor and the group members feel that the students need time between meetings to absorb and test some of the experiences learned it is usual for the counselling groups used in education to meet once, or perhaps twice a week. If the group meets too often, or example more than three times a week, there is the possibility that the frequency of sessions will restrict the group members' external social contacts and limit their opportunities for social reality testing outside the group. The length of each group meeting will be related to the age of the people involved, and the frequency with which the group meets, but sixty to ninety minutes is probably a reasonable time span for college students, thirty to sixty minutes for secondary school pupils and no more than thirty minutes for junior school children.

The composition of a counselling group is another practical consideration which is related to the purpose of the group. Sometimes it is felt that a homogeneous group consisting of students of the same age or sex, or students who seem to have similar problems is the most helpful, whilst other counsellors find that the wider talents of a heterogeneous group make for a better counselling situation. It is necessary to look carefully at the desired outcomes for the group, and to try to ensure that the purposes of the counsellor and those of the students are the same. It is important to recognize that groups can be homogeneous only in certain limited respects. A group chosen for homogeneity in sex or age is likely to be heterogeneous in other factors such as socio-economic background, maturity, motivation and, of course, temperament. It has been suggested that it is unwise to include in a counselling or therapy group people who are excessively aggressive or hostile because they are likely to destroy the atmosphere of acceptance in the group; people who are psychologically sophisticated or those who are not sufficiently in contact with reality have also been seen as undesirable group members, but it is difficult for the school or college counsellor to exclude students on these grounds unless they know them personally. A preliminary interview can help, though this may be more appropriate as screening for therapy groups than as a means of choosing members for a counselling group in an educational setting.

The size of a counselling group, like that of any guidance group, is related to the methodology used. A directive counsellor or one who prefers task oriented discussion may choose to work with a larger action. A group of six to eight students is probably the best size for maximum group interaction.

There are two basic assumptions upon which a counsellor may choose to build her role. One is that it is the task of the counsellor to work with the group to encourage the students to be more self-sufficient and self-directed, so that the counsellor herself may then become another group member and the interaction of the group itself will provide any help which members need. An alternative assumption is that the counsellor works towards the development of the students' self-sufficiency, but because she considered that the group members are not always able to help each other she does not abdicate her special helping role

Glantz and Hayes offer six phases which they believe are involved in group counselling., and offer a basis from which to consider the work of a counselling group:

1. rapport.
2. acceptance.
3. listening and observing.

4. promoting group and individual understanding.
5. problem solving skill development.
6. closing evaluation and procedures.

Whilst the counsellor's acceptance of all the group members and their problems is assumed in the nature of the role of the counsellor, as is the acceptance of the student in individual counselling, the creation of rapport and acceptance within and amongst the group members themselves, and between them and the counsellor is a unique experience which differs from the one-to-one counselling relationship in its patterns of development.

Rapport involves the gradual building of an association of mutual respects and trust and it can be introduced by initial discussion of the group, whether the group should be 'open', so that members may leave when they wish or new members may be brought into the group as it proceeds, or whether it could be 'closed', retaining its initial membership for a specified period of time. Questions directed at the counsellor can be referred to the group for discussion and decision by means of a counsellor response such as 'What does the group feel about this?' If multiple counselling is being done, the role and function of the co-counsellor may be discussed. The structuring of the group by the counsellor in the early stages may also help in the growth of rapport. Structuring should be brief and should focus attention on the particular goals of the group, which may be self appraisal, to encourage the free expression of feelings by group members to each other and to the counsellor, and the avoidance of purely intellectual discussion. The limits of the group may be expressed, for example, in terms of the permitting of verbal but not physical expression of hostile feelings. The emphasis of the observance by all group members and the counsellor of confidentiality about the proceedings of the group is also a part of structuring which can help to bring about trust.

Initial resistance is a natural phenomenon of groups and the creation of an accepting climate is a gradual process which the counsellor tries to encourage by her own acceptance of each student's feelings and his expression of them. From the counsellor the students learn to accept and help one another. Listening and observing actively and intensely are two of the essential skills of the counsellor, and a group situation gives an added complexity to the use of these in order to promote both group and individual understanding. 'The counsellor's task is more complicated in group counselling. He not only has to understand the speaker's feelings and help him become aware of them, but he must also observe how the speaker's comments influence the group members. The counsellor must not only be aware of the discussion, he must be perceptive of the interplay of relationships among the members.' The counselling group can make little significant progress in developing the skills for solving problems until the initial stages of rapport, acceptance, understanding and insight have been established. It may be that the process of group counselling itself will uncover more problems that it actually solves, but if it is effective it also helps to bring about the attitudes and draws out the resources which will enable students to work at these problems themselves once they have been brought to conscious awareness. Alternatively it may lead them to seek individual counselling help for these.

The Result

As a result of research carried out into group counselling among pupils in a secondary school Ohlsen reports that, with varying degrees of depth, each client discovered:

1. that expressing his own real feelings about people, things and ideas helped him to understand himself;
2. that at least one adult could accept him and that this adult, the counsellor, wanted to understand him;
3. that his peers had problems too;
4. that, in spite of his faults, which they wanted to help him ot correct, his peers could accept him;
5. that he was capable of understanding, accepting and helping others;
6. that he could trust others.

Group counselling in education is not group instruction nor is it group therapy, but it is an experience which uses peer group support and identification in the social setting of the group to encourage students to accept and to learn more about themselves and at the same time to learn to accept and help others. Group counselling is characterised by experience not by words, by being something not by talking about it. If one can experience sense of reality about one's self, it is more towards emotional maturity which is the goal of group counselling.

8

Counselling on Social Matters

Social problems relating to the youth and students in particular arise from faulty socialisation and improper nurturing of social qualities by parents, teachers and peers. The purpose of social guidance is not only to assist in resolving social problems like sociopathic personality, delinquency, social maladjustment etc., but also to help in the development of social maturity, healthy habits and desirable attitude and to eradicate prejudices and acquire a set of values.

Many of the opportunities to fulfil social needs are generally lacking in homes and educational institutions. Qualities such as honesty, cooperation, courage, loyalty, kindliness, feeling of identification, etc., do not get proper nourishment, resulting in maladjustment of students. Social guidance programme is mainly directed to meet all these inadequacies. A well organised social guidance programme in educational institutions can be expected to take care of the following:

- Provide assistance to students for social adjustment.
- Help to develop proper attitude towards life and society.
- Assist students in acquiring desirable set of values and developing a positive life philosophy.
- Assist students to maintain good, harmonious relationship with members of the family, peers and other members of the society of which they are members.
- Assist students to understand their rights and obligations to the society.

Three groups of social needs have been identified which are vital for social and emotional well being of the individual.

- The need for interpersonal satisfaction
- The need for group status
- The need for self-development

Socially motivated students can get along well with themselves and with others. Such students generally do not have problems of social adjustment. Students studying in polytechnics have a variety of social needs which are vital for their well being. These include security, affection, recognition, support, belongingness, esteem and social acceptance. These can be classified as :

- need for interpersonal relationship.
- need for group status.
- need for self-development.

Students seek love and affection from those individuals who are close to them and who matter much to them. If the needs for love and affection are fulfilled, they feel warm and socially accepted. This increases their internal strength to interact and communicate freely with fellow beings. In order to get the much needed love and affection from others, students should be capable of maintaining harmonious interpersonal relationship.

Students have to develop a system of interpersonal relations in their social sphere for purposes of satisfying their social needs.

As members of a group every student is assured of being accepted by his peers. If he is not a member of some group he becomes lonely, loses self-confidence and starts to question his own adequacy. It has been proved experimentally that when students are cut off from social and perceptual stimulation for a long time, they experience intellectual deterioration, hallucination and impairment of problem-solving abilities.

Due to a growing awareness of their potentialities and capacities students have a compelling urge to engage in some activities to test and use their potentialities. They pursue self-initiated and self-directed activities which give them a feeling of personal worth. If the self-development needs like achievement, independence, personal recognition, adequacy, self-respect are not properly fulfilled social problems are likely to occur.

Students of today are different from those of earlier times due to the changes in the society and their exposure to a variety of intellectual pursuits. Advancement of technology has brought us together beyond space and time.

Competition has enormously increased in all fields. Old values and beliefs are facing a lot of challenge in the fast changing technological era. Polytechnics as a miniature society are not free from the impact of the outside world.

Social changes and rapid technological developments also get reflected in the polytechnic environment. Students have to adjust to the social climate of the polytechnic which is different from their earlier school climate. This demands a mature behaviour on the part of students.

Students studying in an institution have different cultural backgrounds as they come from different family backgrounds and these affect the interactions in group situations. In the polytechnics existing social norms exert pressure on students to abide by the norms. Deviation from the norms by any of the group members will mean rejection by the group.

Various Problems

(i) Inferiority complex.

(ii) Eccentricism.

(iii) Overdependency.

(iv) Asocial behaviour or Delinquency.

(v) Deviant sexual behaviour;

(vi) Amoral behaviour,

(vii) Social outbursts.

A student having inferiority complex has a deep seated feeling of inferiority which reflects in his curricular and co-curricular activities. He is apologetic and tends to annoy people with his whining and self-deprecating tactics. He feels nervous and uncomfortable at social gatherings and he quickly withdraws from social contacts. Some students develop certain types of compensating behaviour. They develop a type of forced aggressiveness to cover up their feeling of inferiority.

The eccentric students show their characteristics in mannerisms, appearance and habit pattern. They show disregard for what others think of them. They are highly prejudiced persons. This category of students know that they are different from others.

Students who exhibit characteristics of overdependency are dominated by fear and insecurity. They lack confidence for undertaking any activity and seek protection from others in carrying out the work. The overdependent students are mostly emotionally immature. They behave like emotionally unstable students. They get relief from their tensions through physical expressions such as tremors, stuttering, nail biting, ear pulling and other nervous mannerisms.

The behaviour of the asocial group endangers not only their own personality but also the welfare of others. Students belonging to this category are impulsive, emotionally immature, irresponsible and unethical.

Some students attempt to release their tension through socially disapproved forms of sexual gratification. Such as they may pass remarks on the members of the opposite sex and get pleasure in teasing. In extreme cases they develop the habit of faulty differentiation and sexual perversions.

Students whose behaviour is amoral exhibit traits such as dishonesty, stealing, etc. Students having social problems of this category do not keep up their promises. They may be restless, jumpy, greedy and pessimistic. Such behaviour can be attributed to a lack of moral development in them. Development of super ego i.e., morality is very important for healthy social adjustment. Sometimes, students exhibit social outbursts in the form of strike, protest, boycott of classes, etc. These are common nowadays, which cause a lot of disturbance to the activities of the institution. Students at this stage are very sensitive due to their social and emotional development.

At the same time, due to lack of experience they cannot think of the pros and cons of their involvement in such antisocial activities. They feel excited in taking part in activities like strike, demonstration, etc. They let out their tension by shouting, blaming, and sometimes by damaging institutional property. The following table gives the general manifestations of certain behavioural disorders.

The Reasons

A number of causes could be attributed to social problems of adolescents. One common cause for almost all the social problems is social environment. It is difficult to identify a set of causes for a particular social problem because most of them may be responsible for other social problems also. Therefore in the following paragraphs an attempt has been made to discuss the general causes of social problem:

Every student is a member or the society and lives in the social milieu. As such, it is to be normally expected that the adolescent is adequately adjusted and has no adjustment problems whatsoever. However, it ought to be remembered that the adolescent is in the process of getting himself into society and this experience of becoming independent is a traumatic one.

There will be problems due to his expectations, roles, influences, etc., and we shall look into a few such areas. Adolescents have, a tendency to always behave like adults in social relationship with regard to their attitude and behaviour with the opposite sex, speech, dress, religion etc.

Adults set their own standards of expectancy from adolescents, while the adolescents have their own standards. They are interested in such activities which give them immediate satisfaction and peers acceptance. They are not so much bothered about the after effects of their action nor do they care much for adult approval. Thus, this gives rise to a clash between social ethos and the adolescent behaviour. The adolescents have another tendency to think in terms of very fast social reformation. While the philosophy is very much laudable the means by which they would like to accomplish the same hardly gets the desired social approval.

Adolescents are to encounter another very taxing problem of having to adhere to or following the adult example. But we find a position wherein adults seem to say "Do as I say but not as I do". This would naturally give rise to a number of problems that arise in the life of the adolescent as he tries to adjust himself to the social relationship. A need extends as a state of tension which leads a person towards the activities which will relieve tension. Needs can be of two categories—Primary needs such as food, water, cloth, shelter, etc., and secondary needs (mostly psychological) such as love, affection, need for success, need for freedom, need for recognition etc. The non-realisation of the needs leads to frustration. Frustration could be due to several factors: Physical, social, economic, personal, etc. Frustration is often the cause for maladjustment.

Adolescent questions and the failure to get satisfactory answers is often the cause or source for maladjustment. He is faced with such problems as how to make and keep friends, acquire handsome personality, etc. An adolescent's social adjustment is not an exclusive thing but is very closely linked with his home and school relationships. It is known that an individual who has a normal and well integrated home carries wholesomeness of attitude and control of behaviour into many associations. Moreover, the cause of an adolescent's social maladjustment can be traced to a home environment.

Other causes for social maladjustment could be traced to poverty, parental indifference to adolescents, physical and mental disability, delinquency, etc. Lack of congenial environment at home and in the institutions, unsatisfactory bringing up, repressed desires and growing complexity in the environment create conflicts in students. When they fail to manage their conflicts and their coping mechanisms can not reduce or remove tension, they become problematic.

On the onset of adolescence students become increasingly socially conscious which brings radical changes in them. They tend to behave in a more mature way. The group to which they belong may expect to act and think according to group norms.

This also needs change of behaviour on the part of the individual. But from childhood to adolescence, students get very short time, i.e. 2 to 3 years to change their childish behaviour into a mature one. Parents and teachers, most of the time do not realise such difficulties and start criticising students for their mistakes.

As a result of criticisms, students feel themselves inadequate. Whenever a student feels that he is a member of some group, he feels happy and secure. On the other hand, in this process of belongingness, if some gaps are created, students start to feel insecure and that leads to social maladjustment.

As a member of the group, he tries to understand group pattern, tries to behave according to group norm. He wants social recognition through self-assertion. This depends on the approval of the group. But sometimes, social discrimination and resistance by other group members come in the way of social recognition. The students, in such cases, feel embarrassed and unidentified. Many students feel that they are misunderstood or unfairly treated in the family or by their friends. This causes tension in them. Strict discipline in the family, excessive parental supervision, too little independence lead students to disturbed conditions. They feel that their interests are not properly taken care of.

Sometimes, sarcastic remarks by elders, unwelcome advice, unjust behaviour by superiors create conflict and tension in the students. During the adolescent years, students desire to freely interact with members of the opposite sex. Social norms, vague fear, social restrictions, shyness etc., impose severe restrictions in a way in this regard. This built up tension may often lead them towards social withdrawal behaviour. They may often indulge in eveteasing. Thus, they may express their social desire in undesirable ways.

Development of desirable attitude and acquisition of a set of values is important for the individual as well as for the society.

Early social experience determines the attitude of the adolescents. Attitude is "an enduring organisation of motivational, emotional, perceptual and cognitive process with respect to some aspects of individual's work".

The Trends

Attitude is also a tendency to act towards the environment in an appropriate manner. It is always difficult to deviate from the social norms. The members of the group discourage deviation and resist change. The groups want conformity with existing norms. These group norms guide the adolescent in the development of attitude towards that direction. Attitudes are learnt through experiences in the group. Cultural factors are greatly responsible-for the development of attitudes among adolescents. Certain psychological factors like wishes, desires, tensions are also equally responsible for the development of attitudes among adolescents.

Prejudice is a negative attitude. A prejudiced adolescent does not want to moderate his opinion even when there are so many reverse explanations- He does not want to accept new evidence and refuses to take into account the individual differences. Ethnic group based on religion, language, social and cultural traditions help their group members to acquire prejudices.

Their ethnic attitudes give birth to social distance. This ethnic attitude motivates the group members to show unfavourable feelings to other group members. The prejudices emphasise that other group is bad. The prejudiced individual in the group give reasons for his prejudice.

Prejudices also develop because of diverse tradition-, customs and other modes of life. To a certain extent, when one group has the fear of attack from the other group, prejudices arc- strengthened. The other factors like feeling of frustration, cultural repression, complex situation also is responsible for the development of prejudice.

Adolescence is a time when personality becomes increasingly differentiated and hierarchically organised. The self concept develops through interaction with the environment through a series of self-perceptions. Generally all these changes follow the same direction that the adolescent already believes about himself. To achieve adequate self-direction requires sufficient self-differentiation. This makes it possible to realise that an individual himself is the originator of his actions with some measures of freedom, choice and control in directing his life.

Adolescent's sense of identity depends on how the motives are being satisfied. Identity is concerned with whom and what one thinks, and negotiating the meaning of one's life. If a set of desirable values are acquired in the developmental process in interacting with the society, that adds meaning to one's life. In modern life there appears to be two key difficulties in the development of values.

One stems from the complexity and changes of our environment which makes it difficult to acquire and maintain a stable value system. The factors like social status, social roles, frame of reference, interpersonal relationships, group identifications, which are undergoing continuous changes have effect on acquisition of values.

The second difficulty stems from the courage, required to "be oneself". This creates the conflict with the group, and the individual should earn the capacity to bear the responsibility for the consequences of one's action.

An adolescent wants to be self-directing for maintaining the values, but hesitates to give up his security for the sake of independence. This creates a value conflict within him. He is hesitant to accept blindly the established social values and is critical, of evaluating and searching.

Institutions as a whole should take some measures for social guidance activities. The students who join in the polytechnics or colleges have already some preconceived ideas about others. They may be prejudiced and may develop negative attitudes about their classmates.

The existing socio-cultural perspective may also action a barrier in inducing feeling of identification among the individuals. The important thing that demands first attention in social guidance programme is the improvement of polytechnic climate. The success of the faculty in achieving objectives in this regard depends on the type of climate they are able to create in which social problems of students do not lead to mental illness. Teachers have the capability of handling a large variety of social problems.

The Solutions

A variety of strategies like creating congenial atmosphere organising co-curricular activities help in solving social problems. A special strategy viz., classroom meeting model can also be used in solving social problems. Sometimes group counselling sessions are organised for specific type of social problems such as social withdrawal.

The first thing that demands attention in social guidance programme is the improvement of polytechnic climate. The faculty in achieving objectives in this regard depends on the type of climate they are able to create in which students feel secure enough and they are free to present their knowledge and motivate the students to learn.

The socio climate of polytechnic is as important as the air which they breathe. The head of the institution and the heads of the departments should encourage freedom of expression in students and faculty as a whole should nourish free interpersonal interaction among the students.

Another crucial role of the faculty who are actively involved in social guidance activity is inculcating a philosophy of life among students. This is an induction of a system of values which will lead the adolescents towards a satisfying life. Once life philosophy takes shape in the adolescent's this may guide him throughout life. The development of such life philosophy should be in accord with democratic ideas.

To achieve this objective, classes in human relations, moral education may be organised. For moral education classes, religious leaders from different religions may be invited so that they can preach a common philosophy and various principles of life. Conducting group counselling sessions are also helpful for this purpose.

Students have a variety of interests. Provision for different co-curricular activities can meet their interests. It should be seen that majority of students take part in different co-curricular activities which are very much helpful for social development. The co-curricular activities may include sports and games both indoor and outdoor, drama, debates, seminar, musical activities, visit to places, art and sculpture, social services and the like.

Generally in the polytechnic system, the physical education teacher is responsible for organising sports and games activities. But other teachers can help him in organising such activities. They can encourage the students in participating in sports and games by way of explaining its importance. They can see that students are getting enough opportunities for participation.

For cultural activities the teacher can form a team who will be responsible for organising such activities. Students from different classes must be represented in the team. The activities of the team can be coordinated by a cultural secretary duly elected by the students. The team can draw up a schedule of activities in the beginning of the year.

The team as a whole may take the initiative in searching for talent. Various activities under the cultural programmes can be distributed among team members. For example, the student responsible for Wall Magazine can assist others in different activities, but for monitoring Wall Magazine he is accountable to others.

A few students may neither be interested in sports and games nor in cultural activities. On the other hand, they may like to read books outside the scope of their curriculum. There should be provision to supply reading materials to them. Books and journals on mental health, sex and moral education, adventure, political and social histories should be available in the library. Glasser developed a strategy known as classroom Meeting Model for solving social problems. The model, if effectively used can achieve the following objectives.

To reduce loneliness in the students; To promote self identity in students. It has six phases. These are as follows:-

Phase 1: Establishing a climate of involvement. A sort of congenial climate is created where every one is inspired to participate. While sharing opinions group members should not evaluate or find-fault with others.

Phase 2: Exposing the problem for discussion. The issue problem is raised by teacher or students. Examples are given. The problem is discussed elaborately with the probable consequences.

Phase 3: Making a Personal Value judgement. The purpose of this phase is to have the students make a personal value judgement. Considering the social norms, identification of values behind the problem is carried out. Then they are asked to choose between behaviours and make a summary of the values they feel to be applicable for themselves in relation to the behaviour they have screened.

Phase 4: Identify Alternative Courses of Action. Here the students further specify the behavioural alternatives and give consensus on specific ones.

Phase 5: Make Public Commitment. The students are asked to make public commitment to carry out the specific behaviour.

Phase 6: Behavioural Follow-up. After a certain period of time, the teacher asks the students to examine the effectiveness of the new behaviours. If found effective, he reinforces them for future action. The above strategy has moderate structure and the teacher behaviour is controlled by three principles.

- Involvement
- Non-evaluative attitude
- The class as a whole identifies, selects and follows through, with alternative courses of action.

Students should develop healthy interpersonal relationships. Several strategies may be used in developing interpersonal relationship. One such strategy is Sensitivity Training. The objective of sensitivity training is for individuals to understand (i) how they function in a group situation (ii) how a group functions. It is concerned with sensitivity to one's feelings as well as the feelings of others. Sensitivity training is based on some assumptions. One is that individuals should not go back into the past to analyse the effect of events on their lives. "Here and now" provides sufficient experience to work on. In sensitivity training a safe environment is provided in which feelings can be unmasked and shared. The chief qualities of the classroom teacher as expected in this strategy are warm personality and skill in interpersonal and discussion techniques.

9

Counselling for the Disabled

As a group they comprise the most heterogeneous group of exceptional children. They may have a wide range of medical diagnoses and greatly varying special education and support services needs. Some will not be classifiable as handicapped for special education purposes. Many will be educationally retarded, usually due to lack of experiences or suitable adaptations. They may have problems of personal, social, and emotional adjustment possibly related to the physical impairment, that is, somatopsychic, although the presence and degree will depend on the makeup of the individual pupil. There are also some myths associated with this heterogeneous subpopulation. One is that they possess special educational gifts to compensate for the physical impairment.

Obviously, such gifts would be a matter of individual differences related to aptitude, compensation, and availability of time. Another myth is that the physical impairment is accompanied by a mental limitation. It is easy to generalize the handicap because it is so visual and, at times, limiting in terms of participation in school activities.

With this subpopulation it is not uncommon to differentiate between a disability and a handicap. The disability is the measurable constant condition and the handicap is a consequence of the disability. This distinction is probably useful for his group in that many do not, or do not want to, qualify for special education programming. As pointed out by Sirvis, "it is not the actual physical variation but, rather, the individual's attitude in relation to society's view of physical conditions that determine the extent of the handicap"

All classification systems rely heavily on medical diagnosis and degree of functional defect. P.L. 94-142 yields the following classifications and descriptions.

"Orthopedically impaired" means a severe orthopedic impairment which adversely affects a child's educational performance. The term includes impairments caused by congenital anomaly and impairments from other causes.

"Other health impaired" means limited strength, vitality, or alertness, due to chronic or acute health problems such as a heart condition, tuberculosis, rheumatic fever, nephritis, asthma, sickle cell anemia, hemophilia, epilepsy, lead poisoning, leukemia, or diabetes, which adversely affects a child's educational performance."

A more specific breakdown can be made into the broad categories of neurological, orthopedic, infectious disease, and other health impairments. There is always a danger in generalizations made from inclusion in broad categories due to overlap, but the technique is useful as a point of departure for purposes of educational planning.

The Disabilities

Neurological impairments involve the nervous system and generally prove to be more educationally handicapping than other kinds of physical disabilities since the nervous system is the activation of the whole organism. Pupils so impaired present a particular challenge to pupil services staff due to the fact that impairment of learning may compound the physical disability.

1. Cerebral palsy describes a number of neuromuscular disabilities that may range from mild motor incoordination to almost complete helplessness. Prevalence estimates vary according to definition and classification but a reasonable estimate would appear to be three per thousand. In addition to the motor problems there are usually secondary handicaps that impede sensory and receptive functions. The most prevalent secondary handicaps are speech impairments and mental retardation.

2. Epilepsy is a convulsive disorder that results in some kind of seizure. Brain lesions result in uncontrolled neuron firings in the brain or idiopathic and may be either permanent or temporary, depending on etiology. The seizures are usually described as grand mal, petit mal, and psychomotor. The latter form has been of interest to youth workers because some deviant behaviours, including antisocial behaviour, has been traced to this malady. Epilepsy can be controlled by medication but may have as sequelae some drowsiness, poor concentration and incoordination, Prevalence is about one per hundred.

3. Multiple sclerosis is a disorder of the central nervous system characterized by the hardening of the protective covering on nerve fibres. Symptoms include muscle weakness, unsteady gait, and sensory complications. It is a disease of older adolescents and adults and tends to progressive deterioration. Management of the condition involves interpretation of the condition to the individual, provision of a protective regimen, and appropriate treatment.

Orthopedic handicaps comprise musculoskeletal conditions that effect the limbs, spine, and joints. These conditions may handicap a pupil in terms of mobility or coordination, either gross or fine. Such conditions may be either congenital or acquired. A partial listing follows.

1. ***Scoliosis*** is a condition involving curvature of the spine which can cause limited movement. It will most likely require casting and bracing.

2. ***Rheumatoid arthritis*** involves inflammation of the joints, tendons, and muscles. Frequently, there is severe inflammation of the eyes. It represents one of the few conditions where the incidence for girls is higher than for boys. It is more common in children than is generally recognized.

3. ***Muscular dystrophy*** is a disease characterized by the weakening of the skeletal muscles. In children the form of the disease is called pseudo-hypertrophic or Deschesne.

Muscle weakness becomes so pronounced that the pupil becomes confined to a wheelchair. This form of the disease is hereditary and is rarely seen in girls.

4. *Spina bifida* is a term that describes a congenital condition that takes a variety of forms. Basically, the disorder is caused by a failure of closure in the spinal column. This damages the spinal cord and nerve roots in a variety of ways and may result in neurological, sensory, and organ problems. Orthopedic care usually begins at birth and continuing physical therapy is often necessary.

5. *Limb deficiencies* may be congenital or acquired after birth. Successful prosthesis and adaptability to normal routines are dependent on the location and severity of the loss. Pupils who are handicapped in this way often make excellent adjustments due to the long-standing nature of the condition.

6 *Miscellaneous crippling conditions* result from accidents, both vehicular and home. Included in this category would be instances of child abuse that results in impairment of function. The latter is a situation that will often involve investigation and intervention by members of the pupil services staff.

The Diseases

These are conditions that may be either acute or chronic depending on time of onset and subsequent treatment. Some may be transmitted in the school situation.

1. Hepatitis is manifested by a jaundiced appearance which is caused by swelling and soreness of the liver. It has the highest incidence rate, including all diseases, among children of school.

2. Nephritis is seen as puffiness about the eyes and other body parts due to disease of the kidneys. It tends to occur most often in young males.

3. Mononucleosis is most prevalent among high school and

college age youth. The disease is caused by a virus but can be brought on by fatigue and stress.

Other Problems

1. Cystic fibrosis is a hereditary disorder found most often among whites. The condition is characterized by dry coughing and frequent bowel movements. In recent years, medical advances have improved prognosis.

2. Cancer takes the form of leukemia and tumors of the eye, brain, bone, and kidney in children and youth. The various forms of cancer in children tend to be acute and progress rapidly. Treatment of the disease may result in symptoms like fatigue, weight changes, and nausea. The emotional sequelae may necessitate intervention by pupil services staff.

3. Asthma is one of the allergic conditions, often triggered by emotional stress. This illness results in spells of coughing and difficulty in breathing. Although those with mild and moderate involvement will be able to be mainstreamed, there will often be frequent absences from school.

4. Rheumatic fever follows a streptococcus infection and is characterized by chronic infection of the connective tissues. Prolonged attacks may result in heart damage. In the latter instance, the pupil services specialist will want to participate in decisions as to program modifications.

In case involving physical disabilities one often encounters the phenomenon of the multiple handicap. Friedman and MacQueen in the survey of physically handicapped school-aged children found that many had secondary handicaps.

Muitihandicapped means concomitant impairments, the combination of which causes such severe educational problems that they cannot be accommodated in special education programs solely for one of the impairments. The term does not include deaf-blind children.

Unfortunately, pupils who are so characterized often find themselves shunted into special education programming based on the primary presenting school-related handicap. This means that if a neurological impairment causes school assessment and performance results that appear to be at the level of mental retardation, this then becomes a case for attention. The challenge to the pupil services administrator and staff is to insure that the total pupil is considered in such placement decisions. The parents who have lived with a diagnosis of cerebral palsy from birth do not want school personnel to inform them that the child is mentally retarded. Physical disabilities will often cause secondary handicaps and this should be recognized. Appropriate diagnostic services will probably reveal that there are a number of variables that impact performance. It is short-sighted and less than humanistic to ascribe a handicapping condition to the result of one test score or series of observations.

The visually impaired, frequently listed under the sensorihandicapped, are a group that has captured popular interest. A visual impairment is a malfunction of the eye or optic nerve which prevents normal vision. It is standard practice to define visual impairment by degree of visual acuity and field of vision. The term blindness implied sightlessness but the definition refers to severe limitation in visual functioning. The legally blind are those who have central visual acuity of 20/200 or less in the better eye with correction or whose peripheral field is no grater than 20 degrees. The partially sighted have visual acuity between 20/200 and 20/70 in the better eye. Thus, most legally blind people can see some things but they may look dim, blurred, or out of focus. In addition, they may see only part of an object. The blind usually need braille systems while the partially sighted will require large print books.

It is estimated that approximately 0.1 per cent of school age children are visually handicapped. In translation, this means that a school district population of 5,000 will have only five pupils so designated. They represent a small number of pupils and according to statistics comprise the smallest group of exceptional children. Etiologically, the visually impaired are the result of events that occurred prior to, during, or shortly after birth. Some have cataracts or retrolental fibroplasia. The diagnosis is usually as follows:

1. Refractive disorder: myopia, hyperopia, cataracts, astigmatism.
2. Muscle disorder: strabismus, nystagmus, amblyopia.
3. Receptive disorder: retrolental fibroplasia, optic atrophy.

Methods of Teaching

Over the years, instruction for the physically disabled has moved increasingly from the hospital to the school setting. In the school setting, as a result of P.L. 94-142, there is also movement from the self-contained special class to the specially adapted regular classroom. In perhaps no other exceptionality is the need for multidisciplinary planning so crucial. The team may frequently involve specialists from social work, psychology, speech therapy, nursing, rehabilitation counselling, and physical and occupational therapy as well as recreation. Whereas the other handicapping conditions involve essentially mental and emotional components, the physically disabled subpopulation will often entail these in combination with physical limitations. In many school districts, this range of services may not be readily available; therefore, these services must be rendered on a consultative basis. Providing for the full range of services poses a particular problem for the pupil services administrator. However, once the team is assembled, there should be a focus on four developmental goals.

1. Physical independence, including mastery of daily-living skills
2. Self-awareness and social maturation.
3. Academic growth
4. Career education, including constructive leisure activities.

These components should become an integral part of the Individualized Education Program. The team will be assisted by the parents in the development of the IEP, an ingredient that was lacking in the pre-P, L. 94-142 era.

There is probably nothing more important to the physically disabled pupil than physical independence. It has been noted that one of the prime targets for professional personnel is to move the physically disabled person from dependence to independence. Not surprisingly, one of the cornerstones of independence is freedom of physical movement from place to place. If one must depend on others for daily living activities, it is bound to foster dependence or frustration in the best adjusted person. Key personnel in the attainment of physical independence are physical and occupational therapists. The importance of occupational therapy is specified in the 1977 P.L-142 regulations under related services.

1. Improving, developing, or restoring functions impaired or lost through illness, injury, or deprivation.
2. Improving ability to perform tasks for independent functioning when functions are impaired or lost.
3. Preventing, through early intervention, initial or further impairment or loss of function.

Prior to the advent of P.L. 94-142, these services were rarely seen in the schools. Physical and occupational therapists have been traditionally hospital-bound personnel and individuals have been referred to these settings for evaluation and treatment. This still obtains for only a limited number of school districts which employ physical and occupational therapists. However, more are being hired on a consultative basis to serve the schools. One of the persistent problems for the pupil services administrator is to locate such personnel for employment particularly if the district is removed from metropolitan areas or areas that have comprehensive medical facilities.

In the attainment of physical independence during the school hours, there is need for adaptive physical sites, equipment, and materials. The emphasis in the Rehabilitation Act of 1973, P.L. 93-112, Second 504, has increased sensitivity to barrier-free locations but adaptive equipment and materials remain the responsibility of educators who wish to implement least restrictive environments. Although not all locations have to be adapted, most existing buildings with heavy concentrations of physically disabled pupils could make modest modifications without exorbitant costs. A partial list of some minor changes is as follows:

1. Ramps as well as steps for wheelchairs and crutches.
2. Handbars by drinking fountains, toilet stalls, and blackboards
3. Removal of desks to make room for a wheelchair.
4. Modification of furniture to provide for the pupil with braces.
5. Rubber mats over slippery floors.
6. Wide doorways.

While only a general statement can be made about the adaptation of equipment and materials, there should be available to the teaching staff a variety of devices to meet individual pupil needs. Each disability, or combination of disabilities, requires its own adaptations. Some of these adaptations are as follows:

1. Availability of pencil-holding devices or other modification of pencils to assist holding.
2. Provision of trays to keep pencil and crayons from falling to the floor.
3. Provision of book holders or mechanical page turns.
4. Modification of electric typewriters with cutouts for keys.
5. Installation of foot rests.

Some of these approaches may seem minor, but sometimes small steps taken toward the achievement of independence can lead to greater self-confidence and a desire for more physical independence.

Practical Aspects

In terms of self-awareness and social maturation nothing is more important than the development of a positive self-concept. The development of a positive self-concept may be difficult because the physical disability can engender feelings of inadequacy and insecurity. In addition, the physically impaired pupil may experience an attitude of rejection from parents and peers. Not only is self-concept derived from interactions with others but from self-image which, in turn, may be influenced by body image. In essence, the physically disabled pupil must be assisted to feel good about himself or herself which can lead to self-awareness and social maturation. Physically disabled pupils will have their share of adjustment problems but there is nothing in the literature to indicate that this subpopulation is automatically maladjusted. Meyerson states that the physically disabled may be more vulnerable to emotional disturbance than the non-disabled for two reasons:

1. Being placed in more "new" situations than their non-disabled counterparts.
2. Being forced to live in overlapping psychological worlds- one for the disabled and the other for the "normal".

Meyerson suggests solutions to these problems (1) lie in increasing frustration tolerance and teaching adaptation skills and (2) reducing pressure that cause one to seek inaccessible and unobtainable goals that one tends to exclude. Certainly, the physically disabled must learn more about their potential and limitations so that coping mechanisms can be at their highest level. As part of the self-awareness process, physically disabled pupils must be assisted in the exploration of feelings so that they can deal with both frustration and criticism.

Academic growth is important because, as previously pointed out, the physically disabled as a group tend to be educationally deficient. If a pupil loses much time for school it may be necessary to offer tutorial instruction. Obviously, comprehensive diagnostic assessment is necessary in order to determine educational and sensory deficits. However, the curricular approach to the physically disabled must be flexible in the realization that some pupils, particularly at the secondary level, must learn survival skills. Individual academic growth will be facilitated by the new electronic technology which will provide support for missing or defective body parts as well as sensory and motor deficits. Individualization of instruction will revolve around the IEP and annual growth will be charted and monitored through this vehicle. The pupil services specialist should be alert to the need for innovative approaches to the instruction of the physically disabled. Beyond this the pupil services specialist should ensure that needs and strategies are introduced at the team meeting. In this endeavour he or she must have the active support of the pupil services administrator for there is prone to be resistance to such suggestions on the grounds of time and costs. Pupil services staff will be reluctant to assume an activist stance in these matters without administrative support.

The area of career education received heavy emphasis during the 1970s in the schools with all subpopulations. By the mid seventies, there was an awareness that this concept should also be applied to the handicapped. It is particularly relevant for the physically handicapped because over the years they have been systematically excluded from a variety of options in the work place. Related to career education is career development which cannot take place. What has hampered the career development of the physically disabled is the presence of stereotypes that the general public, and perhaps, the physically disabled themselves believe. These stereotypes have been summarized by Osipow.

A discussion of stereotypical assumptions about the disabled have also been discussed by Beane and Zachmanoglou and Humes, Stereotypes must be combated because they tend to be internalized by the physically handicapped and result in self-fulfilling prophecies. The starting point for comprehensive career development is a sequential, systematic program of career education. Career education is intended to help the handicapped as well as the non-handicapped. There are five psychosocial components to career education and they all have relevance for the disabled.

1. Career education assists individuals in becoming aware of the relationship between their maturity and their evolving aspirations, values, and potentialities.
2. Career education assists individuals in developing a sense of worth, purpose, and direction in life.
3. Career education assists the individual in becoming a part of rather than apart from society. This sense of participation

leads to direct application of the principles of normalization.

4. Career education provides the individual with the security of legitimation in relation to the norms of achieving adult status.
5. Career education enables individuals to become fully capacitated to perform all of life's roles more effectively.

The Difference

Assumptions About Career Development in the Handicapped

1. Career development is unsystematic, i.e., the handicapped had better take what is available.
2. Career development is not psychological since the handicapped don't have much psychological life.
3. Career development in one's life is not important for the handicapped.
4. The handicap overrides other career behaviour characteristics.
5. The career options of the handicapped are very limited.
6. The career development of the handicapped is arrested or retarded.
7. The career development of the handicapped is stressful at all points.

At the same time that career education is going on, there is a concurrent growth in career development. Career development of the physically disabled should have as its goal the "preparation for all meaningful and productive activity, at work or at leisure, whether paid or volunteer, as employee and employer, in private business or in the public sector, or in the family". Career development activities for the physically disabled should have a K-12 emphasis. At the secondary level, a period of exploration should embrace the following elements.

1. Exposure to occupational information via lectures, books,

pamphlets, films, and filmstrips, and multimedia kits. Occupationally field trips and resource speakers afford excellent opportunities for the student both to acquire occupational information and to become aware of work opportunities available in the community.

2. Exposure to physically disabled adults is representative of a wide variety of semiskilled, skilled and professional occupations.

3. Exposure to job-related equipment and devices that can assist a physically disabled individual in overcoming his/her physical limitations. Ideally the exposure should include opportunities to (a) observe others use these devices and (b) engage in "hands-on" experience in the classroom, vocational or scientific laboratory, or at the work site of a disabled person.

4. Opportunity to acquire knowledge about one's occupational interests, strength, and weaknesses via comprehensive educational-occupational assessment that should include work samples and/or other forms of simulated work experiences.

5. Opportunities to participate in a wide variety of a academic-occupational classroom, laboratory and work-training experiences. It is especially important that the physically disabled not be arbitrarily excluded from such "nonacademic" subjects as art and music, physical education, laboratory science, and homemaking/industrial education at either the elementary or secondary level. For some of the more severely disabled individuals, specially organized classes or an individualized program in these subjects may be needed. Supervised work experience also is important for the physically disabled since they typically have more difficulty than the able-bodied in obtaining part-time or summer employment.

Characteristic of many of the physically disabled reflect the absence of work-related and social experiences that are part of the every day lives of the non-disabled adolescent. These experience deficits put the physically disabled at a severe disadvantage in relationship to their non-disabled counterparts. Some of the physically disabled have been so sheltered that they do not realize that lower echelon jobs usually precede higher level responsibilities and that one earns vacation time only after a period of successful employment. Pupil services workers should not take for granted the existence of back-ground and experience that contribute to an understanding of the work world.

The aforementioned goals, while not all-inclusive, should provide a blue-print for pupil services workers and administrators as they approach the delicate task of providing an appropriate educational experience for physically disabled pupils. Developmental goals such as these must be believed and subscribed to by those who promote them. To this extent, pupil services specialists and administrators must examine their own attitudes toward the physically disabled.

Counselling strategies with the physically disabled will not be markedly dissimilar from those used with the non-disabled. Client-centered, behavioural, and cognitive-oriented techniques may be equally applicable depending on the pupil, counsellor, and setting. It is important that the counsellor know something about the nature of physical disabilities and have some coursework or practical experiences. As an entry point the counsellor must be cognizant of some of the characteristics of the physically disabled. They are as follows:

1. Many have had few of the social experiences and as a result may be immature and lacking in self-confidence.
2. Some will have aspirations that are too low, while others may have aspirations that are much too high.
3. Many will be reluctant to trust their own judgment and will be inclined to take on a planning role.
4. Much of career planning may be unrealistic or stereotypic.
5. Many will focus on their limitations rather than abilities.
6. Some will feel that educational weaknesses are due to mental limitation rather than lack of opportunity.

The counsellor in assisting physically disabled pupils must be oriented to individual coping levels particularly as they affect career and vocational issues. The coping levels must zero in on the areas of work-accessibility, work performance, and work rewards. Various questions must be posed by the counsellor both to himself or herself and to the counsellee. However, in order to make the counselling process meaningful, the pupil must assume a participatory stance in order to resolve the questions. The physically disabled are so conditioned to having things done to them or for them that it is difficult to reverse this expectation and assume responsibility for their own actions. The ultimate goals is to permit the physically disabled to assume responsibility for their own lives. However, this cannot happen unless all avenues and opportunities have been made available at the appropriate time and place.

General Trends

One of the problems facing the pupil services administrator and staff deals with attitudes of the non-disabled toward disabled peers. As pointed out by Siller, most individuals coming into interaction with the physically disabled feel anxiety or even aversion. Numerous studies can be quoted to confirm that physically disabled persons are often regarded less favourably than the non-disabled. One can reasonably expect this range of feelings from the regular education staff. If the teaching corps cannot view the disabled in a reasonably positive fashion, one can expect a limited range of interest at the IEP team meetings. Modification of such negative attitudinal components involves the necessity of comprehensive staff development and in-service efforts. A number of techniques have been used to produce positive attitudinal changes toward the physically disabled. They can be placed in categories as follows:

1. Direct or indirect contacts between the disabled and non-disabled.
2. Provision of information about disabilities.
3. Persuasion and exhortation.

4. Analysis of the roots of prejudice.
5. Simulation exercises.
6. Discussion in groups.

Some of the techniques are not as effective as others. One of the more successful is actual contact but it works best in structured situations when the participants have equal status. Mere information and persuasion have a limited effect. Any effort to produce attitudinal change should be spearheaded by the pupil services administrator by virtue of his knowledge about the dimensions of the problem. In planning such programs the administrator should remember the following:

1. Attitudinal components toward the physically disabled can be identified and measured.
2. A generalization of attitude components appears to exist across all disabilities.
3. The separate components of attitude within physical disability are positively correlated.
4. Demographic variables are important in the way that attitudes are expressed.
5. Negative attitudinal components are recognized by persons holding to them.

One may expect negative attitudes in some pupil services staff and even in some pupil services administrators. When these occur, it will undoubtedly be necessary to provide intensive and well-organized seminars, for the feelings may be deep and not readily retrievable. The pupil services administrator with negative attitudes will have to work especially hard to bring the reasons for the devaluation to awareness.

In dealing with the physically disabled a method of work sampling is crucial if the pupil services worker is to have some direction for training and placement. Work sampling is particularly important when the vocational prospects for the pupil are not clearly evident. Work sampling or assessment can be accomplished in on-job-training or in workshop settings. The objective is to expose the pupil to a variety of work stations where practical job skills can be demonstrated. Work station experiences can include paper-and-pencil tests, commercial exercises, or job simulations with step-by-step instructions. In work sampling experiences in workshop or rehabilitation settings it is customary to use one of a variety of commercially produced work sample packages. Among them are:

1. *Jewish Employment and Vocational Service System.* Measures potential in industrial categories and includes 28 work samples for hands-on assessment of skills, behaviour, and interests. Work activities of assembly/disassembly, binding, clerical, display/printing, electrical, mail handling, structural development, and metal work are included.

2. *Testing, Orientation, and Work Evaluation in Rehabilitation:* It is the oldest and perhaps best-known work sample system for the disabled. Consists of 94 work samples clustered into 14 occupational areas. Work activities include jewellery manufacturing, drafting, drawing, sewing, and electronics assembly. Personality dimensions of work habits, work tolerance, attitudes, speed, and motivation are also assessed.

3. *Social and Prevocational Information Battery.* Developed for use with retarded individuals and includes knowledge areas in employability, economic self-sufficiency, family living, personal habits, and communication.

4. *Singer Vocational Evaluation System.* An audiovisual approach to work activities in areas of bench assembly, electrical wiring, plumbing and pipe-fitting, cooking and baking, and cosmetology.

5. *Valpar Component Work Sample System.* Has 16 individual assessment units which have been standardized for both able bodied workers and the physically disabled. Units measure skills of size discrimination, clerical comprehension and aptitude, independent problem-solving, eye-hand-foot coordination, and money handling.

This sampling helps the pupil services workers to plan the training and placement.

10

Counselling on Sentimental Issues

There are the most deserving people. There is no one group that will need and receive more counselling and support assistance than the emotionally troubled. Assistance will be rendered along the entire spectrum of the handicap and will include those who are designated as emotionally disturbed and eligible for special education. The need for counselling or therapeutic intervention with this subpopulation is greater than for any other. The stakes are not only immediate but life-long. According to Dimick and Huff the lack of intervention with those who have emotional problems will result in more disabilities than all other health conditions in combination. This is most surprising when one considers that success or failure in life is contingent on an individuals' reservoir of adaptive responses.

Counselling activities with the emotionally handicapped may be either indirect or direct. Pupils being seated therapeutically by outside practitioners will usually be seen by a pupil services specialist in only a consultative or liaison role. On the other hand, pupils with mild handicapping conditions may have no other service but the efforts of the school counsellor, school psychologist, school social worker, and so forth. Eyde has developed a descriptive figure which relates the level of emotional handicap to degrees of counselling involvement.

Severe disorder. This is the group of emotionally handicapped pupils who fit the P.L. 94-142 definition of "severely emotionally disturbed". These pupils will, and should be treated by psychiatrists, clinical psychologists, or mental health treatment teams. The pupil services specialist will generally perform a liaison function between the outside clinical service and the school. It is a rule of thumb that counselling within the school will not take place simultaneously with treatment rendered by an outside source.

Moderate disorder. Pupils within this grouping may be in a resource room situation or in regular classes. It is practically certain that these pupils will require counselling from either outside sources or school personnel. If counselling takes place within the confines of the school, there may be need of a counselling IEP. These pupils may manifest conflicts in the areas of affect, anxiety, and impulse control.

Mild disorder. This relatively large group comprise the group who will remain in the regular classroom. They may not qualify for special educational services but will yet appear emotionally troubled. The pupil services workers' role will be consultant to the teacher in the realm of classroom management. It is likely that most referrals will come from impulse control problems which will be shown through disruptive behaviour and aggressive reactions.

Marginal adjustment. The marginally adjusted pupil is the one who can benefit from preventive measures. The pupil services worker, and specifically the school counsellor, serves as a developmental specialist for this group of pupils. The counsellor will often alert both the teacher and home about a potential problem that may be avoided through the structuring of learning experiences.

Sound mental health. The pupil services specialist may focus on the developmental needs of the "normal" population and will function essentially as a mental health educator. The pupil services specialist will endeavour to promote group and individual activities which will reinforce sound mental health. The pupil services worker will also attempt to develop an ecosystem that will be conducive to sound mental health. With this group the staff member functions as a curricular adviser, teacher trainer, and parent educator.

Along this spectrum of degree of handicap the pupil services administrator may see the opportunity to parcel out areas of responsibility so that territorial concerns are minimal. The school counsellor would have prime responsibility for those with sound mental health., marginal adjustment, and mild disorders. The school psychologist and school social worker would have principal responsibility for dealing with those pupils who manifest moderate and severe disorders. Naturally, this division of labour will be dependent on availability of staffing and philosophy of the district.

It is possible to identify three supportive counselling services for the pupil services worker which can be considered indirect services. These are consultation, collaboration, and conceptualization. The consultant attempts to achieve a match between the pupils' developmental needs and the learning environments. In order to serve as an effective consultant to the providers of instructional services to the emotionally handicapped the pupil services workers must deal with issues of lack of information, lack of skills, lack of confidence, and lack of objectivity. As collaborator the pupil services specialist will assist in the coordination of IEPs which for the emotionally handicapped pupil will probably involve considerable contact with regular classroom teachers due to the fact that many of these pupils will be mainstreamed.

The pupil services specialist as conceptualizer is somewhat more difficult to delineate because it entails observation of the total or "big" picture and reaching some conclusion as to what may be the cause or cure of an individual or institutional problems. If the conceptualizer role does not fall to the pupil services specialist, it may fall to no one. The conceptualizer must determine what areas are impacting the pupil, whether school, home, or community, and how these forces may be modified.

Direct services may include behavioural change counselling, biofeedback training, life-space interviewing, affective education classes, leisure education and therapeutic play, peer counselling, and parent education. The latter is a particularly useful form of counselling to ameliorate the problems of the emotionally handicapped. It has been often observed that part of many emotional disturbance situations is a disordered parent-child relationship. If parents can understand their own adjustment problems, the dynamics of the home situation may change and in doing so the interactions with the pupil may improve. All direct services with emotionally handicapped pupils and their families require special personal qualities and personal commitments. Establishing a relationship and conveying a sense of caring is a must. Typically, the emotionally handicapped pupil and his/her parents have felt frustrated, neglected, isolated, and misunderstood. In order to overcome these feelings of rejection it is necessary to focus on the individual rather than the problem. It is not easy to work with those who experience emotional problems. Those who need the most help often engage in self-defeating behaviour in an effort to reinforce feelings of self-rejection and to encourage hostility on the part of those who seek to help. It goes without saying that every pupil services specialist is not equipped to engage in direct services with this subpopulation.

Practical Problems

Next to learning disabilities the emotionally handicapped represent the newest category. As such it is still in a process of growth and redefinition. While P.L. 94-142 served to delimit the number of pupils who could be so categorized, it remains a fact that the emotionally troubled are still out there. They must be served, either through special education avenues or some modification thereof It remains the category of most concern to teachers and administrators because of the daily challenges. posed by this subpopulation. Some of the issues to be dealt with by a pupil services administrator will be discussed in further detail.

Supporting Structure

An issue of considerable interest to pupil services administrators and staff is the role of support personnel in identification, placement, and follow-up of the emotionally handicapped. The pupil services specialist is usually the first person, after the initial referral, who sees the pupil suspected of being emotionally disturbed. Undoubtedly, the pupil has emotional problems, as perceived by another person, but the task of the pupil services worker is to conduct an initial "screening" to determine whether the pupil is within normal limits in terms of adaptive behaviour. Such screening will depend on many situational variables, for example, adequacy and philosophy of the district, competency of the teaching staff, socioeconomic climate of the school, and so forth. Accordingly, it is not as simplistic as many classroom teachers and general administrators would like it to be. The pupil services worker must make a decision either to go forward with diagnostic instrumentation, a costly procedure, or refer back to the teacher. Unfortunately, the initial introduction is just like in nature, a heavy role indeed. This role will be especially difficult in small schools or districts where the pupil services worker cannot talk with colleagues about prediagnostic impressions. During the placement or IEP process the pupil services specialist who reviewed and prepared the case materials will be expected to make a recommendation based on diagnostic impressions. This will probably be easiest for the school psychologist, due to the availability of test instrumentation, but even here the problem is exacerbated by the fact that test instrumentation is imprecise in terms of diagnosis of emotional disturbance. Once a pupil is placed, there is more need for follow up of the emotional handicapped than for any of the other subpopulations because emotional handicaps are dynamic and reversible. If possible, a pupil service worker should remain in contact with every pupil who has been designated as emotionally handicapped and determined by the IEP team to be in need of special education. If there are staff shortages the pupil services administrator must try to design alternative strategies to make the consultive approach work. Adult education programs might be considered as an alternative.

Related to the role of support personnel is the question of diagnosis The federal IEP regulations are quite specific as to who should be classified as "severely emotionally disturbed." Should such a classification be assigned by a group of school professionals, based on demonstrated behaviour, or should the designation be reserved for clinic personnel? The answer rests, in part, on whether one chooses to follow an educational or medical model. It is possible to mount compelling arguments on both sides. While the education model will tend to move pupils in and out of special education programs more readily, clinical diagnosis is more apt to result in treatment and parental acceptance. If a given district chooses to use a categorical model, it may be expeditious to utilize outside clinical personnel for consensual validation. The designation "emotional disturbance" is a heavy label to assign to any pupil for it may convey more to the parent, community, and society than school staff intend. For example, there is evidence that behavioral disorders have both a sexual and racial bias in that minority males are often overrepresented. Conversely, it has been suggested that the moderately disturbed child is being denied services due to regulatory exclusion.

The Other Side

While it is debatable as to whether emotional disturbance or mental retardation has the most negative image, there is no doubt that emotional disturbance is a label that few people cover for a pupil. The label suggests disordered and unacceptable behaviour that is a threat to others. From a parental point of view, it is usually construed as an indictment of the parent-child relationship. The negative stereotypes associated with this handicap have prevented many pupils from getting needed help. In most districts, IEP teams must either label or describe behaviour before goals and objectives can be finalized. In the process such labeling or description of behaviour must be interpreted to parents who may have habituated an avoidance mechanism. In recognition of this eventuality, a pupil services specialist may decide not to label or describe the pupils as "seriously emotionally disturbed" for fear that the parents will reject the diagnosis and withdraw support of any treatment and placement considerations. In many districts attempts have been made to devise a short-form of the IEP so that parents will not have to face the narration of the uncomfortable details of a full-blown disturbance. The pupil services administrator must seek ways to make an emotional handicap more respectable and palatable. Such strategies may include parent seminars, teacher in-service programs, and pupil self-awareness.

Young Criminals

While the P.L. 94-142 regulations exclude the "socially

maladjusted" it is a fact that a higher proportion of social offenders show behavioural disorder than nonoffenders. Although it is widely accepted that the phenomenon of juvenile delinquency-that is, minors who have violated the law and have been apprehended-is largely in the eyes of the beholder, the fact remains that young people who are so designated have a wide range of emotional problems. Whether the problems are autoplastic or alloplastic, there is no doubt that this group poses a considerable problem for pupil services staff and administrators There is mounting evidence that juvenile delinquents have a high incidence of learning disabilities. This finding is remarkable only in that it took so long to establish the linkage. Juvenile offenders are typically school failures and early dropouts. Aside from other socio-economic factors these youth obviously never found learning to be either relevant or simple. Certainly, the likelihood of school failure can lead to emotional problems and-depending on intrapsychic, family, and community pressures-can precipitate juvenile delinquency. Although juvenile offenders are hardly a homogeneous group, a large measure of hostility may be expressed in socially unacceptable ways. These are the "acting out" pupils who plague the lives of many teachers. Such pupils will be a constant source of referrals to pupil services staff, In order to deal with the phenomenon the pupil services worker will have to assume a change-agent role. That is, there must be a recognition that many of the causes are alloplastic in nature which necessitate going to the community or family for modifications in the environment. The high dropout rate with this subpopulation indicates the need for more intensive effort in the area of primary prevention.

It is a truism that most emotionally troubled youth will be served in the regular classroom by regular teachers. A relative handful will be categorized as emotionally disturbed and therefore eligible for special education of some kind. Those who remain in regular classrooms will continue to be troubled or to trouble teaching staffs. Pupils who are not designated as in need of special education will probably receive no extra assistance unless pupil service specialists choose to intervene. Such intervention will support the regular class placement and may involve counselling, consultation, community mobilization, and the like. In such situations no team meetings are required nor is an IEP necessary. On the surface, this procedure would seem to make the possibility of service more flexible and less bound to bureaucratic restrictions. However, the pupil service specialist will be under great pressure to serve first those who have an IEP. By virtue of traditional job roles intervention can probably best be carried out by the school counsellor. The school counsellor, serving the developmental needs of all youth, is nor restricted by special education parameters. The fact that the school counsellor receives scant mention in the P. L. 94-142 regulations will allow the counsellor to provide services to those who do not qualify for special education benefits. The concept of mainstreaming does receive a lot of publicity and was in the forefront of special education thinking even before P. L. 94-142 was enacted. When it has succeeded, it has usually been through the efforts of special education teachers and a selected few regular education teachers. There is evidence that pupil services workers and special education teachers are more in agreement on behavioural objectives for this subpopulation than regular class teachers.

The Requirement

A recent report by the Children's Defense Fund indicates that two-thirds of the nations' seriously emotionally disturbed pupils are not receiving appropriate special education and related services. The researchers for the Fund, an advocacy group, reviewed the statutes and litigation involving emotionally disturbed children and adolescents and reached the following conclusions:

1. Implementation has been hindered by confusion about how severe a disturbance must be to have been covered by the regulations;
2. The schools' responsibility for psychotherapy, often a needed adjunct service, remains unclear;
3. Resistance to the obligation to pay for residential treatment, when needed, where documented by the schools inability to provide;

4. School psychologists spend practically all their time testing and do not have enough time left for counselling pupils and consulting with teachers;
5. Emphasis on serving the seriously emotionally disturbed has reduced mental health intervention strategies for early attention,
6. Some schools are not referring emotionally disturbed pupils for services;
7. States have been remiss in not encouraging the development of training programs to increase the pool of qualified teachers.

The need for counselling is obvious when one is aware that early recipients of learning disabilities services were found to need supportive and vocational assistance as adults. Practically all pupil services specialists may become involved in counselling SLD pupils. Counselling has proven effective with this subpopulation. Due to the fact that behavioural and adjustment problems often overlap cognitive deficits, there is a need for the counsellor to deal with coping and self-control skills. In dealing with these strategies, the helper may choose to use either a counselling or consultation model. In addition to the student the counsellor will work with the teacher(s) and parent(s).

Students with long standing SLD problems will demonstrate a variety of behavioural symptoms, chief among them will be low self-esteem, anxiety, anger and frustration. Counselling strategies which apply particularly to the adolescent, should :

1. Offer a chance for success, no matter how small.
2. Build an inclination to try by structuring small segments of assigned tasks.
3. Minimize situations where threats, punishment, and strong reactions of adults are prevalent.
4. Keep the student to a reasonable time schedule once he begins to make progress.

5. Alleviate deep-seated fears that he is somehow mentally subnormal.

Counsellors who deal with students who have ambivalence over intelligence may find it useful to use Lloyd Thompson's book entitled *"Language Disabilities in men of Eminence"*. In this provocative piece, Thompson uses a psycho historical approach to illustrate that some great men in history probably had SLD. Among the people described are Thomas Edison, Harvey Gushing, Auguste Rodin, George Patton, Woodrow Wilson, Paul Ehrlich, Albert Einstein and George Washington. Adolescents can identify with these eminent people and realize that all is not necessarily lost because one had a learning problem in school.

Counselling techniques will differ on the basis of behaviour problem. However, Edge, Brawm, and Brown suggest some that may be generally

1. For inadequacy, try "strength bombardment" in a group setting.
2. For anxiety, try relaxation training.
3. For anger, try a cognitive approach, perhaps rational-emotive counselling, or "I messages."
4. For frustration or inappropriate interactions try' "time out".

There is also need for parent and family counselling. Stress and sibling rivalry are commonly found in families of learning-disabled students "parents feel ambivalence, guilt, fear...but....must always subside to the reality that theirs is still a handicapped child who seems normal, but doesn't appear to learn and/or behave normally". This is the essence of the parental frustration, namely, trying to understand how a child who is normal in most ways can fail to learn in school, even with massive amounts of tutoring and family support.

As is true with most mildly handicapped adolescents, the youth who make up this subpopulation will most likely enter the competitive work force after graduation from high school. Of course, some will advance to higher education but it is apparent that an academically delimiting handicap like SLD will dictate circumscribed horizons. Too little attention has been paid heretofore to the post secondary future of the SLD pupil. Part of the problem is related to the difference between career and vocational education/development. Vocational development has a narrower focus and in terms of special education populations has tended to emphasize a limited clientele. Vocational education programs, albeit sorely limited in some parts of the country, have been targeted primarily at those pupils categorized as educable mentally retarded. This targeting developed, in part, from the belief that the mildly retarded had very few choices. The learning-disabled, however, comprise a heterogeneous group with much broader options. Accordingly, the concepts of career preparation and development are highly applicable. If a career is the totality of work or activities over a life time, then a more comprehensive approach is necessary with SLD pupils. However, before strategies are instituted there must be a realization that the SLD pupil required career development assistance.

Due to the fact that the SLD pupil has the given "normal" intelligence it is often assumed that he or she can move through the secondary school situation in lockstep with non-handicapped pupils. The implication is that SLD pupils will somehow absorb incidental career information that will be self-utilized upon graduation. While this rationale is difficult, at best, for even the non-handicapped pupil, it is disastrous for the SLD pupil. A SLD pupil is typically exerting every ounce of energy to survive the academic demands of the secondary school. If one accepts this restraint it is easy to see why little attention will be given to incidental types of learning that are part of the repertoire of informal career preparation and development. Bingham has observed that boys with SLD are less mature in their responses on the Carrier Maturity Index and require planned experience to develop vocational maturity Kendall found that subjects enrolled in vocational-training classes were superior in social maturity and career attitudes.

Another hurdle for school counsellors who are concerned with career development is the often unreasonable expectations of the parents. This hidden handicap will sometimes lead parents astray and arouse expectations of educational and occupational choices that are far beyond the proven capabilities the SLD pupil. This can be a particular problem for youth who come from college-educated or professional families. Although some youth have internalized these parental expectations, most will feel relieved to be guided toward more realistic choices. An additional variable is the actual range of possibilities that may be available. It has been pointed out previously that some colleges are now opening their doors to the identified learning-disabled motivated, successfully-coping pupil. However, the range of possibilities between vocation and college education is much less appealing. Technical schools and related occupations have yet to feel the need to adapt to the needs of the learning-disabled.

The pupil services administrator and staff must be alert to the need for career preparation and development for the SLD adolescent at these times. If quantity and quality of academic programming were the issues of the seventies then post secondary career issues will be the frontier of the eighties. It should be reiterated that P.L. 93-112. the Rehabilitation Act of 1973, does recognize specific learning disabilities as an adult disorder. The SLD person is entitled to the same considerations as others with more visible handicaps. The pupil services staff must forge a linkage with rehabilitation counsellors and employers. This is a task that will fall to school counsellors, school psychologists, and school social workers.

Problems Ahead

There arc a number of issues conforming the pupil service administrator within the domains of both development and management. The problems may differ depending on the maturity of the department, but the problem areas have similarities atinitial development problem centres around the instructional delivery system that is best for the district and the student configuration. For example, it is better to go with a tutoring program as opposed to the resources room concept? Once a procedure has been initiated, it is difficult, but not impossible, to change. The pupil services administrator must examine the nature of the SLD staff/parental expectations and financial resources and act accordingly. A development or redevelopment should utilize the needs-assessment technique so all parties are in agreement. Another development issue to be faced in the 1980s is when expansion should cease. During the 1970s the objective was to increase services so as to meet the needs of an unserved population. The time will come when not only will it be appropriate to limit expansion but also to reduce services. At a time when general school enrolments are decreasing and regular class teachers are being dismissed, can one in good conscience continue SLD services at the same level? This issue must be resolved through analysis of caseloads and the generation of "hard data" for justification,

Specific management problems may revolve around the maintenance of identification standards, standardization of caseloads, interstaff relationships, least restrictive environment, and evaluation/accountability.

11

Counselling on Mental Issues

Of lates different views of mental health counselling have evolved, including those that are developmental; relationship-focused; and treatment-centered, advocacy-based, or slanted toward personal/environmental coping. CACREP has developed a detailed description of this speciality, along with requirements for course work, basic knowledge, and skills. There is still some question about what mental health counselling encompasses.

To help the profession better define itself, Spruill and Fong suggest the following interdisciplinary definition: "Mental health counselling, a core mental health care profession, is the aggregate of the specific educational, scientific, and professional contributions of the disciplines of education, psychology, and counselling focused on promotion and maintenance of mental health, the prevention and treatment of mental illness, the identification and modification of etiologic, diagnostic, and systems correlates of mental health, mental illness, and related dysfunction, and the improvement of the mental health service delivery' system." Whether or not this definition stands the test of time, it is clear that mental health counselling is interdisciplinary in its history, practice settings, skills/knowledge, and roles performed. Its interdisciplinary nature is an asset in generating new ideas and energy. At the same time, however, it is a drawback in helping those who identify themselves as mental health counsellors distinguish themselves from some closely related mental health practitioners.

There are many practitioners within the counselling profession who use the title mental health counsellor. They work in a variety of settings, including mental health centers, community agencies, private practice, health maintenance organisations (HMOs), employee assistance programs (EAPs), health and wellness promotion programs (HWPs), geriatric centers, crisis control agencies, and child guidance clinics. They counsel a diverse group of clients, including rape victims, spouse abusers, depressives, families, potential suicide victims, substance abusers, and those with disorders from anxiety to dissociation. In addition, they consult, educate, and at times perform administrative duties. They often work closely with other helping professionals, such as psychiatrists, psychologists, clinical social workers, and psychiatric nurses, and become part of a team effort. Thus, it is crucial that mental health counsellors know the DSM-IV so they can converse intelligently with other health professionals and skillfully treat dysfunctional clients. Mental health counsellors have general counselling skills as well as speciality skills related to the needs and interests of particular populations or problems.

Wilcoxon and Puleo found that, as a group, mental health counsellors are interested in professional development related to applied areas of counselling such as marriage and family counselling, substance abuse/ chemical dependency, third-party reimbursement, and small-group counselling. Such interest is understandable in light of the fact that most mental health counsellors are practitioners and earn a living by offering services for remuneration.

Mental health counsellors are as diverse as rehabilitation counsellors in the ways they use theories and techniques in their practices, in part because mental health counsellors work in such varied settings and have widely varying functions. Their responsibilities and the theories they choose to follow depend on the needs of their clients. Brief reports in the *Journal of Mental Health Counselling* reflect mental health counsellors' interests and activities, featuring information on everything from marketing mental health counselling services to ethical issues surrounding sliding fee scales.

Dingman suggests that topics ranging from counsellor involvement in disasters to mental health counsellor's roles in school settings will be covered in the future. The literature about mental health counselling focuses on two major issues:

1. prevention and promotion of mental health and
2. treatment of disorders and dysfunctions.

Both topics are likely to continue attracting attention because they are considered primary roles of mental health counsellors.

A primary philosophical emphasis throughout the history of mental health counselling has been on prevention and promotion of mental health services. Many mental health counsellors are actively involved in primary prevention types of programs through the schools, colleges, churches, community health centers, and public and private agencies where they are employed. Primary prevention is characterised by its "before the fact quality"; it is intentional and "group or mass, rather than individually oriented". It may be directly or indirectly implemented, but it ultimately results in healthier and better-adjusted individuals.

Hershenson suggests an approach to mental health counselling that emphasises healthy development—that is, positive coping and growth. He points out that "insofar as counselling derives from a model based on healthy development it can reasonably hope to achieve its purpose of promoting healthy development in its clients". He notes that Erik Erikson and Abraham Maslow offer two solid bases from which mental health counsellors can work, The work of these researchers was based on observations about human development and emphasised the promotion of healthy life-styles.

New Trends

The integration of these two systems yields six personal development trends: survival, growth, communication, recognition, mastery, and understanding. The first two trends focus on the self, the middle two on interpersonal functions, and the final two on the accomplishment of tasks. Mental health counselling is geared toward the improvement of the self in interpersonal relationships and task performances. In an important and related article on healthy personal development. Heath outlines a comprehensive model of healthy maturation. He points out that research demonstrates that the psychological maturity of an adolescent is a major predictor of adult mental health and vocational adaptation and that the degree of adult maturity is related to marital sexual adjustment and vocational adaptation.

Following are the practical general principles that counsellors can apply in promoting client development :

1. "Encourage the anticipatory rehearsal of new adaptations," such as those that deal with jobs and intimate relationships.

2. "Require constant externalisation of what is learned and its correction by action." In essence, Heath believes practice makes perfect the accomplishment of all human tasks. Learning is accomplished through feedback.

3. "Allow a person to experience the consequences of his or her decisions and acts." Heath agrees with Alfred Adler on this idea. He notes that inappropriate or excessive rewards may have an unhealthy effect on a person's development.

4. "Appreciate and affirm strengths." Reinforcement, according to Skinner, is crucial to new learning. Heath agrees and says that the acknowledgment and acceptance of people's strengths can bolster self-confidence and help them take risks necessary for new learning.

Focusing on person's environments is another preventive emphasis of mental health counsellors. Huber sums up the research in this growing area of interest, noting that environments have personalities just as people do. Some environments are controlling and rigid, whereas others are more flexible and supportive. To make effective use of this social-ecological perspective, mental health counsellors should do the following:

- Identify the problem as one essentially connected with a particular setting. Some environments elicit or encourage specific behaviours that may not be healthy.

- Gain the agreement of clients and significant others that the environment is the client. It is much easier for most people to see a difficulty as simply a matter related to the individual.

- Assess the dynamic variables within an environment. Moos developed a number of ways to evaluate environments. Counsellors can work with clients to determine how environments function in favour of or counter to the client's needs.
- Institute social change. The counsellor helps the client with specific methods for improving the present environment.
- Evaluate the outcome. There is no one way to do this; but the more clearly the client states his or her criteria for the ideal environment, the better the evaluation possibility.

Related to the social-ecological perspective is ecosystemic thinking: "thinking that recognises the indivisible interconnectedness of individual, family, and sociocultural context". Mental health counselling is enlarged to consider the cultural contexts in which people relate and communicate in this view. Marriage is an obvious example of a situation that illustrates the importance of both personal and environmental factors in individual's well-being. Wiggins, Moody, and Lederer conducted a study on marital satisfaction and found that the most significant predictor was the compatibility of couple's tested personality typologies. They concluded, as did Holland that individuals express 'satisfaction with and seek intraction in environments that meet their psychological need? In interracial marriages, which are increasing, mental health counsellors can be therapeutic in helping couples identify and address predictable stressors in their lives, such as prejudice or identity issues regarding biracial children, and helping them find support or marriage- enrichment groups.

The number of people who need and seek mental health services cannot adequately be dealt with by the nation's mental health providers, even if the treatment of clients were the only activity in which these professionals were engaged. To address societal needs, mental health counsellors concentrate on secondary, prevention (controlling mental health problems that have already surfaced but are not severe) and tertiary prevention. In such cases (in contrast to primary prevention), mental health counsellors use theories and techniques developed by major theorists such as Rogers. Ellis, Skinner, and Glasser to treat symptoms and core conditions. Thus, mental health counselling becomes more like other helping disciplines, such as psychology, social work, and psychiatric nursing.

Mental health counsellors have a stronger tendency to deal with treatment in their discussions of the essence of mental health counselling than they do prevention. This emphasis on treatment links mental health counselling to allied health professions rather than traditional counselling. In addition, an emphasis on treatment presents a problem in regard to politics and inclusion within health systems. Unless mental health counselling is seen as distinct it may not be universally included as a core discipline for reimbursement from third-party sources beyond the state level.

There are several ways to rectify mental health counselling's tendency to concentrate on treatment. They include teaching prevention in mental health counselling programs, supporting legislation that funds preventive counselling, promoting prevention through interprofessional collaboration, establishing primary prevention as the principal mode of counselling for mental health counsellors, and encouraging the publication of more articles on primary prevention in the *Journal of Mental Health Counselling*. An emphasis on prevention will not diminish mental health counsellor's need to address secondary and tertiary prevention for children and adolescents as well as older persons. Nor will it dissuade mental health counsellors from focusing on the treatment of other general and specific life-span disorders, such as mild depression; smoking cessation; obsessive-compulsive behaviour; and bulimia. But if mental health counselling pursues the treatment of pathology and dysfunctionality too vigorously, it will most likely become a pale imitation of the medical profession and offer services that do not address an unfilled, nonmedical niche: promoting mental health. The speciality areas of rehabilitation counselling and mental health counselling have much in common, yet they are quite distinct.

Despite its recent inception, this profession has had a powerful influence on the lives of individuals and communities. It has helped the disabled gain employment and greater self-sufficiency and become productive members of the society. Although mental counselling is among the youngest counselling specialities, it has made a major impact on the general public and counselling profession. Rehabilitation activities focused on the physically disabled, but now they include work with emotional, mental, and behavioural disabilities. Bitter and Porter list a number of disabilities that rehabilitation counsellors commonly deal with: alcoholism, arthritis, blindness, cardiovascular disease, deafness, developmental disabilities, cerebral palsy, epilepsy, mental retardation, drug abuse/ neurological disorders, orthopedic disabilities, psychiatric disabilities, renal failure, speech impairments, and spinal cord conditions.

Steps have been taken in recent years to provide services for the economically disadvantaged, public offenders, and other less-obvious and often neglected groups. With such a heterogeneous population, rehabilitation counsellors typically work with other service agencies to provide needed programs for their clients. An example of this cooperative approach occurs between rehabilitation counsellors and school counsellors on behalf of children with disabilities.

Mental health counsellors have also been strongly influenced by federal and state legislative acts that have set standards for the delivery of mental health services. Members of AMHCA (American Mental Health Counsellor Association), in turn, have been active in supporting federal and state legislation that recognises Certified Clinical Mental Health Counsellors as core practitioners (recognised main providers) within the mental health profession. They have also been involved in defining the areas in which they work and establishing guidelines for how to function in them. Seiler and Messina, in keeping with these efforts, define the essence of mental health counselling as promoting healthy life-styles, identifying and eliminating stressors; in individual's life-styles, and preserving or restoring mental health. Wilmarth notes that mental health counsellors are engaged in assessing and analysing background and current information on "clients, diagnosing mental and emotional conditions, exploring possible solutions, and developing treatment plans."

Preventive mental health activities and a recognition of the relationship between physical and mental health have become very prominent since the mid 1970s. At that time the President's Commission on Mental Health was created, and initial government entitlements were directed toward prevention of mental disorders and promotion of wellness. Attention to these aspects of mental health counselling continues to increase. A final similarity between the development of rehabilitation and mental health counselling is the setting in which counsellors are employed. Traditionally, most rehabilitation counsellors have been hired by federal, state, and local agencies. Since the late 1960s, however, more have moved into for-profit agencies and private practice. In 1985 the majority of mental health counsellors were employed in private practice; but in the early years of AMHCA, most worked in community mental health centers. The movement from the public sector into private employment is the result of several developments, such as economic changes, new emphases by businesses and insurance companies, national professional certification requirements, and state licensure laws that have affected all counsellors.

Counselling as Treatment

Rehabilitation counselling's focus on serving individuals with disabilities provides a clear-cut conceptual distinction for differentiating rehabilitation practice from the practice of other counselling specialities. The speciality differs from habilitation primarily in its emphasis on education. Rehabilitation stresses reeducation of disabled individuals who have previously lived independent lives; habilitation focuses on educating clients who have been disabled from early life and have never been self-sufficient. Rehabilitation counsellors also distinguish between having a disability and being handicapped. Official definitions of what constitutes a disability are crucial in the work of the rehabilitation counsellor. A person with a disability has either a physical or a mental condition that limits that person's activities or functioning. Between 10 and 15 percent of the U.S. population is disabled. The Americans with Disabilities Act, however, projected that there are up to 43 million people with disabilities in this country. When describing this population, counsellors must avoid language "that portrays people with disabilities in imprecise, stereotypical, or devaluing ways". Such language is demeaning and places these persons in a negative light. A handicap, which is linked to but distinct from a disability, is "an observable or discernible limitation that is made so by the presence of various barriers". It is the cumulative result of obstacles that disabilities interpose between persons and their maximum level of functioning. An example of a disabled person with a handicap is a quadriplegic assigned to a third-floor apartment in a building without an elevator or a partially deaf person being given instructions mainly through verbal means. Rehabilitation counsellors help clients in these and similar situations overcome handicaps and effectively cope with their disabilities.

An interesting aspect of rehabilitation counselling distinguishes it from other forms of counselling: its historical link with the medical model of delivering services. The prominence of the medical model is easy to understand when one recalls how closely rehabilitation professionals are involved with the physically challenged. "Rehabilitation counselling practice requires knowledge in areas of medical terminology, diagnosis, prognosis, vocational evaluation of disability-related limitations, and job placement in the context of a socioeconomic system". Although the medical model originally dominated this counselling speciality, more pragmatic models of helping seem to be emerging. For instance, the minority model assumes that persons with disabilities are a minority group rather than people with patholosies. The peer-counsellor model assumes that people with direct experience with disabilities are best able to help those who have recently acquired disabilities.

Stone lists three ways in which rehabilitation counselling differs from other types of counselling. First, there are differences in the nature of clients served. Rehabilitation counsellors work with a much more impaired population than do other counsellors. Most rehabilitation clients have severe physical, mental, or behavioural disorders. Second, rehabilitation counsellors are responsible for providing clients with educational information and remedial and therapeutic treatment. Unlike other counsellors, rehabilitation counsellors traditionally focus their efforts on helping clients obtain employment. Many beginning rehabilitation counselling students embrace the Protestant work ethic. As Sinick observes, the word vocational is incorporated into the name of many state agencies and job titles that relate to the field. Third, clients expect rehabilitation counsellors to be professionals who provide a wide range of services, especially those connected with disabilities and employment. All clients expect much of counsellors, but rehabilitation clients have more specific needs and hopes than most.

Rehabilitation Counsellors

Rehabilitation counsellors use a wide variety of counselling theories and techniques. Almost all of the affective, behavioural, and cognitive theories reviewed in this text are employed by those who work in this field, Recently, there has been an emphasis on social-systems theories in rehabilitation practice and with it has come renewed research on comparing psychologically based hypotheses with those that are more systemic. The actual theories and techniques used in rehabilitation counselling are dictated by the education and style of counsellors as well as the needs of clients, For example, a disabled client with sexual feelings may need permission, information, and suggestions on how to handle these emotions while another disabled client who is depressed may need other forms of attention and input. Ideally, theories and techniques are chosen with regard to specific situations and are aimed at enhancing the overall functioning of clients. This approach is in keeping with Rusalem's observation that one of the main tasks of rehabilitation counsellors is to help their clients accept and adjust to disabilities and the attitudes and reactions of society at large. Livneh and Evans point out that rehabilitation clients who have physical disabilities ;for example, blindness or spinal cord injuries, go through 12 phases of adjustment: shock, anxiety, bargaining, denial, mourning, depression, withdrawal, internalised anger, externalised aggression, acknowledgment, acceptance, and adjustment/ adaptation. Livneh and Evans believe that there are behavioural correlates that accompany each phase and intervention strategies appropriate for each one. For example, the client who is in a state of shock may be immobilised and cognitively disorganised. Intervention strategies most helpful during this time include comforting the person, listening and attending, offering support and reassurance, allowing the person to ventilate feelings and referring the person to institutional care if appropriate.

Affective and insight strategies are appropriate for the early phases of the adjustment process and that action and rational orientations work best in later phases. They also contend that disabled clients with low intelligence or low levels of energy may best be served by more direct, action-oriented counselling theories and techniques, such as Bandura's modelling and Skinner's operant conditioning, Krumboltz's behavioural counselling, and Glasser's reality therapy. On the other hand, rehabilitation clients with relatively high levels of energy and intelligence may respond better to more indirect counselling strategies: Rogers's person-centered approach, May's or Frank! s existential therapy, Adler's individual counselling, and Perls's Gestalt therapy. Covens notes that there is little support in the research literature for the effectiveness of indirect counselling methods in rehabilitation counselling.

Rehabilitation counsellors use more action-oriented approaches, such as those generated by behavioural and Gestalt theories. Coven believes that Gestalt psychodrama can be especially powerful in helping rehabilitation clients become more involved in the counselling process and accept responsibility for their lives. Techniques such as role playing, fantasy enactment, and psychodrama can be learned and used by clients to help in adjustment. A few examples will illustrate some specific ways in which rehabilitation counsellors provide services. Hendrick points out that physical injuries such as spinal cord damage produce a major loss for an individual and consequently have a tremendous physical and emotional impact. Rehabilitation in such cases requires concentration on both the client's and the family's adjustment to the situation.

Everyone involved needs help working through the mourning

process, and all need to be included in developing detailed medical, social, and psychological evaluations. A long-term counsellor commitment involves carefully timed supportive counselling, crisis intervention, confrontation, life-planning activities, sex counselling, and group counselling. In short, the rehabilitation counsellor must help the person with an injured spinal cord develop an internal locus of control for accepting responsibility for his or her life. In addition to serving as a counsellor, a professional who works with the physically disabled must be an advocate, a consultant, and an educator. The task is comprehensive and involves a complex relationship among job functions.Some children with disabilities are also mentally limited. In these cases, the counsellor's tasks and techniques may be similar to those employed with a physically disabled adult or adolescent (supportive counselling and life-planning activities). But young clients with mental deficiencies require more and different activities. Norton advocates that counsellors who work with this population first work through personal feelings about the children. Only then can counsellors begin to be helpful. Huber asserts that counsellors must also help parents assess feelings, ideally in a group setting. While working with adolescents who have mental difficulties due to head injuries, a counsellor must address social issues as well as therapeutic activities.

As a general rule, increased time and effort in attending to psychosocial issues is required for working with anyone who has been mentally impaired, regardless of the cause. Rehabilitation counsellors also provide services for persons with HIV/AIDS. HIV is now considered a chronic illness, and people with AIDS are classified as disabled under the Americans with Disabilities Act.

A large percentage of people in these two groups are already socially stigmatised, so rehabilitation counsellors must first examine their own attitudes and feelings before attempting to deal with this special population. Then their tasks are to assist clients in dealing with psychosocial tasks, such as maintaining a meaningful quality of life, coping with loss of function, and confronting existential or spiritual issues.

Common client emotions include shock, anger, anxietv, fear, resentment, and depression. Therefore, counsellors must help clients face these emotions as well. In addition, practical considerations such as preparing for treatment or death must be handled in a sensitive and caring way. Hollirngsworth and Mastroberti point out that in dealing with minority groups, such as women workers with disabilities, counsellors must be aware of the developmental processes typical in such populations and be prepared with appropriate counselling techniques for the problems peculiar to each group. Counselling disabled women, for example, involves four interrelated elements: (a) job or skill training or education; (b) family support services; (c) trait-and-factor job matching and placement services; and (d) soft counselling support services. The rehabilitation counsellor must be a jack of all trades. He or she must not only provide services directly but also coordinate services with other professionals and monitor client's progress in gaining independence and self-control.

Rehabilitation counsellor must be a person with a clear sense of purpose. There are several competing, but not necessarily mutually exclusive, ideas about what roles and functions rehabilitation counsellors should assume.

In the late 1960s, Muthard and Salomone conducted the first systematic investigation of rehabilitation counsellor's work activities. They found eight major activities that characterise the counsellor's role and noted a high degree of importance attached to affective counselling, vocational counselling, and placement duties Rehabilitation counsellors reported spending about 33 percent of their time in counselling activities, 25 percent in clerical duties, and 7 percent in client placement. In 1970 the U.S. Labour Department listed twelve major functions of rehabilitation counsellors, which are still relevant:

Personal counselling. This function entails working with clients individually from one or more theoretical models. It plays a vital part in helping clients make complete social and emotional adjustments to their circumstances.

Case finding. Rehabilitation counsellors attempt to make their services known to agencies and potential clients through promotional and educational materials.

Eligibility determination. Rehabilitation counsellors determine, through a standard set of guidelines, whether a potential client meets the criteria for funding.

Training. Primary aspects of training involve identifying client skills and purchasing educational or training resources to help clients enhance them. In some cases, it is necessary to provide training for clients to make them eligible for employment in a specific area.

Provision of restoration. The counsellor arranges for needed devices (for example, artificial limbs or wheelchairs) and medical services that will make the client eligible for employment and increase his or her general independence.

Support services. These services range from providing medication to offering individual and group counselling. They help the client develop in personal and interpersonal areas while receiving training or other services.

Job placement. This function involves directly helping the client find employment. Activities range from supporting clients who initiate a search for work to helping less motivated clients prepare to exert more initiative.

Public relations. The planning process requires the counsellor to include the client as an equal. The plan they work out together should change the client from a recepient of services to an initiator of services. The counsellor is an advocate for clients and executes this role by informing community leaders about the nature and scope of rehabilitation services.

Evaluation. This function is continuous and self-correcting. The counsellor combines information from all aspects of the client's life to determine needs and priorities.

Agency consultation. The counsellor works with agencies and individuals to set up or coordinate client services, such as job placement or evaluation. Much of the counsellor's work is done jointly with other professionals.

Follow-along. This function involves the counsellor's constant interaction with agencies and individuals who are serving the client. It also includes maintaining contact with the clients themselves to assure steady progress toward rehabilitation.

In an extensive examination of the professional duties of 1135 Certified Rehabilitation Counsellors, Rubin and associates identified six major job functions that are essential in any work setting. First, counsellors prepare and monitor a client's progress in attaining specified rehabilitation objectives. Counsellors and clients need to be sure of goals and how well they are being achieved. Second, counsellors must make client referrals and coordinate services with other agencies. Rehabilitation counselling is a multidimensional task whose success is dependent on a strong system of interconnection. Third, counsellors must offer vocational counselling, which includes discussing a client's assets, limitations, and possible occupations. Fourth, a rehabilitation counsellor focuses on affective counselling. He or she must be able to hear a client's feelings about employment or achievement of goals. Fifth, counsellors interpret tests and integrate rehabilitation planning. It is essential that goals and plans be based on realistic data. Finally, counsellors must continually read the professional literature to keep up with current business and legal trends. This knowledge is essential for helping clients to the fullest. The similarity is striking between what rehabilitation counsellors actually do and their formal job descriptions. Rehabilitation counselling has a strong, clear identity. Counsellors within the profession do not engage in certain activities, such as developing or administering tests or accompanying clients to job interviews. Their roles are limited to assure functionality and efficiency.

To help counsellors perform their tasks even better, Hershenson has proposed a practical way to conceptualise a disability and provide services. He contends that disabilities result from one of four forces: supernatural, medical, natural, or societal. Therefore, treatment can be based on explanations and techniques emphasising faith (for the supernatural), logic (for the medical and natural), and power (for the societal).

12

Counselling for Vocations

There are reasons to treat vocational guidance as a subject of importance in this book. We have seen that in fact the separation of a man's vocational life from his personal life is a false distinction, then again, it is in his vocation that a man often takes on the stereotypes of his time, and of his society, as William James so graphically described it many years ago. Finally, it is the case that both in Britain and the United States, specialised guidance emerged out of vocational guidance-curiously enough, both systems started at almost the same time, with the publication of Frand Parson's book in 1909 and the rise of his Vocation Bureau at Boston; and in Britain, with the attachment of juvenile departments to some of the Employment Exchanges in the same year. Again, in Eastern Europe, we shall see that the new appearance of specialist counsellors, as they are called, is very largely to help the efficient development of the national economies. Even in Sweden, where pupil-centered systems of thought dominate educational reform, the importance of the Labour Market Board in the formulation of policy about counselling, has been and remains very real.

Man's attitude to something which takes up much, if not most, of his waking hours, has rarely been neutral. Work has been seen as a necessary evil, as one of the virtues that pave the path to heaven, as the most important way in which an individual contributes to his society, and as a major instrument of self-realisation. But many discussions about work beg the question of what it is, and this distinction is important. If we define work as 'what you do to earn a living,' then a distinction between work and leisure becomes possible. If we say that work is 'doing anything which you would rather not do' then the distinction becomes a little blurred, since when a man builds a sailing-dingy for pleasure, for example, he may engage in many hours of painful toil in his leisure time to gain a distant goal. Making a rather cautious start, however, let us take this preliminary position about work and its significance; work is the purposeful expenditure of mental or physical effort resulting in fatigue. The purposes may be legion: to propound a doctrine, to build up a stamp collection, to avoid punishment, to play football. This is, after all, implied in the common uses of the word. The labourer straightening his back after a hard spell of digging, the schoolboy closing his books after a nights' homework, the mountaineer lying exhausted above the cliff-face he has just conquered, may all say 'that was hard work.' The concept of fatigue is necessary: we expend a small amount of energy in eating, but this is hardly work; on the other hand, work and pleasure may be inextricably mixed; and the very act of love can be an exhausting experience.

One of the most satisfying experiences in human life is that of creativity; the creative process is essentially that of a search, and this search is inseparable from a process of work as we have so far defined it. It is impossible to avoid the suggestions of sexuality in this: to create is to give birth, whether physically in woman after her labour; or to new ideas after a period of creative disturbance; or to an object after mental and physical labour on it. It is also associated with the release of aggression and even with the concept of war: to gain victory after struggle and after sustaining intermittent defeats in which the individual may have felt not only his self-confidence, but his personal integrity, threatened. A successful outcome to a creative struggle is in fact the outward projection of part of the individual's life force; in the newly born child, the completed boat, the beautiful garden, the individual sees a material assurance of his own identity, and even at times a kind of immortality. Just as work is central to the creative process, so this in turn provides the context within which work takes on its deepest significance. Boris Pasternak once wrote: "the fabulous is never anything but the commonplace by the hand of genius," and genius itself has been described as a capacity for taking pains." Even at its highest level, the transformation of the mundane involves a process of work. These thoughts give us the possibility of refining our definition of work: in its most significant form – work is the sustaining of tensions, or risks, and intermittent failures, inseparable from the process of forming new ideas and giving them material reality.

Seen in this light, then, work should always be involved in some way with the realisation of at least some part of the worker's dream: it should express, however imperfectly, some aspect of that world of fantasy that once gladdened his childhood's play; it should symbolise, from time to time, the deeper values of the worker's life. The idea, sometimes heard, that a child passes in adolescence from a fantasy view of the world of work, to a reality view of it, seems to miss the fact that human development is normally a continuous, unfolding pattern in which the past can never be dismissed or neglected. When an individual is required to work for long periods of time, usually out of economic or social necessity, at tasks which afford him the opportunity whatever for any expression of his personality, both the concept of work and the individual are thereby degraded, and the destructive effects are no doubt proportional to the length of time over which such a situation continues.

Much, but not all, of peoples' work takes place in the context of earning a living, or following a career, and for ease of discussion let us call this 'employment'. A man's employment of course includes its social setting: the people he meets in the course of his employment, and the social recognition which his employment affords, both of which are important influences on his attitude towards it.

Employment roles usually require a fairly massive commitment of work, and this is a good point at which to examine some of the broad possible consequences of this. The most satisfying employment is one which presents challenges that we can meet by a deep and creative personal involvement. This is usually seen as a good thing, and we are apt to forget some negative sides of it. Success here, as elsewhere in behaviour patterns generally, is likely to be followed by a deeper involvement. This can usually be justified, if the need arises, but the requirements of 'earning a living[1] or 'following a career.' If progressive improvements are accompanied by increasing success, the employment may begin to draw in too much available energy, and insidiously to attenuate the private life, which may become correspondingly shallow. Too much work now take place in one setting only-the employment role is not sufficiently distributed over the broad spectrum of life. Whether this is seen as a good or a bad thing depends greatly on the social values that are accorded to private life, the family, religion, and so on. These may well vary from one society to another. A friend of mine, who once worked in Africa, found that the attendance of his labour force was rather erratic. One day, when very few men had turned up, he went out and found one of them, a huge negro, lying on the side of the road with his hands behind his head. "Why are you not at work?" He asked. And got the reply: "for a long time now we have had very hot, wet, unpleasant weather: this is the first good day, and any sensible man will lie on his back in the sun."

One specific aspect of a deepening involvement with a employment role is however, worth a special mention; a tendency to use it to compensate for failures in private life, and to evade the need for more effort there. Work-especially creative work-can take the mind off other things, and release the tension generated by frustration elsewhere. Persistent evasions of this sort may well amount to a rejection of life itself, impossible to justify except by rare creative genius in the employment role.

At the other extreme are employments which are potentially creative, but in which the individual has failed in the sense that he cannot involve his deeper life with the work, whose functions he discharges in a mechanical way; and employments which are basically sterile, such as many forms of factory labour. In the first of these we may find the imitator-the individual who conforms over-closely to the style of clothing, the turns of speech, the ways of thought, the patterns of activity appropriate to his employment role, as a compensation for a deeper failure there. 'Action', wrote Canard, 'is consolatory. It is the enemy of thought and the friend of flattering illusions.' This over-identification with the trivia of the employment stereotype may extend into many distant and apparently irrelevant areas of life, so that in extreme cases we may say with the scathing words of Voltaire about an acquaintance: 'he was born a man, and died a grocer.'

If, on the other hand, the work offered by the employment role is both demanding and boring, the concept of work itself may be rejected wholesale, leading to the use of non-creative, non-demanding leisure activities upgraded out of all proportion to their value Harold Entwhistle has emphasised the high likelihood that boring employment leads to the dull and unimaginative use of leisure: a man whose brain has been dulled by eight hours of monotonous toil can hardly be expected to burst into creative leisure activity: in short his ability to work has been damaged. It is perhaps significant that throughout history we see examples of those sections of the population engaged in the dullest, most routine work, putting a high value on non-demanding 'viewing' activities, from the circuses of ancient Rome to the football stadiums of today.

How far does vocational guidance, as practised in our schools, stand up to examination from this viewpoint? Nearly everywhere, in the practice of vocational guidance, it is assumed that work means employment, and this is particularly clear in the description of the various offices and activities in this field, such as 'careers officers,' 'careers teachers,' 'careers convention,' 'careers literature,' and 'work experience'. The over-emphasis on this association of work with employment reflects a general failure to think deeply enough about the meaning of work; and implies an acceptance of the popular idea that work and leisure are different things. Perhaps this is partly the price of an empirical approach to guidance generally, with its unwillingness to explore concepts at the abstract level. The idea of a clear distinction between work and leisure certainly needs to be broken down, perhaps by more attention in training programmes and conferences in counselling, to the definition and discussion of goals and assumptions. If it is not, there may be some future danger of the spread of courses and programmes of 'education for leisure', carrying further the artificial distinction already present in the terms we looked at earlier. Where pupils can be encouraged to relate ideas which they find personally exciting, to those which they associate with work, the basis of a new approach exists, meaning, in effect, the marriage of vocational guidance to counselling.

However, the question of how far children should be encouraged to express their creative energies through employment alone is very complex, and illustrates the impossibility of separating vocational guidance from the need an overall philosophy of life. At one extreme is a certain view of employment as a 'job' void of anything worthwhile; a daily interruption of life; at the other extreme is the obsessively employment-dedicated man to whom nothing but a career matters. Proponents of the first viewpoint sometimes take a 'realistic' or 'tough-minded' approach to the formation of employment-attitudes, and hence to vocational guidance. They argue that at the present time, and in the foreseeable future, many forms of industry will require large reserves of manpower for the dullest and most routine jobs. For such people education should concentrate on the creative use of leisure, and in any case, not encourage a false view of the world of work, among those most likely to fall into routine employments. Such unimaginative attitudes ignore the onrush of automation, the increasing geographical mobility of urbanised societies, and the whole background pattern of change, which, however materialist its methods and aims, is swiftly changing the approach of many young people towards their vocational futures The question which adolescents increasingly ask, in Britain and elsewhere, is not how to find a good job or to make a career, but whether to bother about such things. I have little sympathy with those who dismiss such young people as being simply lazy: their problems seem to me to arise out of a deeply sincere questioning of the worth of modern urban civilization. The spread of cynicism about accepted values, the rejection of the establishment, of authority, seem to go wider than the characteristic and temporary rebellion in adolescent development against the older generations; and as we shall see later, even in communist countries there is some evidence of a similar trend, masked by lip-service to stereotype ideals. The drift of this wind through our societies further illustrates the change of separating vocational guidance from counselling.

Fundamental Issues

Why in fact has the development of guidance in semi-specialised form in British schools, been so closely identified in the past with careers work? Why have these simple and essential ideas about the relationship between work, leisure, and personal development not been sufficiently considered to lead guidance away from a narrow pre-occupation with employment, to a wider view of life goals? The answers probably lie in the tendency in British society, which we have looked at, to concentrate on processes rather than on concepts; on immediate problems rather than on long term goals. Thus, the earliest government intervention, represented by the Employment Acts of 1909 and 1910, set up juvenile departments in some Employment Exchange to help place boys and girls in jobs, and to allow Local Education Authorities to do this also. To be fair, the wording of the Acts and official memoranda at this time indicate a recognition of the need for guidance on a wider basis; but in practice the provision becomes one of job-placement, predominantly for the children of the poor. The excessive concentration on job-placement has remained as part of the official attitude towards vocational guidance, in spite of various attempts at improvement, and in spite of being drawn much more closely into the framework of L.E.A supervision since 1948. Why did the concept not evolve faster? There are several possibilities. One is the fact that guidance structures existed outside and independently of the schools; the contact between Youth Employment Officers and school staff was too fleeting for serious discussion of deeper issues in guidance. The fact that an organised structure existed outside the schools; and school heads, often tending to think of the successful pupil as one who made the ascent into a university or teacher-training college, may, as we have suggested earlier, have thought of an early leaver looking for a job, as an educational failure. Also, for many years, the use of psychological tests was almost totally unknown among teachers, so that no independent pointer to the relationships between personal, educational, and vocational needs of children was available.

But the main reason why for so long the idea of guidance lay at the level of job-placement in Britain is almost certainly to be found in the social stratification of education. The acceptance of new ideas in guidance and the rise in the numbers of careers teachers, and the emergence of the counsellor as a new figure in schools, coincide closely with the rise of comprehensive secondary schools. We have already emphasised the tendency of grammar and public school heads to judge success in terms of educational attainment. This limited the development of the concept in those areas. In the secondary modern schools which emerged after the 1944 Education Act, a large number were situated in industrial slum areas, where the prospects, career or otherwise, were too grim to think about. Here there was little or no incentive to start thinking along sophisticated lines about guidance. But the comprehensive schools which emerged a few years later were in a different position; they offered a diversity of educational opportunity at the secondary level unknown in the other kinds of school, and extended deep into adolescence the problems of educational, vocational, and personal choice. In such circumstance, especially in the larger schools, sense of uncertainty, even of being lost, can easily emerge, and for the young pupil soon grow to formidable proportions among so many new faces, both of pupils and staff, most of them stranger. In such a situation, the development of an effective guidance system, able to make contact with such pupils is completely necessary if the main aims of the school are to achieved: one can go further and say that it is the presence of such a system, and its efficient functioning, that largely holds the balance between a comprehensive school approaching its ideals, and an 'education processing factory' of the kind described by opponents of the comprehensive school principle.

In fact, the sort of situation we have suggested here has involved fairly specific problems, and their solution has encouraged the emergence of techniques. The newcomer has to be introduced to the school; at its simplest this means making certain that the pupil understands what opportunities are open to him, and how to use the main lines of communication. Pupil records have to be developed beyond the simple report-card stage, in order to record as much as possible of the kind of information which, in a smaller community, would be casually picked up by teachers in getting to know their pupils. The advantages of using psychological tests as a short-cut to objective information have begun to be recognised, and teachers involved in guidance work in comprehensive schools frequently seek courses at which they can build up their knowledge and experience with such instalments, and so improve the quality of the record system. There has been considerable attention to the formation of guidance teams, and to the use of team work techniques to help overcome the communication problems in big establishments, and to deal with the wide diversity of problems encountered. These developments, as Moore emphasised in his study of five such systems, have given rise to immediate problems, and, judging by the growing importance attached to them, seem to have met with a good deal of success. As we have already seen, movements of this kind tend to call for role-differentiation, and specialists of the kind or another tend to appear in the teamwork, leading naturally to the question of appointing a personal counsellor, or counsellors, for the pupils, The tradition of guidance, as employment-centered vocational guidance, was of course inadequate to meet this need, and hence the importation wholesale of the American theories and practices of counselling.

But the solutions worked out from the 1950's onwards, and increasingly throughout the 1960's, were in terms of how to develop and integrate new areas of guidance to meet the peculiar problems of big schools, and not generally in terms of deep thinking about the existing concepts-especially, of vocational guidance. The goals were seen in terms of the solution of immediate problems. Thus, it happens that we can only say that vocational guidance in Britain has evolved during the last two decades, if by 'evolution' we mean the expansion and refinement of provision, not of concepts. This means that a difficulty is sometimes found in how to relate the specialist in vocational guidance to the specialist in personal counselling, in the organisation of school guidance teams. In some such patterns the careers teacher actualy appears as an additional specialist outside the main guidance team, itself organised around a system of personal counselling, Again, in some schools, counselling is dominated by a concept of vocational guidance crudely centred on helping the adolescent to make a happy 'first-job' choice, which of course means that the emphasis is on the early leavers rather than over the whole school population. Again, at least some of the confusion that exists about the difference between "counselling' and 'guidance' stems from the fact that there has been a continuous development of provision in this semi-specialist area, but as a result of the failure of the concept to evolve, there is now a split between a concept which began in Britain, and a similar one, which evolved in a totally different fashion in North America, and was then imported into Britain in its matured form, as counselling, in the 1960's. As an example of this difficulty, an authoritative article in *New Era* in 1968 stated that vocational guidance was essentially informative, and should be handled by careers teachers, whereas personal guidance was essentially problem centred, and constituted the main role of the counsellor in secondary schools. Likewise, vocational guidance is still seen by the Youth Employment Service in terms of employment-guidance. In this however the Service is not to blame, being hamstrung by its terms of reference.

Underlying all these questions about the relationship of vocational guidance to counselling are of course big questions about the relationship between the individual and his society, and about social duties.

Aims and Objectives

1. People differ in abilities, interests and personalities. No two people are exactly alike; each has. a characteristic pattern of traits and abilities.

2. They are qualified, by virtue of their characteristics, for a number of occupations. An individual has the potential for success and satisfaction in many occupations. Occupational multi-potentiality is found among men and women. Research has also shown that physically and mentally handicapped people can satisfactorily perform many occupations.

3. Every occupation requires a characteristic pattern of abilities, interests and personality traits, with tolerances wide enough, however, to allow for some variety of occupation for each individual and some variety of individuals in each occupation. Just as an individual has

the potential for achieving success and satisfaction in a number of occupations, so each occupation can be performed satisfactorily by diverse individuals. Studies indicate that abilities and interests fall into patterns which distinguish one occupation from another, and it has been found that people prefer, enter and succeed most consistently in occupations for which they have appropriate patterns of traits. These occupational ability patterns are much broader.

The purpose of vocational guidance is:

(i) ***To serve the individual and society:*** For the individual, the objective is to help him in occupational choice, which is a developmental process taking place over a period of years. It ends in a compromise between interests, capacities, values and opportunities which are available. There are three periods of occupational choice: the early period of fantasy choice, governed largely by the wish to be an adult; the period of tentative choice determined largely by interests, later to be modified in the light of knowledge about capacities and values; and finally, the period of realistic choice in which exploration, crystallization and specification phase succeed each other.

(ii) ***To prevent maladjustment and dissatisfaction:*** The process of occupational choice is irreversible. So it is essential that vocational guidance facility is made available to the individual to prevent maladjustment and dissatisfaction.

(iii) ***To ensure efficient use of manpower:*** For society and the nation, vocational guidance aims at efficient use of manpower and greater economy in the execution of work in industry, business and government offices.

The primary aim of vocational guidance is the promotion of personal satisfaction with life as a whole. As such, the process of vocational guidance will consist of the following factors:

(a) Enabling the individual to discover information about himself/herself, his/her abilities, interests, needs, ambitions, limitations and their causes.

(b) Providing him/her with information about his/her environment, the advantages and disadvantages of different occupations and educational courses, the qualifications necessary for entry into them, and the total range of opportunities available to him/her in theory and practice.

(c) Providing him/her with a frame of reference in which to see himself/herself in relation to these educational and vocational opportunities; to orient him/her to the helping agencies available and to alert him/her to future decision-making points in his/her career.

(d) Providing counselling in order to promote self-understanding and to develop educational and occupational plans.

(e) Providing a placement service to help him/her to implement those plans.

(f) Providing a follow-up service to help him/her if necessary, when faced with future decision-making situations.

Certain emphases implicit in the process of vocational guidance are :

(a) Vocational guidance is essentially a developmental process concerned with anticipating crimes and future decision-making situations.

(b) It is client-centred, that is, counsellor's prime responsibility is to his client.

(c) In practice it is difficult to distinguish between educational and vocational guidance as most educational decisions will have their vocational implications.

(d) Vocational guidance must concern itself with the total life of the individual. In practice, his/her working life cannot be separated from his/her non-working life. In fact, vocational guidance is concerned with developing the individual's self-concept, his occupational self-concept and his extra-occupational self-concept.

(e) Values and choices are not imposed upon him/her. He/she is encouraged to define his/her own problems and to make his/her own decisions.

Role of Education

The two terms are closely related but are not synonymous. Vocational education begins where vocational guidance, in a way, ends. Vocational guidance without vocational education is a waste. Vocational education is a necessary preparation or training undergone before an individual enters a vocation chosen through vocational guidance.

Educational and vocational guidance are so closely akin that they are almost always discussed together in professional writing and research. The student's choice of courses and his/ her vocational plans are functionally interrelated. Educational guidance becomes fruitful only by keeping an eye on the vocational implications of subjects and the field of occupations they will lead to. Similarly, a plan of vocational guidance must be followed or accompanied by educational guidance. Both are parts of the total guidance process, "by which an individual's potentialities are discovered and developed, through his own efforts for his/her personal happiness and social usefulness."

Educational guidance is often influenced by vocational considerations and vocational guidance is incomplete without educational guidance preceding it. The distinguishing mark between the two is the character of the dominating purpose. In vocational guidance, the vocational consideraiions dominate, whereas in educational guidance "making a life in school" is more important than "making a living" after the school years.

The primary stage: The primary school period is the most formative period in which habits, skills and attitudes develop. It can be used as an exploratory period for locating the special aptitudes and inclinations. Students who do not hold any promise of benefiting from secondary schooling can be diverted elsewhere. About twenty percent of the students who are likely to step into working life will have to be guided to the avenues and opportunities available. Similarly, about 20 per cent students who take up vocational courses will have to be guided to the institutions offering these courses. About 60 per cent of the students have to be prepared for high school education. Through well known guidance techniques, the incidence of misfits can be reduced to some extent and right course of action made possible. Proper guidance is required to improve quality as low standards of achievement are not always related to low intelligence quotient or other forms of mental backwardness but also to a wrong course of action adopted.

The purpose of vocational guidance at the primary stage is to help the child through the curriculum and the extra-curriculum to develop his/her basic skills and attitudes which are important for successful work. There are essential requirements of a good worker, whatever be the field, for example, doing the job earnestly in a neat and systematic manner, using what one possesses to an optimum extent, doing it in co-operation with others. Habits of doing work and proper attitudes towards work may be developed.

The potentialities of the different subjects can be tapped for developing the required qualities. Subjects like social studies, science, languages, mathematics, work experience—all are useful in this direction. Information about the occupational divisions and occupational families these courses lead to, the special skills they require, and the relationship at school achievements to employment, may be pointed out.

Besides, through an organised programme of co-curricular activities, the students may be helped to explore and understand themselves. These activities should be provided in the regular time-table and must be continued throughout the primary stage with necessary changes in the form and content. The aim is to enable the child to know his/her capacities and limitations. The knowledge is very useful for future planning.

Since many pupils leave school at the end of Class VIII, it is necessary that occupational information suiting their needs is provided to them at this stage. Sufficient information about jobs and vocational courses which might be of use to them, should be given to them through talks and visual aids.

The secondary stage : In the new pattern of education, there will be general education up to the secondary stage. The following will be the objectives of vocational guidance at the secondary school level:

1. ***Helping pupils according to their vocational assets and liabilities.*** Through a student informalion service, the guidance programme should assist the pupils to appraise their abilities, aptitudes, interests and personality qualities. The pupils should be helped to 'measure' themselves, their assets and liabilities.

2. Helping pupils to be familiar with vocational implications of different subjects to be studied in the secondary school.

3. ***Helping pupils to be familiar with occupations and their requirements.*** For successful adjustment to the world of work, pupils should be helped to be familiar with occupations and their requirements. The pupils should be made familiar with the employment situation in the country, the job trends, requirements of different jobs as period of training, emoluments, conditions of work and future prospects. This knowledge will be of great help in making adjustments, and preparing proper plans for his future.

   One of the major responsibilities of the guidance worker is to bring the complex reality into focus and to help the individual to evaluate both his opportunities and his limitations, so that the transition from secondary school to the academic or vocational stream of higher secondary school or junior college is facilitated.

4. ***Helping pupils to prepare themselves for entry into the careers of their choice :*** As students step into the working life, they will have to be provided with information about the training facilities sufficiently in advance to avoid inconvenience.

5. ***Helping pupils to get suitable jobs :*** *A good programme of vocational guidance should help the pupils in "getting a good start in the profession."* For this, it is necessary that schools

keep themselves in touch with employment exchanges so that they are in a. position to give adequate information to school leavers about the jobs available.

The function of vocational guidance at this stage is :

1. To carry on the work started in the earlier stages more intensively and vigorously. The pupils should be made aware of the opportunities open to them.
2. To help pupils relate their studies to the vocations that are open to them.
3. To help pupils make a comprehensive study of the careers on the lines they would like to pursue.
4. To help pupils acquaint themselves with avenues for higher education and the assistance which might be available in the form of scholarships, stipends, grants and fellowships.
5. To help pupils make contacts which would be helpful in putting their plans into successful operation.

Main Objectives

The following are the objectives of vocational guidance:

- To assist students to acquire knowledge of the characteristics, functions, duty requirements of occupations in which they are interested.
- To enable students to get relevant information about abilities and skills in terms of related qualifications and competencies required to take up the identified occupation.
- To enable students to understand their potentials and to identify occupations which they may take up.
- To assist students in developing abilities to analyse occupational information and make suitable choice by using appropriate career information effectively.
- To assist students in getting information about various post-educational and training facilities and apprenticeship schemes.

- To enable students to choose the right type of jobs.
- To develop entrepreneurship qualities in students for taking up self employment.

There has been a phenomenal growth of industries during recent times. Rapid industrialisation implies a higher manpower requirement.

While industries both in the public, organised and unorganised sectors are concerned about recruiting the "right type of personnel" to carry out a variety of challenging and productive job, every student is bothered about getting the right job after successful completion of his education. The selection of the right person for the right job is a key factor in the technological progress of a country. Students desire to earn their livelihood after successful completion of their education. They consciously work towards this.

For this purpose, they need to get adequate information about the job opportunities, job availability in the area of their study. Assistance provided in getting such information can be expected to go a long way in enabling students to enter the world of work.

Students after completion of their study face many problems in the choice of an appropriate career due to inadequate information about career growth and development opportunities, suitability of the job to match their interest/ aptitude, vocational preparation etc. With the limited information available through, newspapers and employment advertisements, some students may be fortunate enough to get a job while others may not. This results in frustration in those who do not get some suitable placement.

A person's performance for a vocation is influenced by the aspirations and choice of their parents. This may result in an unsatisfactory placement of the student. However, it is important to note that the vocational choice should be decided more on the individual's ability, interest, aptitude, rather than on parental aspirations alone. Some individuals are often found to be dissatisfied in the work they are doing and are not properly adjusted to the work environment leading to frustration, state of stress, diminished productivity, etc.

An unfavourable attitude of any individual is not conducive for the work culture in any organisation. Efforts must consciously be made by educational institutions to work towards developing a positive attitude towards work in their students. If this can be done in the institution, it can be expected that there would be a transfer of this in the work situation.

The success or failure of a person in a vocation depends upon, many other factors including satisfaction one derives from the vocation. Satisfaction results from working in harmony with one's own potentialities, strengths, weaknesses, etc.

Lack of an awareness of the self with regard to perception of reality, self-esteem, interest, personality etc., often leads to the setting up of unrealistic and unachivievable goals to work. This in turn may lead to frustation in the work situation. An organised vocational guidance programme in the institution may be of great: help to meet these problems. Through this programme students get necessary information about different careers. The world of work remains no more unfamiliar to them. Students get all sorts of information needed for a particular career or a group of careers in the vocational guidance programmes. Improper selection of courses of study , in the institution, inadequate information about job prospects, lack of knowledge of job training, unfavourable attitude towards work, mismatch of interests, aspirations to the job obtained are some of the factors which contribute to vocational problems.

Vocational guidance services offered on the basis of a proper understanding of the potentialities of the students in terms of their aspirations, acquired knowledge and skills in relation to the nature of the job can be expected to be of immense assistance to students in the choice of their careers.

It is known that students have individual differences in relation to their vocational choices. The nature of vocations are different from one another in terms of the nature of work, outputs, growth potentialities, etc. Whenever any attempt is made to place a person in a job not suited for him, the result will be disastrous both to the individual and the job. In deliberately organising vocational guidance programmes, teachers must be careful enough to consider data about the students.

The data may include the training obtained (knowledge and skills acquired), level of intelligence, special abilities, interests, aptitude, personal health details, personality details, economic status, etc. Information regarding these and other relevant aspects must be collected objectively using suitable methods.

In the process of vocational guidance the individual is assisted to understand his abilities and limitations and accept them. Once he is aware of his potentialities, he is helped to make use of the available opportunities. For the effectiveness of vocational guidance, the students' goals, needs and interests are also taken into account.

A well organised system of vocational information readily available to students and a set up which encourages students and trains them to find out the available information about careers form the basis for the choice of vocational guidance strategies.

Students may face many difficulties in the choice of vocation, vocational persuasion and vocational adjustment. This often leads to several ills such as students not getting proper jobs, encountering difficulties in getting on well with the job, etc. This implies that students should discover their capabilities. They must relate the information they acquire about their career to their own capabilities.

Vocational guidance strategies should be based on the following principles:

– Occupation is to be looked at as a source of income to people and a major source of satisfying needs and optimising aptitudes, competencies and interests.

– The individual needs to understand the total perspective of a vocation for which he has decided to prepare himself.

– The selection of a particular vocation is not confined to a single, fixed decision but a time extending process, involving a series of social and personal factors.

– Vocational guidance services should be based on the principle of individual differences.

– Different strategies need to be used to cater to the individual vocational needs of students.

- Vocational guidance service must fulfil the vocational needs of every student.

Vocational guidance can be given to an individual as well as to a group. When an individual faces any vocational problem like selection of a vocation, adjustment in vocation etc., individual guidance is given to him. On the other hand, if a similar vocational problem is faced by a group, a group guidance programme can be organised.

Group guidance in vocational area can not only be organised in problem cases but also, to prepare individuals for vocation. Various approaches are followed in organising vocational guidance. These include, career corner, career talk, career conference, industrial visit, simulated interview and vocational counselling.

Career corner is a display place for imparting vocational information. A talk by a professional on various aspects of an occupation or a group of related occupations is career talk. A panel of speakers invited for discussion on a variety of careers in engineering, accountancy, agriculture etc., is a career conference.

The purpose of visit to industry organised in a vocational guidance programme is to enable students to get first hand experience on practical aspects of jobs.

In vocational counselling the assistance is given to the individual to understand and solve, his vocational problems. Simulated interview sessions are intended to train students to acquire the necessary skills for facing Interview for jobs. Career corner is a display centre of different career books, pamphlets, posters and notices related to career information. The objectives of a career corner are:

- To enable students to get various information about occupations from a variety of career literature.
- To enable students to analyse their employment opportunities by consulting a career index.
- To enable students to get latest information about various job opportunities.

Various Stages

- Selection of a suitable place for the career corner.
- Collection of career literature.
- Career Index preparation.
- Display of career literature.
- Periodical updating of literature.

A suitable place for setting up a career corner is very essential. The place should be such that it is easily approachable by students and that it is in a prominent place in the institution. An ideal situation would be to have an independent room. The room should have adequate furniture such as display tables, book racks, chairs, display boards.

If an independent room is not available, a portion of the library may be utilised for the purpose. Necessary career literature for display must be collected from various sources. These display materials may be in the form of career information booklets, pamphlets, advertisements in the form of paper cuttings, posters, charts, photographs of industries, etc. Each of these type have specific purposes. The career literature may provide information to students about career opportunities, job requirements, caree growth opportunities, knowledge and skill requirements, job' pay package, work conditions, etc.

The large number of materials collected must be attractively displayed to catch the attention of the students. These are to be arranged in a systematic manner. All the career literature available in the career corner is to be arranged systematically. For this, a group of literature under a particular corporation, services, organisation may be placed together. For example, all the career literature available in railway services may be placed together.

Similarly all the career literature available in defence services may be placed together. Students usually demand easy and quick reference about job avenues and opportunities. This can be facilitated through Career Index Cards. Career Index Cards are cards which give information about the educational qualification, age, experience essential for a job.

It also contains information about the salary, promotional chances, etc. Teachers must prepare these cards by collecting relevant information from the industries and store them in card catalogue. These must be arranged in a suitable manner.

The growth rate of industries is vary fast The nature of the jobs available changes with the growth. With modernisation forming the backbone of industries knowledge and skill requirements by the industries from job aspirants will not remain the same. Hence it is imperative that the career literature available must be constantly updated. Periodical updating of literature and discarding the obsolete one must be a continuous process.

Students can get information about vocation and career not only from different printed materials, but also directly from experienced persons in the field. Career talk is one of the methods of providing career information through lectures, seminars, and talks by professionals in the field. The value of books and pamphlets which are the principal sources of vocational information increases, if students get a chance to interact with professionals who are actually on the job. The following are the, objectives of career talk.

– To enable students to get information about careers directly from an experienced person in the field.

– To enable students to get opportunity to clarify their doubts related to career through direct interaction with experts.

– Decide the topic which has got importance.

– Prepare a brief note about what is expected from the visitor and send it to the speaker.

– Choice of suitable themes.

– Selection of the speaker.

– Decision of date and time.

– Preparation of career brief.

– Coordination of the career talk programme.

Success of career talk depends upon the care with which the theme for the programme is selected. The theme should be one of interaction and useful to a majority of students. The theme identified should cover all details about job opportunities. It is essential to note that the theme must cover a wide range of jobs instead of narrowing the same to any one job. Some of the themes for career talk are "Career in Banking Services for Technical Diploma holders" "Career in Army Engineering Corps", "Start your own Small Scale Industry". The fact that appropriate speaker should be identified to give the career talk needs no overemphasis. The key to the realisation of objectives of career talk is the expert chosen for the talk. In choosing a person it is necessary to look for the following characteristics:

- should have worked at different levels.
- have a thorough knowledge of all details of the job.
- be conversant with the latest developments in the industries.
- be a good speaker.

The next important step is to fix the schedule for the programme. One of the usual criteria for deciding the date and time would be the convenience of the identified speaker. Further the schedule must be such that most of the students will be able to attend the programme. It will be useful to arrange the same during the working hours of the Institute rather than after the institutions hours in order to ensure the attendance of a maximum number of students. The talk, should be considered as an integral part of the institutions activity to be deliberately organised. It may be useful to involve the student's union in organising this activity.

Careful preparation is essential for making the career talk useful to students. Both the institution and the identified speaker must make adequate preparation for this programme. In order that the speaker makes necessary planning he should be provided information such as the background of the institution, discipline of students attending the programme, number of students, their areas of interest, aspirations, total time set apart for the session, content expected to be covered etc.

The institution could prepare a brief note on the talk covering the details of time, date, speaker's name, objectives of the programme, content and points of discussion. Such a brief be made available to students in advance. The speaker may be requested to use audio visual aids for presentation.

Any photography, that he may want to exhibit may be collected well in advance and arrangements for their display. It will be useful and appropriate if teachers who are in charge of the programme meet the speaker and discuss with him all details of the programme. Coordination of the programme is very vital if students should derive maximum benefit from it.

Some of the tasks of the programme may be, left to the members of the Student's Union. These may be arranging the lecture hall, receiving the speaker, arranging the display materials, distributing the programme brief etc. There should be a thorough follow up after the programme. The follow up may be in the form of visits to industries by a group of students, discussion sessions on identified themes.

As the very name suggests it is a conference of a few persons from various industries, teachers and students for the purposes of discussing the identified themes for vocational guidance. The main objectives of the career conference are given below:

- To enable students to get opportunity to collect information about different careers of their choice from a panel of experts
- To enable students to get the opportunity to have a direct interaction over a group of careers.
- To enable students to get a broader perspective on various career opportunities.
- Identifying the speakers
- Finalising the date, venue and time
- Monitoring the programme
- Evaluating the programme

– Constituting a organising committee

– Preparing a plan of activities

In order to facilitate smooth and effective organisation of the career conference programme, it is necessary to constitute an organising committee in the institution. This committee may consist of a teacher counsellor, one teacher from each of the disciplines, chairman of the student's union and two student representatives. This committee will be responsible for planning, conducting, monitoring and evaluating the programme. The various tasks of the committee include selection of the theme for the conference, (give examples of themes) identifying the participants for the conference from the industries to talk on different aspects of the theme, fixing the date, time, meeting identified speaker and getting their acceptance extending invitation, etc. The schedule of the conference activities must be prepared well in advance. It is essential to organise a few career conferences and not just one. Each conference may focus on a discipline or a group of related disciplines. The schedule may be properly spaced out during the academic year. For each programme the .plan of activities must be prepared.

Role of Industries

Industrial visit helps the student to get first hand information about the different aspect of the industry such as the tradition of work culture, organisational hierarchy facilities provided.

– Students get first hand information about their future working place.

– Students get the opportunity to come in contact with their future employers.

– Select the industry to be visited.

– Write to the Personnel Manager of the industry/firm for fixing the date and time.

– Prepare the students for the visit.

– Conduct the visit.

– Organise the feedback session after the visit is over.

For industrial visit, the firm or industry may be selected from the nearby locality or from a distant place, depending on the purpose of the visit and the group which is going to visit. For example, if the visit is organised for electronics diploma students, there is no justification for visiting a fertiliser factory, which is situated very near to the industry. The visit to the same fertiliser factory by a group of chemical engineering diploma students will be very much useful. Therefore the selection of the industry or firm should be on the basis of the needs of the students.

Students who are going to visit the industry need some preparation. They are instructed to take necessary kits like note book, camera, etc. The instruction, the uniform or dress is also given. Students are also asked to follow certain instructions like, they should not touch any machine without permission, they should not talk in the shop floor, etc.

During the time of visit, the students are asked to note down the pertinent information. The personnel manager of the industry or firm is requested to give systematic briefing of jobs from employees' point of view. The details of machines and equipment can be heard from the foreman of the respective section. After the visit is over, the students are asked to submit a report on the industrial visit. A discussion session is organised for getting the necessary feedback.

Simulated Interview

Simulation means artificial creation of the real situation. Sometimes it may not be possible to provide a real setting to the students for training to face interview. Interview is one of the methods followed by some organisations/ industries to recruit the most appropriate persons for various positions.

The selection of the aspirants to jobs depends on how they perform in such interviews particularly if there are a large number of them with similar qualifications and experience. In such cases, candidates after short listing will be invited to appear in an interview by a staff selection committee.

In such cases, one who performs well in the interview will be selected. It implies that students must know how to take an interview. Facing an interview and performing well by way of impressing the interviewing committee is an art. They should be necessarily trained in this so that they may learn all the behavioural requirements therein.

- To enable students to get opportunity to acquire the necessary skills of facing an interview
- To enable students to get over complexes like frightening behaviour which come in the way during the interview performance.
- Select the interviewer (s) and the interviewee.
- Brief the interviewer (s) and interviewee about specific roles to be played.
- Organise the simulated interview session.
- Obtain feedback from the candidates.

Interview is a personal meeting between two individuals. The purpose of this may be evaluation, counselling, selection etc. In the meeting situation one is the interviewer and the other the interviewee.

It has been found that one interviewer is not sufficient in conducting interviews like selection interview and evaluation interview. Therefore a panel of interviewers is required to interview the candidate. This panel of interviewers form the interview board and conducts the interview.

In simulated interview, interview session is organised, in an artificial situation. Here, one or more persons play the role of the interviewer. While some other individual plays the role of an interviewee. Through simulated interview session, the interviewers try to explore the capacity of the interviewee in relation to a particular job. As soon as the interviewee presents himself before the interview board, the chairman of the board takes the initiative to start the session by asking him to take the chair.

To develop opening structure, the chairman may ask the candidate about his name, qualification, etc. He then, invites other members of the board to ask questions. In the development phase of the interview, the interviewers skilfully ask probing questions.

This explores the capacity of the interviewee gradually. When the interviewers feel that the purpose of conducting the interview is achieved, the chairman once again takes the initiative to close the interview session. This he does by offering thanks to the interviewee for his participation.

In vocational counselling, problems such as selection of vocation, preparing for a vocation and progress in vocation are handled.

Every counselling session has specific objectives. Situational development influences every counselling session a lot. The major structure of any counselling session depends on the problem of the counsellee. However it may follow a general structure of activities. Phases are given below:

- Fix the time and date for the counselling session
- Begin the session as per schedule
- Create a congenial atmosphere through easy communication
- Assist the counsellee to explore his needs and potentialities
- Review the world of work with counsellee
- Assist counsellee to choose relevant occupation
- Get the feedback from the counsellee
- Terminate the session slowly.

In vocational counselling, the assistance is given by an individual to another to solve the latter's vocational problems. The individual who undergoes vocational counselling discovers his potentialities relevant to a particular vocation or a group of vocations. Several items of information like requirements and conditions of success in a vocation, advantages and disadvantages, compensation opportunities and prospects in several lines of work may also form part of the vocational counselling.

Through vocational counselling the self-awareness of the individual who comes for assistance is enhanced. The counsellor in vocational counselling, assists the individual to discover and evaluate his personal needs. Once the client realises his needs, it is necessary on the part of the counsellor to nurture his needs which make him more alert.

As a result of the counselling process, a sense of personal identity in relation to the world of work grows. The counsellor and counsellee, review occupations and works. In this review phase of the counselling process, only those occupations are considered which the counsellee feels relevant to him. The counsellee discovers himself in the light of his new experience.

Rapid Development

Vocational development is a mark of maturity. In a complex society such a development is in itself an achievement. Vocational planning precedes vocational experience, but competence in planning also requires abilities, which come with maturation. Vocational choice is a process of growth reflecting other phase of development.

Right of Choice

It is a very important decision a person must make for himself and this choice is a long process rather than a simple incident. Vocational interests and choices do not appear all of a sudden during adolescence, they appear as a result of developmental process. A number of theories have been advanced by psychologists and occupational analysts on occupational choice.

An individual never reaches the ultimate decision at a single moment in time, but through a series of decisions over a period of many years. The period during which the individual makes what can be described as a fantasy choice; the period during which he is making a tentative choice; and the period when he makes a realistic choice.

The period of fantasy choice coincides in general with the latency period, between six and eleven, although residual elements of fantasy choice frequently carry over into preadolescent years.

The period of tentative choice coincides, by and large, with early and late adolescence; with few exceptions, realistic choices are made in early childhood.

There are three basic elements regarding occupational choice:

(i) occupational choice is a developmental process; it is not a single decision made over a period of years—a process which takes place over a minimum of six or seven years, and more typically over ten years or more.

(ii) since each decision during adolescence is related to one's experience upto that point, and in turn has an influence on the future, the process of decision-making is basically irreversible.

(iii) since occupational choice involves the balancing of a series of subjective elements with opportunities and limitations of reality, the crystallisation of occupational choice inevitably has the quality of a compromise.

Vocational choices take place as a result of a developmental process. Very often this development can be traced to the influences exerted before birth. Child development studies have proved the powerful influence which the thwarted ambitions and frustrations of the parents have on the vocational choice of the individual. Vocation being the implementation of the self-concept, when the parents have failed to achieve it during their own career, they have sought it through the choice of career for their children.

Vocational development may be conceived of as beginning early in life and as proceeding along a curve late in life. Thus, a four year old child who plays the policeman or soldier is in a very early stage of vocational development and the old man of sixty who does not work for money but still keeps himself busy with writing books in the field of his specialisation is going through the late stage of vocational development.

Buehler has classified the vocational life stages as:

1. growth (birth to 14 years)
2. explanatory (15 to 24 years)—with the sub-stages of fantasy

which may be tentative or realistic with appropriate attitudes towards work and occupation;

3. establishment (24 to 44 years)—beginning with trial and progressing into a stable position as the individual begins to make his place in the world of work;
4. maintenance stage (45 to 64 years)—characterised by stability in the field in which establishment has taken place earlier in life; and
5. decline stage (65 onwards)—characterised by deceleration during the early part and progressing into one of retirement.

The process of vocational development is continuous and ongoing and is essentially that of developing and implementing a self-concept; it is a compromise process in which the self-concept is a product of the interaction of inherited aptitudes, neural and endocrinal make-up. Opportunity to play various roles, and evaluations of the extent to which the results of role playing meet with the approval of supervisors and fellows.

The process of compromise between individual and social factors, between self-concept and reality is one of role-playing whether the role is played in fantasy, in the counselling interviews, or in real life activities, such as school classes, clubs, part-time work and entry jobs.

The opportunities of exploring the occupational roles available in the world of work through actual participation are obviously limited-while part-time and trial jobs offer some real experience, only a very few occupational roles can be sampled in this way.

The material for these role playing activities can come from a number of sources: the home, peers, friends and acquaintances who are in employment, the mass media, school/college/university, the career masters, counsellors, recruitment literature, and so on. The inadequacies of these indirect sources and the unrealistic occupational perceptions which are gained from them often frustrate the most determined attempts to achieve a realistic compromise.

Work satisfaction and life satisfactions depend upon the extent to which the individual finds adequate outlets for his abilities, interests, personality traits and values; they depend upon his establishment in a type of work or work situations and a way of life in which he can play the kind of role which his growth and explanatory experiences have led him to consider congenial and appropriate.

Vocational preferences and competencies, the situations in which people live and work, and hence their self-concepts, change with time and experience, making choice and adjustment a continuous process. The vocational preferences of the developing child are subject to continual change.

For the young child, the chosen occupation is often one which is identified with adults. The process of occupational choice and adjustment does not end when a youngster enters his or her first job.

Occupational expectations will rarely be fully realised and some adjustment to the unexpected will be necessary. Even when such adjustment is achieved, the process is not complete. Regular work activities may facilitate the development of latent skills which the individual may subsequently want to utilise more fully.

A growing awareness of the world of work and the opportunities available may also motivate the individual to seek out what to perceive in better jobs. Even where a person remains in the same job for much of his life, a series of adjustments will be necessary to meet with the individual's changing concept of himself.

Factors at Work

The nature of the career pattern is determined by the individual's parental socio-economic level, mental ability, and personality characteristic and by the opportunities to which he is exposed. Occupational choice and subsequent vocational development is greatly influenced by the experience a child undergoes. The individual is a product of his environment, his inherent aptitudes and neural endocrinal make-up.

Role of Individual

The most important social system which impinge upon the individual and influence his development, is the family in which he happens to be born and reared. The vocational development of the individual, which is a continuous process, beginning in early childhood and continuing into the late years of life, appears to be as much influenced by his family as are other aspects of his development.

The abilities, interests, physique and personality of the individual, which play such an important role in his vocational development, are partly determined by hereditary factors and the particular constellations of genes which the individual inherits depends upon his parents and ancestors.

Physical factors such as the geographical location of the home, the physical conditions prevailing in the home, and the health of various members of the family may, at times, have a significant effect on the vocational development of the individual. A boy coming from a home in a remote village will have much more difficulty in obtaining a college education than a boy residing in a town.

A person residing in a town which does not offer facilities for specialisation in a particular field will have to seek admission in another town, which obviously involves additional expenditure on board and lodging. If the family budget cannot accommodate this extra expenditure, the student has to change his educational-vocational aim and specialise in a different field or compromise by taking up a course of training at a lower level in the same field, if such training is available in his home town.

The location of the family residence also determines the type of vocational activities which the individual may take up. A person who has spent the formative years of his life in a project area—which is the centre of engineering activity—is likely to have more information about engineering, develop an interest in it, and see himself as playing a role in it, than a person who has lived far away from such type of activity.

Physical conditions in the family such as overcrowding, noise, lack of proper light and ventilation, and an inadequate diet may all have an injurious effect on the health of the individual as well as on his ability to concentrate on studies or work, and thus may adversely affect his vocational development.

Health of the members of the family may also have an indirect effect on vocational development. Crippling, ill-health or death of the breadwinner of the family may make it necessary for a youngster to discontinue his studies, no matter how bright he may be, and take up the first available job, whether it is suitable or not. Similarly, ill-health or death of the mother may make it necessary for a girl to spend so much of her time on household chores, that her studies or job are neglected, or, even to relinquish her studies or job altogether.

The social economic level of the family appears to exercise the most potent influence of all. The level and quality of education available and aspired to, as well as the level of work aspired to and accessible, are greatly affected by the family's finances and social contacts. Thus, their children have higher aspirations either as a result of pressure from the parents or as a result of internalising parental pressures or both. If their intellectual endowment is good, their higher level of aspiration may be achieved. But if intellectual endowment is not commensurate with level of aspiration, conflict will arise; the individual will not be able to have an integrated self-concept, and vocational maladjustment is likely to follow.

At times, however, the reverse is true. Among very affluent families, the level of educational and vocational aspirations may be low, and a person with good abilities may not be sufficiently motivated to concentrate on studies and strike out a vocational path for himself, thus may fail to actualise his potentialities.

Persons who belong to families from the higher economic strata also have better chances of finding employment at a higher level because their parents, and they themselves, have more contacts with people who are well-to-do and influential, people who are employers rather than employees.

In setting up a professional practice or business, too, individuals from the higher socio-economic strata are at an advantage because of the capital available to them as well as the well-to-do friends and acquaintances who are potential clients.

The occupation information which a person picks up from his family will influence his vocational thinking and eventual choice of occupation. The types of occupations concerning which a family can provide information will vary with its socio-economic level—a person from a higher level family is in a better position to obtain more information about professional, business and administrative work, and one from a lower level family about skilled, semiskilled and unskilled work.

The types of cultural stimulation prevalent in the family, and the types of equipment available, which depend considerably on the socio-economic level of the family, will play a part in facilitating or hindering the development of the youngster's abilities and interests in certain directions, providing or failing to provide him with opportunities to test his self-concept through explanatory activities.

Identification of the individual with the socio-economic class to which his family belongs may also influence his self-concept. A person from a higher class family may find it difficult to work as a peon or clerk; while a person from a lower class family will tend to see himself in these or similar roles-if his vocational thinking is reality-oriented and not dominated by fantasy-and may find it difficult to see himself as a professional man or business man; an administrator or manager.

Family as a mediator of culture also influences vocational development. Caste and religion, mediated through the family, at times have a profound influence on vocational development. Caste often restricts the occupations open to its members.

This restrictive effect will play a greater part in the vocational development of a person who comes from an orthodox family in which conformity and obedience have been stressed than in the vocational development of a person whose family is unconventional and regards its membership of a particular caste as a chance factor to which no importance need be attached. Family's religion too at times gives a bias to the choice of occupation. For example, the frequent choice of martial career by the Sikhs appears to be related to the militant nature of their religion.

Family is also instrumental in helping the individuals develop attitudes and values. It has been proved through researches that children are not born with attitudes but they acquire them gradually through various experiences and influences. Parents wittingly or unwittingly transmit attitudes and values to children.

Attitudes towards various types of occupations as well as towards work itself are learnt in the home, and play their part in developing in the individual preference for certain occupations and dislike for others. This is how people come to consider occupations as ranking high or low in prestige, as clean or dirty, as safe or risky, as purposeful or frivolous.

For example, the individual who has grown up in a home where manual work is looked down upon as being uncultured and dirty, is likely to develop the attitude that manual work is beneath his dignity and to think that society will set less score by him if he takes up an occupation which involves manual work. This single factor is responsible for most of the people in our country seeking white collar jobs, and remaining unemployed while jobs requiring skilled and semi-skilled work go abegging.

Work values learned in the family can have a farreaching effect on vocational choice and adjustment. For example, if concern for the welfare of people has permeated a home, the personality of an individual growing up in such a home cannot but be influenced by it, and he is likely to seek and find fulfillment in one of the social welfare occupations. If, on the other hand, monetary considerations have been predominant in his family, he will tend to go in for a type of work in which the monetary rewards are attractive.

A family in which aesthetic values play their part in daily living, children in that family will prefer artistic occupations. Children who come from a family in which intellectual activities and achievements are valued, are likely to be drawn towards intellectual pursuits in adulthood, whereas children who come from a home in which intellectual activities are not valued will tend not to be attracted towards such activities, or if there be an attraction on account of high intellectual abilities seeking an outlet, the attraction will not be without conflict.

Emotional currents in the family also have a subtle influence on vocational development. Inter-personal relations which prevail within the family, particularly during the individual's formative years, play a great role in shaping his entire personality and behaviour, including vocational behaviour.

Conditions such as parental neglect or rejections, overprotection, parental disharmony or intense sibling rivalry can create insecure, unintegrated persons who find it difficult to make a good vocational adjustment; they find it difficult to make vocational decisions. Even when they make decisions, they are often unwise, and unstable; they have work inhibitions or an overbearing urge to achieve which defeats its own purpose.

Personality difficulties are the most frequent cause of vocational inefficiency and dissatisfaction and also of discharge from environment. Emotional needs fostered in the early interpersonal relations in the family tend to motivate the individual to seek their satisfaction through vocational activities. For instance, a child who has been over-protected by his family and grows up to have a strong need for security and dependence, will tend to avoid occupations involving outdoor life, leadership, taking risks, and so on.

Another person whose needs for self-expression and recognition have not been gratified within his family, may either seek a vocational situation in which needs can be gratified or he may become so cowed down and lacking in confidence that he may choose an occupation considerably below his ability level, or even drift into an occupation without planning. An exaggerated need of independence, developed in the course of his relationships with his parents, may make it difficult for a person to accept any salaried employment and impel him towards setting up his own business or go into some other independent venture.

Family provides the earliest adult role models with whom the individual may ider.tity or whom he may reject. Normally the boy wants to be like his father and incorporates within himself the characteristics of the father, including his occupational role, work values and attitudes. As a child, he plays games in which he acts out the occupational role of the father, and later he wishes to take up the same occupation in earnest.

However, for the girl, the mother is a sex model rather than an occupational model, whereas for the boy the father is both a sex model and an occupational model. The bright girl who is aiming at a career thus often finds a suitable feminine occupational model lacking in her family; she may then identify with some female outside the family or with her father, or other male member of the family. In the latter event, the conflicting identifications may cause maladjustment in the vocational as well as in the personal-social sphere.

Frequently, such a girl compulsively seeks fulfillment through a career and is unable to seek fulfillment in the normal psycho-biological female roles of wife and mother. The boy, too, at times has conflicts arising out of identification with his mother as well as his father. The individual's self-concept emerges from and is greatly influenced by his family.

Their judgement of his capacities and characteristics, the status and role he experiences in his relations with them, their acceptance or rejection of him as a person; it is from a myriad of such perceptions that the individual develops a concept of himself as a worker which he tries to implement in the course of his vocational development.

Ability is another important factor which matters in vocational development. Adolescents with higher intellectual ability tend to seek and prepare for jobs which require higher kind of intelligence, while the ones with lower mental ability go in for semi-skilled jobs and continue in positions of almost no importance. The individuals who do not choose their careers according to their level of ability, land in failure because of poor competence.

Though no systematic and thorough study made on Indian samples is available, some foreign studies have produced results to illustrate the difference in vocational success of the intelligent and dull individuals. In one of the studies it was possible to follow-up eight individuals who had been diagnosed as feeble-minded or of borderline intelligence.

Some eighteen years earlier, when their vocational achievement was studied, two of them were working as truck drivers; another was a taxi driver; a welder; a shipping clerk; a train repair man, and an assembler at an air plane factory. All of these persons were earning meagre money but each one of them was self-supporting and a productive citizen. Many of them were university teachers, physicians, lawyers, architects, authors, engineers and artists.

A social and an extrovert in all probability, would make a successful public relations officer but not a scholar or a librarian. Similarly, a quiet and an introvert would be unhappy if placed on the job of a salesman. Every job can be described in terms of the personality characteristics it requires for the person to be happy and satisfied in it. For example, good teachers are usually social, communicative, self confident, self-sufficient and aggressive.

Attempts have been made to measure people's personal suitability to a particular job through the study of their interest patterns., through their responses to questions in interest inventories and interest blanks.

Prediction of the most suitable career for an individual is based on the numerous profiles of successful individuals in various jobs. The profile of the individual wanting guidance can be compared with those who have already been successful in that particular field.

The similarity and divergence between their personal qualities is a reliable guide for prediction of a career for the individual tested. Studies of reliability of these predictions have proved that young people changing a particular career have interest profiles markedly similar to those of the successful persons in that particular line. Study done by Norton has also shown that persons most stable in their jobs showed interest patterns most suitable to work of their choice.

A significant difference has been found in the earnings of persons in jobs most suited to their personality characteristics and the ones who have been placed in jobs not suited to their interest patterns.

In addition to the job satisfaction, suitable personality and interest patterns provide the individual with an opportunity for the development of vocational drive. Mere work skills and abilities are not the sole determinants of success of the individual on the job; good personal adjustment and skills of inter-personal communication are also a must.

Role of Economy

Economics plays an important role in the vocational choice and development of an individual. While planning the career, the individual, naturally, avoids the vocations with low wages and low prestige even though these may be the ones in which he is interested the most.

Business cycle is another economic factor affecting the vocational development of young persons as well as the vocational pattern and adjustment of older adults. It is an established fact that business completes a cycle of success and failure. The business expands and brings the society to the condition of complete prosperity followed by another period of prosperity.

This cycle has definite effects on the vocational development and employment of the individual. A young adult who completes his education during depression is faced with the strain of scarcity of employment which is unfamiliar to another young man who may have passed college during more prosperous times. The two are forced to make very different vocational adjustment.

During depressions, there is a general downgrading which results in dissatisfaction among the workers. During prosperous times, on the other hand, there is scarcity of suitable individuals, so there is a trend of upgrading. Persons with ordinary qualifications, are able to secure good and above-expectation jobs.

Another factor which influences vocational development of an individual is industrialisation. Many new jobs come up due to industrialisation. The people are not usually familiar with these jobs. They had never aspired for them neither have they had the opportunity to explore their interests and aptitudes for these jobs. Industrialisation also effects the workers already settled in jobs. For many it may mean getting uprooted and looking for the main jobs; for the others it may mean acquiring new skills to fit into the positions requiring skilled labour.

Official Policy

Public policy has its effect on the vocational development of the individual. Reservations both in admission and jobs proves an important factor for Scheduled Castes to go in for particular vocations—in spite of the fact that they are not well-qualified. Similarly, those from other castes may not be able to go in for medicine or engineering in spite of fairly good merit as compared to the Scheduled Castes. Hence change in vocations in spite of interest, aptitude and ability for these lines.

State patronage for a particular industry in a backward area acts as a boost while similar industry in an advanced area may suffer an obvious setback. Changes in fashion and style also affect the vocational development. New styles of dresses, hair-cuts, make-up, furniture and household equipment, create new vocations and may affect the vocational development. Natural calamities as floods, earthquakes, droughts also affect the vocational development.

The aim of all vocational guidance programmes and activities is vocational adjustment. As far as adjustment to a vocation is concerned it is necessary that the individual should have a pleasant feeling and tone while doing his occupational work and that he should acquire a reasonable amount of facility in that work. Vocational adjustment in case of some individuals also means that the individual should be able to express his personality adequately through his work.

The occupation should provide him with enough remuneration to meet his economic needs. The work should also enable him to enjoy some social status and allow him to play a certain type of role in society in conformity with his values and personality needs. Vocational adjustment cannot be judged merely by satisfaction and facility in work.

Such criteria of adjustment tends to be narrow and neglect the "global" aspects of adjustment. Vocational adjustment means adjustment not only to work involved in the occupation but to all social, economic and physical situations connected with the occupation.

An occupation brings with it many social relationships with colleagues, superiors, subordinates and the public. An occupation also creates for the individual a social atmosphere in which he lives and works. Hence vocational adjustment means adjustment not only to work but to these social relationships and the social atmosphere prevailing in the place of work.

A good deal of satisfaction is derived from social relationships. A worker may be very good in his work but if he is not adjusted to the social atmosphere, he should be considered as vocationally maladjusted.

Conversely, a worker may not be quite competent by virtue of his aptitudes in the work but if he is able to derive satisfaction from the social relationships he may be well-adjusted to the work situation as a whole. Social status is considered a factor more important in occupational adjustment than economic gain.

Professional and technical competence is not enough for vocational success or adjustment. There are many occupations— professional and technical in nature— which call for the qualities and competencies other than those required in the technical execution of work.

People lose positions or fail to attain positions even when they are competent to perform the technical duties involved in their jobs. Conversely, technically incompetent persons may be retained or achieve advancement because other qualities offset the lack of technical competence.

Vocational adjustment also involves the implementation of a part of the individual's self-concept in the world of work. By self-concept is meant the complex of ideas and attitudes which an individual has about himself and to the world around him.

Thus, self-concept defines the locus of the individual in the field of his relations to the social and physical world. In simpler words, it is the picture of the individual as it appears to him or the way he looks at himself.

Super in his memorable article "Vocational Adjustment—Implementing a Self-Concept" explains how the self-concept is involved in vocational adjustment. He redefines vocational guidance in terms of self-concept when he says, "vocational guidance is the process of helping a person to develop and accept an integrated and adequate picture of himself and of his role in the world of work, to test this concept against reality, and to convert it into a reality, with satisfaction to himself and benefit to society".

Individuals vary in the degree of need for implementation of their self-concept in the occupational world, with the result that at the lower extreme, there would be individuals who could obtain satisfaction from several types of work within the range of their capacity. Some thinking has also been directed to the problem of fulfillment of emotional needs of the individual in his occupational world and the role of emotional needs in vocational choice.

Gratification of these needs is regarded to be the psycho-dynamic factor in vocational choice and adjustment. This need may be felt by the individual consciously or may operate from the unconscious as an impelling force. Some of the needs, as stated by Murray, are abasement, achievement, acquisition, affiliation, aggression, autonomy, cognizance, escape, nurturance, recreation, succorance, and so on. It may be assumed that the persons' interests are focused on activities which seem likely to permit the satisfaction of their strongest need.

If so, it may further be presumed that adjustment in a particular occupation involves the satisfaction of a particular need or a particular combination of needs. However, it seems that different individuals tend to satisfy the same need in different occupations. For example, the need for achievement may be satisfied by one individual in medicine whereas the same need may be satisfied by another individual in a technical occupation. Conversely, it may be stated that different individuals or different types of individuals gratify different needs in the same occupation. The need for creativity plays an important part in vocational choice and adjustment.

The Organisation

There has been considerable attention to the formation of guidance teams, and to the use of team work techniques to help overcome the communication problems in big establishments, and to deal with the wide diversity of problems encountered. These developments, as Moore emphasised in his study of five such systems, have taken place as a response to immediate problems, and, judging by the growing importance attached to them, seem to have met with a good deal of success. Movements of this kind tend to call for role-differentiation, and specialists of the kind or another tend to appear in the teamwork, leading naturally to the question of appointing a personal counsellor, or counsellors, for the pupils. The tradition of guidance, as employment-centered vocational guidance, was of course inadequate to meet the need, and hence the importation wholesale of the American theories and practices of counselling.

But the solutions worked out from the 1950's onwards, and increasingly throughout the 1960's, were in terms of how to develop and integrate new areas of guidance to meet the peculiar problems of big schools, and not generally in terms of keeping thinking about the existing concepts, especially, of vocational guidance. The goals were seen in terms of the solution of immediate problems. Thus, it happens that we can only say that vocational guidance in Britain has evolved during the last two decades, if by 'evolution' we mean the expansion and refinement of provision, not of concepts. In some such patterns, the careers teacher actually appears as an additional specialist outside the main guidance team, itself organised around a system of personal counselling. Again, in some schools, counselling is dominated by a concept of vocational guidance crudely centred on helping the adolescent to make a happy,'first-job' choice, which of course means that the emphasis is on the early leavers rather than over the whole school population. Again, some, at least, of the confusion that exists about the difference between 'counselling' and 'guidance' stems from the fact that there has been a continuous development of provision in this semi-specialist area, but as a result of the failure of the concept to evolve, there is now a spilt between a concept which began in Britain, and a similar one, which evolved in a totally different fashion in North America, and was then imported into Britain in its matured form, as counselling, in the 1960's. As an example of this difficulty, an authoritative article in New Era in 1968 stated that vocational guidance was essentially informative, and should be handled by careers teachers, whereas personal guidance was essentially problem centred, and constituted the main role of the counsellor in secondary schools. Likewise, vocational guidance is still seen by the Youth Employment Service in terms of employment-guidance. In this connection, however, the Service is not to blame, being hamstrung by its terms of reference.

Underlying all these questions about the relationship of vocational guidance to counselling are of course big questions about the relationship between the individual and his society, and about social duties. While we shall touch on some of these issues in the second part of this book, we can immediately turn to look at the institutional framework within which the various guidance functions take place, and by which they are also partly shaped and limited.

One of the most satisfying experiences in human life is that of creativity; the creative process is essentially that of a search, and this search is inseparable from a process of work as we have so far defined it.

It is impossible to avoid the suggestions of sexuality in this regard, to create is to give birth, whether physically in woman after her labour; or to new ideas after a period of creative disturbance: or to an object after mental and physical labour on it. It is also associated with the release of aggression and even with the concept of war: to gain victory after struggle and after sustaining intermittent defeats in which the individual may have felt not only his self-confidence, but his personal integrity, threatened. A successful outcome to a creative struggle is, in fact, the outward projection of part of the individual's life force; in the newly-born child, the completed boat, the beautiful garden, the individual sees a material assurance of his own identity, and even at times a kind of immortality.

Just as work is central to the creative process, so this in turn provides the context within which work takes on its deepest significance. Boris Pasternak once wrote: 'The fabulous is never anything but the commonplace by the hand of genius' and genius itself has been described as a capacity for taking pains. Even at its highest level, the transformation of the mundane involves a process of work. These thoughts give us the possibility of refining our definition of work: in its most significant from, work is the sustaining of tensions or risks, and intermittent failures, inseparable from the process of forming new ideas and giving them material reality.

The idea, sometimes heard, that a child passes in adolescence from a phantasy view of the world of work, to a reality view of it, seems to miss the fact that human development is normally a continuous, unfolding pattern in which the past can never be dismissed or neglected.

When an individual is required to work for long periods of time, usually out of economic or social necessity, at tasks which afford him opportunity whatever for any expression of his personality, both the concept of work and the individual are thereby degraded, and the destructive effects are no doubt proportional to the length of time over which such a situation continues. Much, but not all of peoples' work takes place in the context of earning a living, or following a career, and for ease of discussion, let us call this 'employment'.

A man's employment, of course, includes its social setting; the people he meets in the course of his employment, and the social recognition which his employment affords, both of which are important influences on his attitude towards it. Employment roles usually require a fairly massive commitment of work, and this is a good point at which examines some of the broad possible consequences of this.

The most satisfying employment is one which presents challenges that we can meet by a deep and creative personal involvement. This is usually seen as a good thing, and we are apt to forget some negative sides of it. Success here, as elsewhere in behaviour patterns generally, is likely to be followed by a deeper involvement. This can usually be justified, if the need arises, but the requirements of 'earning a living' or 'following a career.' If progressive improvements are accompanied by increasing success, the employment may begin to draw in too much available energy, and insidiously to attenuate the private life, which may become correspondingly shallow. Too much work now takes place in one setting only—the employment role—and is not sufficiently distributed over the broad spectrum of life. Whether this is seen as a good or a bad thing depends greatly on the social values that are accorded to private life, the family, religion, and so on. These may vary well from one society to another.

One specific aspect of a deepening involvement with a employment role is, however, worth a special mention: a tendency to use it to compensate for failures in private life, and to evade the need for more effort there. Work—especially creative work—can take the mind off other things, and release the tension generated by frustration elsewhere. Persistent evasions of this sort may well amount to a rejection of life itself, impossible to justify except by rare creative genius in the employment role. At the other extreme are employments which are potentially creative, but in which the individual has failed in the sense that he cannot involve his deeper life with the work, whose functions he discharges in a mechanical way; and employments which are basically sterile, such as many forms of factory labour.

In the first of these we may find the imitator—the individual who conforms over—closely to the style of clothing, the turns of speech, the ways of thought, the patterns of activity appropriate to his employment role, as a compensation for a deeper failure there. 'Action', wrote Canard, 'is consolatory. It is the enemy of thought and the friend of flattering illusions.' This over-identification with the trivia of the employment stereotype may extend into many distant and apparently irrelevant areas of life, so that in extreme cases we may say with the scathing words of Volatire about an acquaintance: 'He was born a man, and died a grocer.'

If, on the other hand, the work offered by the employment role is both demanding and boring, the concept of work itself may be rejected wholesale, leading to the use of non-creative, non-demanding leisure activities upgraded out of all proportion to their value. Harold Entwhistle has emphasised the high likelihood that boring employment leads to the dull and unimaginative use of leisure: a man whose brain has been dulled by eight hours of monotonous toil can hardly be expected to burst into creative leisure activity: in short his ability to work has been damaged. It is perhaps significant that throughout history we see examples of those sections of the population engaged in the dullest, most routine work, putting a high value on non-demanding 'viewing' activities, from the circuses of ancient Rome to the football stadiums of today.

How far does vocational guidance, as practised in our schools, stand up to examination from this viewpoint? Nearly everywhere, in the practice of vocational guidance, it is assumed that work means employment, and this is particularly clear in the description of the various offices and activities in this field, such as 'careers officers,' 'careers teachers,' 'careers convention,' 'careers literature,' and 'work experience'. The over-emphasis on this association of work with employment reflects a general failure to think deeply enough about the meaning of work; and implies an acceptance of the popular idea that work and leisure are different things. Perhaps this is partly the price of an empirical approach to guidance generally, with its unwillingness to explore concepts at the abstract level. The idea of a clear distinction between work and leisure certainly needs to be broken down, perhaps by more attention in training programmes and conferences in counselling, to the definition and discussion of goals and assumptions. If it is not, there may be some future danger of the spread of courses and programmes of 'education for leisure', carrying further the artificial distinction already present in the terms we looked at earlier. Where pupils can be encouraged to relate ideas which they find personally exciting, to those which they associate with work, the basis of a new approach exists, meaning, in effect, the marriage of vocational guidance to counselling.

However, the question of how far children should be encouraged to express their creative energies through employment alone is very complex, and illustrates the impossibility separating vocational guidance from the need, an overall philosophy of life. At one extreme is a certain view of employment as a job void of anything worthwhile; a daily interruption of life; at the other extreme is the obsessively employment-dedicated man to whom nothing but a career matters.

Proponents of the first viewpoint sometimes take a 'realistic' or 'tough-minded' approach to the formation of employment-attitudes, and hence to vocational guidance. They argue that at the present time, and in the foreseeable future, many forms of industry will require large reserves of manpower for the dullest and most routine jobs. For such people, education should concentrate on the creative use of leisure; and in any case, not encourage a false view of the world of work, among those most likely to fall into routine employments. Such unimaginative attitudes ignore the onrush of automation, the increasing geographical mobility of urbanised societies, and the whole background pattern of change, and which, however materialist its methods and aims, is swiftly changing the approach of many young people towards their vocational futures.

The question which adolescents increasingly ask, is not how to find a good job, or to make a career, but whether to bother about such things. I have little sympathy with those who dismiss such young people as being simply lazy: their problems seem to me to arise out of a deeply sincere questioning of the worth of modern urban civilization.

The spread of cynicism about accepted values, the rejection of the 'establishment,' of authority, seem to me to go wider than the characteristic and temporary rebellion in adolescent development against the older generations; and as we shall see later, even in communist countries there is some evidence of a similar trend, masked by lip-service to stereotype ideals. The drift of this wind through our societies further illustrates the change of separating vocational guidance from counselling. Why in fact the development of guidance in semi-specialised form in British schools, has been so closely identified in the past with careers work? Why have these simple and essential ideas about the relationship between work, leisure, and personal development not been sufficiently considered to lead guidance away from a narrow pre-occupation with employment, to a wider view of life goals? The answers probably lie in the tendency in British society, which we have looked at, to concentrate on processes rather than on concepts; on immediate problems rather than on long term goals. Thus, the earliest government intervention, represented by the Employment Acts of 1909 and 1910, set up juvenile departments in some Employment Exchange to help place boys and girls in jobs, and to allow Local Education Authorities to do this also. To be fair, the wording of the Acts and official memoranda at this time indicate a recognition of the need for guidance on a wider basis; but in practice the provision became one of job-placement, predominantly for the children of the poor.

The excessive concentration on job-placement has remained as part of the official attitude towards vocational guidance, in spite of various attempts at improvement, and in spite of being drawn much more closely into the frame work of L.E.A supervision since 1948. Why did the concept not evolve faster? There are several possibilities.

One is the fact that guidance structures existed outside and independently of the schools: the contact between Youth Employment Officers and school staff was too fleeting for serious discussion of deeper issues in guidance. The fact that an organised structure existed outside the schools; and school heads, often tending to think of the successful pupil as one who made the ascent into a university or teacher-training college, may, as we have suggested earlier, have thought of an early looking for a job, as an educational failure. Also, for many years, the use of psychological tests was almost totally unknown among teachers, so that no independent pointer to the relationships between personal, educational, and vocational needs of children was available.

But the main reason why for so long the idea of guidance lay at the level of job-placement in Britain is almost certainly to be found in the social stratification of education. The acceptance of new ideas in guidance and the rise in the numbers of careers teachers, and the emergence of the counsellor as a new figure in schools, co-incide closely with the rise of comprehensive secondary schools.

We have already emphasised the tendency of grammar and public school heads to judge success in terms of educational attainment. This limited the development of the concept in those areas.

In the secondary modern schools which emerged after the 1944 Education Act, a large number were situated in industrial slum areas, where the prospects, career or otherwise, were too grim to think about. Here there was little or no incentive to start thinking along sophisticated lines about guidance. But the comprehensive schools which emerged a few years later were in a different position: they offered a diversity of educational opportunity at the secondary level unknown in the other kinds of school, and extended deep into adolescence the problems of educational, vocational, and personal choice. In such circumstance, especially in the larger schools, sense of uncertainty, even of being lost, can easily emerge, and for the young pupil soon grow to formidable proportions among so many new faces, both of pupils and staff, most of them stranger. In such a situation, the development of an effective guidance system, able to make contact with such pupils is completely necessary if the main aims of the school are to be achieved: one can go further and say that it is the presence of such a system, and its efficient functioning that largely holds the balance between a comprehensive school approaching its ideals, and an 'education processing factory' of the kind described by opponents of the comprehensive school principle.

In fact, the sort of situation we have suggested here has involved fairly specific problems, and their solution has here involved fairly specific problems, and their solution has encouraged the emergence of techniques.

The newcomer has to be introduced to the school; at its simplest, this means making certain that the pupil understands what opportunities are open to him, and how to use the main lines of communication. Pupil records have to be developed beyond the simple report-card stage, in order to record as much as possible of the kind of information which, in a smaller community, would be casually picked up by teachers in getting to know their pupils.

The advantages of using psychological tests as a short-cut to objective information have begun to be recognised, and teachers involved in guidance work in comprehensive schools frequently seek courses at which they can build up their knowledge and experience with such instruments, and so improve the quality of the record system.

Personal guidance is the assistance given to any individual to solve his emotional problems and to assist him to control his emotions. Controlled emotion is the most significant characteristic of a mentally healthy individual. An individual having control over his emotions when threatened with conflicts and frustrations is able the maintain a mental balance by working against stress. Polytechnic students who are in the adolescent period of their growth and development exhibit heightened emotionality. Anxiety and frustration in students also result in emotional tension. These may be accompanied by irritability and tendency for emotional outbursts. Their hightened emotionality may be due to environmental and social factors. Students, at this stage, feel the urgency of breaking down old habits of thought and action. They are upset during the period of adjustment. Once they explore certain coping mechanisms of adjustment, the excessive emotionality usually disappears.

Students greatly need assistance in understanding the various coping mechanisms of adjustment.

When the individual is confronted with a succession of

frustrating situations, the immediate reaction may be one of anger or hostility. In many respects, anger and hostility are difficult emotions to deal with. Both involve tension which demands discharge. But the conditions of civilized living permit only a few direct outlets. The hostile behaviour is expressed through intolerance, aggression, impatience, over excitement and the like, which may be observed in adolescents.

Fear is one of the emotions which may be related to material objects, social relationships or to self. The thing, we fear, are actual or potential sources of frustration. Specific dangers tend to arouse fear. Ordinarily, fear elicits a withdrawal or flight reaction. In the face of intense fear, the individual may panic or freeze and become unable to function in any organised manner.

Many situations give rise to anxiety. Situations causing worry are generally accompanied by anxiety. Stress situations inducing anxiety are often difficult to cope with. This is because the nature of the threat is usually unclear to the individual. Adolescents quite often express this motion.

Jealousy is one of the emotions which is social in origin. In its extreme form, it may take the form of violence. Jealousy and annoyance may arise together. The causes of annoyance have a broader canvas than jealousy. The emotional types discussed above generally have adverse effects on the individual. But like biological drives, emotions may arouse, sustain and direct activity and as such play an energizing role in behaviour. Emotions also may serve as emergency sources of power.

For example, in stress situations where habitual reaction patterns are not adequate, strong emotions make maximum energy resources available and thus help the organism for meeting such emergencies.

The emotions like joy, pleasure, delight, affection etc., are mostly helpful in overcoming the stress situation and thus protect the self from crisis and frustration. These emotions also dominate during the adolescence period. Emotional disequilibrium produces conflict within an individual. When emotional conflicts are unresolved, he becomes emotionally problematic. Emotional conflict is a painful mental state in which opposing and contrary wishes and thoughts are ranged against each other and pull the individual in opposite directions. Conflicts arising out of emotions may vary greatly in their kind and intensity. Frustration is a feeling of inadequacy and tension caused by blocking of desires or pathways to a goal. This may happen consciously or unconsciously.

The manifestation of an emotional problem may be observed in such behaviours as fear of meeting people, psychological withdrawal, upset in minor happenings, anger, hostility, aggressiveness, criticising of everybody and everything. There may be several causes of frustration which is one of the major emotional problems of students. These include disappointment in love, loss of comfort and stability, complicated situation, lack of personality traits, loneliness, rejection by peers, and lack of mental abilities.

Anxiety is frustrated fear. Students suffering from anxiety exhibit feelings of insecurity, lack of self-confidence, fear about their ability to achieve their goals and meet difficulties of life and world. A number of causes for emotional problems have been identified. These are favouritism by teachers, heavy load of home work, lack of concentration, threat of self due to bias, insult, contradiction, being teased, sarcastic comments etc. Emotional insecurity is also one of the major causes of anxiety reaction. Nervousness means a large variety of reaction. The nervous students are restless, unable to concentrate on studies, get upset at the slightest defeat or threat.

On the surface, such a student may show behaviour like biting his nails, playing with his handkerchief or buttons, moping the forehead again and again etc. These meaningless activities help him to get over from the tension. It has been observed that students who suffer from nervousness have gone through great insecurity in their life time. This feeling of insecurity may be due to poverty, neglect, loss of parents, occasional threats and dangers. In some cases, the students may acquire this insecurity from their parents. "Psychological stress is the state of an organism where the student perceives that his well-being (or integrity) is endangered and that he must devote all of his energies to its protection".

In psychological stress, the integrity of the organism is involved and he cannot find a normal adjustive response. Frustration and anxiety produce tension within the individual and prolonged tension causes stress. Almost all behaviour manifesting stress are similar to anxiety. But in stress, their degree of intensity may be more. In the ever changing environment, every individual must change his behaviour to maintain emotional stability. Adjustment to change is a conscious process involving reasoning, imagination and learning new behaviour.

Emotional conflict may arise out of a stressful situation, the degree of which depends on the individual's personality structure. Emotional conflict produces anxiety and tension within the individual and when all the coping mechanisms fail to adjust, the individual undergoes stress. Neurosis is a milder form of mental ailment which generally originates from prolonged emotional strain and emotional conflict. It gives a lot of trouble to the individual in the form of anxiety and causes a number of adjustment problems.

The neurotics are unhappy, anxious, inefficient and ineffective. They are over sensitive, lack maturity, self-centered and always complain of physical ailments like tiredness, indigestion, headaches and sleeplessness. Neurotics believe that they are the victims of misfortunes over which they don't have any control. They are highly suggestible and obstinate.

Case histories of neurotic students reveal the underlying causes such as violent emotional conflicts, distressing emotional experiences, loss and disappointment in life, violent discord in social relationships or some frightening happenings.

Unfavourable early training, non-congenial environment also cause neuroticism. If the life at home and institution are full of tensions, annoyances, fears and anxieties students are likely to develop a neurotic personality. Several strategies depending on the nature of the problem and the purpose can be used for emotional guidance.

Cooperative counselling "is a blend of the direct guidance and authority typical of directive counselling and the non judgmental, active listening behaviour typical of nondirective techniques". In co-operative counselling, the following phases of activities are followed: The data and time of counselling session is fixed by the counsellor with the consent of the counsellee. The counselling session is to start with self-introduction. The counsellor tries to stimulate clients' thinking by asking questions.

When the counsellee remains silent, the counsellor waits for the response.

The counsellor restates the counsellees feelings and message. The counsellor assists the counsellee to choose appropriate coping mechanism. The counselling traits as per prefixed date and time. The counsellor introduces himself with his brief professional expertise. The student who comes for help also introduces himself.

In the bringing of the session, the counsellor asks a few questions to the counsellee. These questions are asked in a non-threatening manner. The purpose of asking these questions is to stimulate the clients' thinking. These questions are specific and related to counsellees' emotions and attitude. Thus, the client is encouraged to express his thoughts. When non-threatening questions work, these stimulate deep communication.

The separation of a man's vocational life from his personal life is a false distinction; then again, it is in his vocation that a man often takes on the stereotypes of his time, and of his society, as William James so graphically described it many years ago. Finally, it is the case that both in Britain and the United States, specialised guidance emerged out of vocational guidance-curiously enough, both systems started at almost the same time, with the publication of Frand Parson's book in 1909 and the rise of his Vocation Burea at Boston; and in Britain, with the attachment of juvenile departments to some of the Employment Exchanges in the same year.

Again, in Eastern Europe, we shall see that the new appearance of specialist counsellors, as they are called, is very largely to help the efficient development of the national economies. Even in Sweden, where pupil-centered systems of thought dominate educational reform, the importance of the Labour Market Board in the formulation of policy about counselling, has been and remains very real.

Man's attitude to something which takes up much, if not most, of his waking hours, has rarely been neutral. Work has been seen as a necessary evil, as one of the virtues that pave the path to heaven, as the most important way in which an individual contributes to his society, and as a major instrument of self-realisation. But many discussions about work beg the question of what it is, and this distinction is important. If we define work as what you do to earn a living,' then a distinction between work and leisure becomes possible. If we say that work is 'doing anything which you would rather not do' then the distinction becomes a little blurred, since when a man builds a sailing-dingy for pleasure, for example, he may engage in many hours of painful toil in his leisure time to gain a distant goal.

Making a rather cautious start, however, let us take this preliminary position about work and its significance: work is the purposeful expenditure of mental or physical effort resulting in fatigue. The púrposes may be legion: to propound a doctrine, to build up a stamp collection, to avoid punishment, to play football. This is, after all, implied in the common uses of the word. The labourer straightening his back after a hard spell of digging, the schoolboy closing his books after a nights' homework, the mountaineer lying exhausted above the cliff-face he has just conquered, may all say 'that was hard work.' The concept of fatigue is necessary: we expend a small amount of energy in eating, but this is hardly work; on the other hand, work and pleasure may be inextricably mixed; and the very act of love can be an exhausting experience.

One of the most satisfying experiences in human life is that of creativity; the creative process is essentially that of a search, and this search is inseparable from a process of work as we have so far defined it. It is impossible to avoid the suggestions of sexuality in this: to create is to give birth, whether physically in woman after her labour; or to new ideas after a period of creative disturbance; or to an object after mental and physical labour on it. It is also associated with the release of aggression and even with the concept of war: to gain victory after struggle and after sustaining intermittent defeats in which the individual may have felt not only his self-confidence, but his persona! integrity, threatened.

A successful outcome to a creative struggle is in fact the outward projection of part of the individual's life force; in the newly born child, the completed boat, the beautiful garden, the individual sees a material assurance of his own identity, and even at times a kind of immortality. Just as work is central to the creative process, so this is in turn provides the context within which work takes on its deepest significance. Boris Pasternaik once wrote: 'the fabulous is never anything but the commonplace by the hand of genius,' and genius itself has been described as a capacity for taking pains. Even at its highest level, the transformation of the mundane involves a process of work. These thoughts give us the possibility of refining our definition of work: in its most significant form, work is the sustaining of tensions, or risks, and intermittent failures, inseparable from the process of forming new ideas and giving them material reality.

Seen in this light, then, work should always be involved in some way with the realisation of at least some part of the worker's dream; it should express, however imperfectly, some aspect of that world of fantasy that once gladdened his childhood's play; it should symbolise, in part or from time to time, the deeper values of the worker's life.

The idea, sometimes heard, that a child passes in adolescence from a fantasy view of the world of work, to a reality view of it, seems to miss the fact that human development is normally a continuous, unfolding pattern in which the past can never be dismissed or neglected. When an individual is required to work for long periods of time, usually out of economic or social necessity, at tasks which afford him to opportunity whatever for any expression of his personality, both the concept of work and the individual are thereby degraded, and the destructive effects are no doubt proportional to the length of time over which such a situation continues.

Much, but not all, of peoples' work takes place in the context of earning a living, or following a career, and for ease of discussion let us call this 'employment', A man's employment of course includes its social etting: the people he meets in the course of his employment and the social recognition which his employment affords, both of which are important influences on his attitude towards it.

Employment roles usually require a fairly massive commitment of work, and this is a good point at which to examine some of the broad possible consequences of this. The most satisfying employment is one which presents challenges that we can meet by a deep and creative personal involvement. This is usually seen as a good thing, and we are apt to forget some negative sides of it-Success here, as elsewhere in behaviour patterns generally, is likely to be followed by a deeper involvement This can usually be justified, if the need arises, but the requirements of 'earning a living' or 'following a career should be present. If progressive improvements are accompanied by increasing success, the employment may begin to draw in too much available energy, and insidiously to attenuate the private life, which may become correspondingly shallow.

Too much work now takes place in one setting only-the employment role-and is not sufficiently distributed over the broad spectrum of life. Whether this is seen as a good or a bad thing depends greatly on the social values that are accorded to private life, the family/ religion, and so on. These may well vary from one society to another. A friend of mine, who once worked in Africa, found that the attendance of his labour force was rather erratic. One day, when very few men had turned up, he went out and found one of them, a huge negro, lying on the side of the road with his hands behind his head. "Why are you not at work?' he asked. And got the reply: 'for a long time now we have had very hot, wet, unpleasant weather: this is the first good day, and any sensible man will lie on his back in the sun.'

One specific aspect of a deepening involvement with a employment role is, however, worth a special mention: a tendency to use it to compensate for failures in private life, and to evade the need for more effort there. Work-especially creative work-can take the mind off other things, and release the tension generated by frustration elsewhere. Persistent evasions of this sort may well amount to a rejection of life itself, impossible to justify except by rare creative genius in the employment role.

At the other extreme are employments which are potentially creative, but in which the individual has failed in the sense that he cannot involve his deeper life with the work, whose functions he discharges in a mechanical way; and employments which are basically sterile, such as many forms of factory labour. In the first of these we may find the imitator-the individual who conforms over-closely to the style of clothing, the turns of speech, the ways of thought, the patterns of activity appropriate to his employment role, as a compensation for a deeper failure there, 'Action', wrote Canard, 'is consolatory. It is the enemy of thought and the friend of flattering illusions.'

This over-identification with the trivia of the employment stereotype may extend into many distant and apparently irrelevant areas of life, so that in extreme cases we may say with the scathing words of Voltaire about an acquaintance: 'he was born a man, and died a grocer. If, on the other hand, the work offered by the employment role is both demanding and boring, the concept of work itself may be rejected wholesale, leading to the use of non-creative, non-demanding leisure activities upgraded out of all proportion to their value.

Harold Entwhistle has emphasised the high likelihood that boring employment leads to the dull and unimaginative use of leisure: a man whose brain has been dulled by eight hours of monotonous toil can hardly be expected to burst into creative leisure activity: in short, his ability to work has been damaged. It is perhaps significant that throughout history we see examples of those sections of the population engaged in the dullest, most routine work, putting a high value on non-demanding 'viewing' activities, from the circuses of ancient Rome to the football stadiums of today.

Nearly everywhere, in the practice of vocational guidance, it is assumed that work means employment, and this is particularly clear in the description of the various offices and activities in this field, such as 'careers officers', 'careers teachers', 'careers convention', 'careers literature' and 'work experience'. The over-emphasis on this association of work with employment reflects a general failure to think deeply enough about the meaning of work; and implies an acceptance of the popular idea that work and leisure are different things. Perhaps this is partly the price of an empirical approach to guidance generally, with its unwillingness to explore concepts at the abstract level.

The idea of a clear distinction between work and leisure certainly needs to be broken down, perhaps by more attention in training programmes and conferences in counselling, to the definition and discussion of goals and assumptions. If it is not, there may be some future danger of the spread of courses and programmes of 'education for leisure', carrying further the artificial distinction already present in the terms we looked at earlier. Here pupils can be encouraged to relate ideas which they find personally exciting, to those which they associate with work, the basis of a new approach exists, meaning, in effect, the marriage of vocational guidance to counselling.

However, the question of how far children should be encouraged to express their creative energies through employment is very complex, and illustrates the impossibility of separating vocational guidance from the need of an overall philosophy of life. At one extreme is a certain view of employment as a 'job' void of anything worthwhile; a daily interruption of life; at the other extreme is the obsessively employment-dedicated man to whom nothing but a career matters. Proponents of the first viewpoint sometimes take a 'realistic' or 'tough-minded' approach to the formation of employment-attitudes, and hence to vocational guidance.

They argue that at the present time, and in the foreseeable future, many forms of industry will require large reserves of manpower for the dullest and most routine jobs. For such people education should concentrate on the creative use of leisure; and in any case, not encourage a false view of the world of work, among those most likely to fall into routine employments. Such unimaginative attitudes ignore the onrush of automation, the increasing geographical mobility of urbanised societies, and the whole background pattern of change, which we look at in the next two chapters, and which, however materialist its methods and aims, is swiftly changing the approach of many young people towards their vocational futures. The question which adolescents increasingly ask, in Britain and elsewhere, is not how to find a good job, or to make a career, but whether to bother about such things.

Their problems seem to me to arise out of a deeply sincere questioning of the worth of modern urban civilization. The spread of cynicism about accepted values, the rejection of the 'establishment,' of authority, seem to me to go wider than the characteristic and temporary rebellion in adolescent development against the older generations; and as we shall see later, even in communist countries there is some evidence of a similar trend, masked by lip-service to stereotype ideals. The drift of this wind through our societies further illustrates the change of separating vocational guidance from counselling.

Practical Aspects

The development of guidance in semi-specialised form in British schools, has been so closely identified in the past with careers work. These simple and essential ideas about the relationship between work, leisure, and personal development have not been sufficiently considered to lead guidance away from a narrow pre-occupation with employment, to a wider view of life goals. The answers probably lie in the tendency in British society, which we have looked at, to concentrate on processes rather than on concepts; on immediate problems rather than on long term goals. Thus, the earliest government intervention, represented by the Employment Acts of 1909 and 1910, set up juvenile departments in some Employment Exchange to help place boys and girls in jobs, and to allow Local Education Authorities to do this also.

To be fair, the wording of the Acts and official memoranda at this time indicate a recognition of the need for guidance on a wider basis; but in practice the provision becomes one of job-placement, predominantly for the children of the poor. The excessive concentration on job-placement has remained as part of the official attitude towards vocational guidance, in spite of various attempts at improvement, and in spite of being drawn much more closely into the frame work of L.E.A supervision since 1948. Why did the concept not evolve faster? There are several possibilities.

One is the fact that guidance structures existed outside and independently of the schools: the contact between Youth Employment Officers and school staff was too fleeting for serious discussion of deeper issues in guidance.

The fact that an organised structure existed outside the schools; and school heads, often tending to think of the successful pupil as one who made the ascent into a university or teacher-training college, may, as we have suggested earlier, have thought of an early leaver looking for a job, as an educational failure. Also, for many years, the use of psychological tests was almost totally unknown among teachers, so that no independent pointer to the relationships between personal, educational, and vocational needs of children was available.

But the main reason why for so long the idea of guidance lay at the level of job-placement in Britain is almost certainly to be found in the social stratification of education. The acceptance of new ideas in guidance and the rise in the numbers of careers teachers, and the emergence of the counsellor as a new figure in schools, coincide closely with the rise of comprehensive secondary schools. We have already emphasised the tendency of grammar and public school heads to judge success in terms of educational attainment. This limited the development of the concept in those areas.

In the secondary modern schools which emerged after the 1944 Education Act, a large number were situated in industrial slum areas, where the prospects, career or otherwise, were too grim to think about. Here there was little or no incentive to start thinking along sophisticated lines about guidance. But the comprehensive schools which emerged a few years later were in a different position: they offered a diversity of educational opportunity at the secondary level unknown in the other kinds of school, and extended deep into adolescence the problems of educational, vocational, and personal choice.

In such circumstance, especially in the larger schools, sense of uncertainty, even of being lost, can easily emerge, and for the young pupil soon grow to formidable proportions among so many new faces, both of pupils and staff, most of them stranger. In such a situation, the development of an effective guidance system, able to make contact with such pupils is completely necessary if the main aims of the school are to achieve: one can go further and say that it is the presence of such a system, and its efficient functioning, that largely holds the balance between a comprehensive school approaching its ideals, and an 'education processing factory' of the kind described by opponents of the comprehensive school principle.

In fact, the sort of situation we have suggested here has involved fairly specific problems, and their solution has encouraged the emergence of techniques. The newcomer has to be introduced to the school; at its simplest this means making certain that the pupil understands what opportunities are open to him, and how to use the main lines of communication. Pupil records have to be developed beyond the simple report-card stage, in order to record as much as possible of the kind of information which, in a smaller community, would be casually picked up by teachers in getting to know their pupils.

The advantages of using psychological tests as a short-cut to objective information have begun to be recognised, and teachers involved in guidance work in comprehensive schools frequently seek courses at which they can build up their knowledge and experience with such instruments, and so improve the quality of the record system. There has been considerable attention to the formation of guidance teams, and to the use of team work techniques to help overcome the communication problems in big establishments, and to deal with the wide diversity of problems encountered.

These developments, as Moore emphasised in his study of five such systems, have taken place in response to immediate problems, and, judging by the growing importance attached to them, seem to have met with a good deal of success. As we have already seen, movements of this kind tend to call for role-differentiation, and specialists of the kind or another tend to appear in the teamwork, leading naturally to the question of appointing a personal counsellor, or counsellors, for the pupils. The tradition of guidance, as employment-centered vocational guidance, was of course inadequate to meet this need, and hence the importation wholesale of the American theories and practices of counselling.

But the solutions worked out from the 1950's onwards, and increasingly throughout the 1960's, were in terms of how to develop and integrate new areas of guidance to meet the peculiar problems of big schools, and not generally in terms of deep thinking about the existing concepts-especially, of vocational guidance. The goals were seen in terms of the solution of immediate problems. Thus it happens that we can only say that vocational guidance in Britain has evolved during the last two decades, if by 'evolution' we mean the expansion and refinement of provision, not of concepts.

This means that a difficulty is sometimes found in how to relate the specialist in vocational guidance to the specialist in personal counselling, in the organisation of school guidance teams. In some such patterns the careers teacher actualy appears as an additional specialist outside the main guidance team, itself organised around a system of personal counselling. Again, in some schools, counselling is dominated by a concept of vocational guidance crudely centred on helping the adolescent to make a happy 'first-job' choice, which of course means that the emphasis is on the early leavers rather than over the whole school population.

Again, at least some of the confusion that exists about the difference between 'counselling' and 'guidance' stems from the fact that there has been a continuous development of provision in this semi-specialist area, but as a result of the failure of the concept to evolve, there is now a spilt between a concept which began in Britain, and a similar one, which evolved in a totally different fashion in North America, and was then imported into Britain in its matured form, as counselling, in the 1960's. As an example of this difficulty, an authorative article in New Era in 1968 stated that vocational guidance was essentially informative, and should be handled by careers teachers, whereas personal guidance was essentially problem centred, and constituted the main role of the counsellor in secondary schools. Likewise, vocational guidance is still regarded by the Youth Employment Service to be an employment guidance service. However, the blame goes to its terms of reference and not the YES.

13

Present Scenario

The pupils, parents, legislators, the community at large, and educators all must view guidance as a profession that provides a need service, available from no other source. Two factors determine whether or not this will occur. The first is the sensitivity and perceptiveness of guidance workers in discerning the real problems and needs, particularly those of which the general public is only dimly aware. The second is the effectiveness in communicating goals and results to this same public. Obviously, something positive has to happen in the lives of those who come in contact with guidance. Identifying needs and publicizing results will not alone accomplish the task of ensuring the support of guidance services. But guidance already has the means to ensure that, it has a significant impact, and the dynamic nature of the profession, documented throughout this book, practically guarantees that it will enlarge and improve on present approaches and techniques.

Thus, the question needs to be faced, will the guidance professions able to respond effectively to the two major tasks? My position is that it will; the motivation, competency, and imagination of those who will do the job are already plentiful.

In fact, a recurring theme in earlier chapters is the inventiveness guidance workers have repeatedly demonstrated not only in dealing with current needs but in anticipating emerging or hidden ones. Failure will come only if enthusiasm falters, and pressures and challenges are allowed to cause a futile search for security through ingratiatingly taking on a myriad of insignificant and irrelevant tasks in the attempt to become indispensable rather than be professional. Predictions are hazardous but necessary. The task is made easier by the post-bicentennial climate of taking stock and looking to the future. A positive orientation towards the future is essential in the midst of the present confusions and dilemmas:

America is wallowing in a period of disappointment and disillusion. The idea of progress is tili alive, but it is not well. There is an emerging 'new pessimism', not only in foreign policy but in domestic affairs. Government is viewed as, inevitably, bumbling and corrupt. Other social institutions are considered obsolete and ineffectual. But, Elam's view is not one of long-term pessimism. Hopeful signs both of society in general and schools in particular can be drawn from the position that ours is a "self correcting society" and the schools are "a major instrument in shaping the future".

The bases for optimism are substantial. Resources are being depleted, but there are avenues available utilizing selective growth and alternative energy resources that can, if used fully and promptly, head off disaster. The nation's collective ingenuity can find new ways to cope with destructive trends. Scientific and social innovations and breakthroughs have served to improve the quality of life in past years and have the potential for equally or greater success in the future.

We are only beginning to use our intellectual potential for progress on all fronts; education, especially, stands to gain enormously from new developments in both the cognitive and affective areas. But we may need to experience a "socioquake" and thus arrive at new ways of viewing man in relation to the environment rather than patching up the old perceptions and practices. With an assumption of constructive and positive changes, what are major directions for the next several decades? A review of even a handful of the significant themes required a look at political, economic, social, and educational aspects.

Constant Process

There is a continuity in the international political alignments among power blocs, even as new nations strive for status and recognition, and energy resources modify relations among countries. International politics will be based on power balances and energy resources, but there will be a greater recognition and acceptance of the concept of interdependence of nations.

The related worldwide problems of growth, crowding, and inadequate resources will be faced: cooperative efforts will be made to slow down the population explosion, increase worldwide food production, and enhance the self-sufficiency of third-world countries. Economic problems, primarily inflation, and unemployment will continue to cause hardships for individuals, while increasing both the cost of services and the need for them. Cooperation among nations will be emphasized, while reduced energy resources and needs of undeveloped countries heighten problems in this country.

The trend of a rising median population age will continue, and the effects will be felt in every aspect of life. Not only will there be a shift in the emphasis of guidance and counselling, but retirement policies and benefits, education, housing, medical care, and the world of work will be dramatically affected. Work and the work setting are changing in ways that will have profound effects in the years ahead.

There will be an increased demand for job security as protection against the fluctuations in the economy. At the same time, however, more humane and stimulating working conditions will be sought. The work week and work day will be shortened, and variations such as splitting job and self-selected work hours will be tested. The increasing age of the labour force and the steady trend for more female participation will affect the workplace in many ways not yet known to us. Changes in education will range from introducing new financing plans to establishing programmes for lifelong learning. As the proportion of school-age individuals decreases, the cost of public education rises, and the needs and political power of older persons become more visible, we may see a higher quality of schooling. It seems certain that there will be provisions for lifelong easy entry and exit in educational and training programmes.

New school models will merge education and life-family, community, and working ways that will make education more significant. Writz predicts that "some kind of provision for enterprising the earning 'and learning of a living, for interweaving for interspersing the earning and learning of a living, for interweaving employment and self-renewal, is going to have to be recognized as the essential còndition for an effective career as worker, citizen, or human being". A host of trends are encompassed by the need. Shane describes as "how to remotivate youth to feel that life is good, that it is worth living, and that it can bring enduring satisfaction". Many of the problems of today stem from the lacks this statement implies; some young people seek solutions in fads, cults, drugs, or deviant life-styles.

The educational institution will play a significant part in building new values and purpose, but the next several decades will be marked more by questions and searching than by answers and solutions. If we translate the societal trends into guidelines for counselling and guidance, a general picture of increased pressure for services emerges. The need to make the most use possible of human and material resources leads to a greater concern for individual awareness of potential and opportunities.

The increasing interdependence among nations could enhance concern for problems that are common to different cultures and bring guidance workers in different countries closer together to pool strategies and techniques.

Developing and underdeveloped countries can profit from learning about what is done in other areas if they have the opportunity to adapt principles and strategies for local uses. It would be well to avoid an attitude that what is done in technologically advanced countries is best for others. A cooperative approach to unique needs of each culture would be true implementation of the spirit of guidance. Many of the cutbacks that appear to be inevitable will very likely cause disruptions in established patterns of travel recreation, and day-to-day living. New modes may actually be growth-producing. There may, for example, be less dependence on commercial entertainment, but the changes may call for difficult adaptations.

The changing age of the population has obvious and important implications for guidance. Not only will there be a shift to include expanded services for those in their middle and later years, but new types of help will be needed, e.g., assisting mid-life and older persons with educational and work planning. The changing world of work offers some of the most direct implications for guidance and counselling of any aspect of life. Even though efforts are being made to adapt work to individuals and to develop new patterns of work hour and sharing jobs, the central problem of finding meaning and fulfillment will demand increased attention.

Perhaps a combination of meaningful leisure activities and income-producing work will needed. Whatever the eventual solutions, it seems that some kind of human development services both the workplace and in the community will be needed. The changing world of work offers some of the most direct implications for guidance and counselling and aspect of life. Even though efforts are being made to adapt work to individuals and to develop new patterns of work hours and sharing jobs, the central problem of finding meaning and fulfillment will demand increased attention. Perhaps a combination of meaningful leisure activities and income-producing work will be needed. Whatever the eventual solutions, it seems that some kind of human development services both in the workplace and in the community will be needed.

The increasing need for accountability and making the most productive use of resources will make education give additional emphasis to helping all pupils understand and utilize their full potential. Questions are being raised about the assumed benefits of large schools, and there is a shift emerging that emphasizes compulsory education, not just compulsory attendance. These and other trends imply that help will be needed to make the school a place for learning and development attuned to the needs of the individual and the community.

The task of helping youth to find challenge, meaning, and stimulation in school programmes, work, and productive community life is made even more demanding by the changing social and economic conditions. This is a school-community problem that demands the best efforts of practically everyone, but it is one in which guidance personnel have a unique opportunity for effective leadership and service. A brief and general review of major trends slights a multitude of specific issues, problems and directions of critical significance for guidance workers (e.g. licensure, ethics, preparation, and affirmative action), but it gives the backdrop against which they will be worked out. Moreover, the major trends contain a formation of an increasing need for guidance and counselling for helping all individuals in lifelong growth and development and to give guidelines for dealing with the specific questions and problems.

A major point of this book is that new strategies, techniques, and technology are vital of effective delivery of services today. The future will make even greater demands on the creativity and inventiveness of guidance workers. Two factors support this prediction-accountability and financing. From the counsellor's point of view, the major reason is to provide better—quality help to more people; improving the quality of life ranks above the demand for hard evidence of effects and adjusting to cope with financial limitations. But the realities of the situation require a consideration of the most effective use of personnel and material resources to achieve desired goals.

Tomorrow may usher in strategies that are unknown today. The past few years have witnessed a proliferating of approaches, technology, and strategies. Some are destined for a brief meteoric life before falling into oblivion. Others are sure to become major styles of guidance in the future. The problem that counsellors face is how to tell the difference. There is no quick or easy way; research and evaluation provide the most valid answers. Intuition may seem a trusty guide, but it is often so entangled in personal commitment to an approach or enthusiasm for a cause that its value is doubtful. Moreover, the attitude that what is new is good and what is old is bad leads to a distorted view that inhibits a thoughtful and perceptive selection of the most effective means. This naive position, coupled with a tendency to partially try-out and quickly dispose of new approaches, not only creates discontinuous development but often relegates to the scrap heap potentially valuable methods and materials. There is much faddishness in U. S. guidance, abetted by an affluence that permits spending of enormous sums on new developments that are discarded even before rigorous testing can be completed. This luxury is fast disappearing. It will take careful evaluation and use of both the old and new to fashion the guidance of the future.

Productive elements that will gain additional use in the years ahead are already reflected. Consultation is one. Together with psychological education and "giving guidance away", it represents a new taking shape for many years. Paraprofessional and computers also have great potential. The needs survey, a new label for holding guidance close to what the public wants, is obviously here to stay.

It has never disappeared since the concept of guidance first surfaced at the turn of the century, but since then it has fallen on hard times. Accountability is of course not new; the only surprising things is that it took so long to emerge as a major consideration in the helping services. A number of other strategies have been endorsed in the preceding pages; the movement toward lifelong learning and guidance, and integrating the school with the community and workplace are the most significant. The separate elements are not new, but the synthesis brings into being a strategy of tremendous importance. One front along which the profession advances does not invoive largescale movements nationwide in scope—it is in the day-to-day work of the counsellor who may, for example, develop a better way to help a counselee explore goals, make decisions, and carry- out plans, or devise a new mode of working with groups of pupils or parents. It could be any of the multitude of things the counsellor does. Shared with colleagues, these activities have a ripple effect that eventually makes a difference in school guidance.

Reflections on programmes naturally lead to speculation about the practice of guidance five, twenty, or thirty years ahead. What will it be like? Is it possible to look into the future with any certainty? Some trends appear to be fairly clearly indicated by current developments. One of these is licensure. There almost certainly will be some type of widespread provisions for licensure, which will have an impact on school counsellors. Effects will be felt more definitely by those in non-school settings, however, as it is predicted that employment in an educational institution will enable the counsellor to practice regardless of licensure status.

Accountability will be given more attention in all settings. Evidence of positive effects will be needed to ensure the continued existence of school guidance services as well as to maintain support for programmes in other settings. Moreover, counsellors will be expected to expand services with little additional financial support.

The counsellor's role will be more clearly defined, partly because of accountability and partly because of the use of new strategies such as outreach and psychological education, which give the work a visible structure and purpose. Increasing attention will be given to the needs of special groups, e.g., mid-life and older persons, minorities, the handicapped, and women. Moreover, we will see at least the beginning of the implementation of lifelong learning and school community cooperative approaches.

New Trends

Changes in public education, particularly the expanded infusion of career education, will make the school a more dynamic and realistic learning environment. At the same time the "basics" will be increasingly emphasized. All of these changes will offer counsellors opportunities to serve in new ways and to build a solid position in education. More processes and personnel will be utilized to expand the reach of guidance services. Paraprofessionals are one example, particularly peer counsellors. After their slow start in the past decade, computers will be used with increasing frequency.

As school budgets are examined, questions will be raised about the necessity for guidance services. The predicted outcome, however, is that there will be an increase in they support for services because the offer ways to deal with the most pressing school and community problems.

The impact of the social, economic, and political trends described will have a more pronounced effect on guidance and counselling than in the immediate future. It is predicted that more definite patterns of those trends given for the next five years will have emerged, e.g., licensure regulations will be crystallized, career education will be the major mode in public education, and guidance roles will be more clear-cut and more widely understood. Computer Technology will be used, and counsellors will have much more time to devote to the personal, effective, and decision-making needs of youth.

Lifelong education and school-community cooperation will be realities, and counsellors will work with all ages in both school and community.

There will be increases in the number of counsellors needed; preparation standards will provide for differential staffing, with high levels of technical and human-relations competency for those in supervisory positions. At the same time there will be increased attention to prevention of problems and the provision of easily available community-wide services. School counsellors will be regarded as logical persons to coordinate all school-guidance and pupil-personnel services, and will provide leadership for community wide coordination strategies.

Disregarding the gloomy projections of those who question the likelihood of civilization lasting into the 21st century—such apprehension would have been equally appropriate in any approach of recorded history—it is not only possible but essential to look ahead to try to discern a reasonably accurate, if tentative, outline of the shape of guidance. Leaders in the field, such as Berdie, Harris, Morgan, and Walz, show a substantial consensus about major developments in the future. Four characteristics stand out. First, the counsellor will go where people are; outreach will be major strategy, and there will be considerable use of support persons. Marple describes a thought provoking fantasy of the future in which "Friendship Centers" alter the lives of people nationally and internationally. But typically, no clear-cut definition of the arrangement of such a center is given; but the implication is that location and type of housing will be of less importance than what happens in the community.

The second major prediction is that services will be available lifelong; the school-age emphasis will have disappeared. Guidance will be provided over the whole range of individuals and groups;

no social strata or subculture will be favoured over any other. Along with this breadth, helping agencies and institutions will collaborate far more than they do today, and guidance workers will have a more comprehensive knowledge of and better working relationships with colleagues in other settings. Much of the counsellor's work will emphasize prevention; while crisis help will be provided, the major thrust will be the change agent's task reducing or eliminating destructive features of the environment that generate problems.

The counsellor's increased versatility will require a sound background in theory, research, and techniques, the quality of preparation will rise. Facilitating personal development, building effective working relationships, and gaining an in-depth understanding of various cultures will be given higher priority. Preparation programmes will utilize input from the school, the community, and the working world, and measure student progress on the basis of competency.

Other aspects of the role in the years ahead involve legal status, ethical practices, professional organizations, and counsellor's supply and demand. Prospects are good for increased professional status and the attendant legal and ethical responsibilities. Professional organizations will again the prestige to induce employers to upgrade hiring standards.

Practical Aspects

The conditions that support the need for guidance have been highlighted well. It is inconceivable that any of them will fade away; recent events in social, economic, and political life show that problems and needs will become more complex and pressing in future.

The viability of guidance as a major helping service depends not only on the profusion of societal problems, complexities, and needs; it must be seen as an effective response. The many publics-pupils, parents, legislators, the community at large, and educators-must view guidance as a profession that provides a need service, available from no other source. Two factors determine whether or not this will occur. The first is the sensitivity and perceptiveness of guidance workers in discerning the real problems and needs, particularly those of which the general public is only dimly aware. The second is the effectiveness in communicating goals and results to this same public.

Obviously something positive has to happen in the lives of those who come in contact with guidance. Identifying needs and publicizing results will not alone accomplish the task of ensuring the support of guidance services. But guidance already has the means to ensure that it has a significant impact, and the dynamic nature of the profession, documented throughout this book, practically guarantees that it will enlarge and improve on present approaches and techniques.

Thus, the question needs to be faced, will the guidance profession be able to respond effectively to the two major tasks? My position is that it will; the motivation, competency, and imagination of those who will do the job are already plentiful. In fact, a recurring theme in earlier chapters is the inventiveness guidance workers have repeatedly demonstrated not only in dealing with current needs but in anticipating emerging or hidden ones. Failure will come only if enthusiasm falters, and pressures and challenges are allowed to cause a futile search for security through ingratiatingly taking on a myriad of insignificant and irrelevant tasks in the attempt to become indispensable rather than be professional.

The Outcome

Predictions are hazardous but necessary. The task is made easier by the post-Bicentennial climate of taking stock and looking to the future. A positive orientation towards the future is essential in the midst of the present confusions and dilemmas:

America is wallowing in a period of disappointment and disillusion. The idea of progress is still alive, but it is not well. There is an emerging new pessimism, not only in foreign policy but in domestic affairs. Goverment is viewe as inevitably, bumbling and corrupt. Other social institutions are considered obsolete and ineffectual.

But, Elam's view is not one of long-term pessimism. Hopeful signs both of society in general, and schools in particular can be drawn from the position that ours is a "self correcting society" and the schools are "a major instrument in shaping the future".

The bases for optimism are substantial. Resources are being depleted, but there are avenues available utilizing selective growth and alternative energy resources that can, if used fully and promptly, head off disaster. The nation's collective ingenuity can find new ways to cope with destructive trends. Scientific and social innovations and breakthroughs have served to improve the quality of life in past years and have the potential for equally or greater success in the future. We are only beginning to use our intellectual potential for progress on all fronts; education, especially, stands to gain enormously from new developments in both the cognitive and affective areas. But we may need to experience a "socioquake" and thus arrive at new ways of viewing man in relation to the environment rather than patching up the old perceptions and practices.

With an assumption of constructive and positive changes, what are major directions for the next several decades? A review of even a handful of the significant themes required a look at political, economic, social and educational aspects.

There is a continuity in the international political alignments among power blocs, even as new nations strive for status and recognition, and energy resources modify relations among countries. International politics will be based on power balances and energy resources, but there will be a greater recognition and acceptance of the concept of interdependence of nations. The related worldwide problems of growth, crowding, and inadequate resources will be faced; cooperative efforts will be made to slow down the population explosion, increase worldwide food production, and enhance the self-sufficiency of third-world countries.

Economic problems, primarily inflation, and unemployment, will continue to cause hardships for individuals, while increasing both the cost of services and the need for them, Cooperation among nations will be emphasized, while reduced energy resources and needs of undeveloped countries heighten problems in this country.

The trend of a rising median population age will continue, and the effects will be felt in every aspect of life. Not only will there be a shift in the emphasis of guidance and counselling, but retirement policies and benefits, education, housing, medical care, and the world of work will be dramatically affected.

Work and the work setting are changing in ways that will have profound effects in the years ahead. There will be an increased demand for job security as protection against the fluctuations in the economy. At the same time, however, more humane and stimulating working conditions will be sought. The work week and work day will be shortened, and variations such as splitting job and self-selected work hours will be tested, The increasing age of the labour force and the steady trend for more female participation will affect the workplace in many ways not yet known to us.

Changes in education will range from introducing new financing plans to establishing programs for lifelong learning. As the proportion of school-age individuals decreases, the cost of public education rises, and political power of older persons become more we may see a higher quality of schooling. It seems that there will be provisions for lifelong easy entry and exit in educational and training programs. New school models will merge education and life-family, community, and work-in ways that will make education more significant. Writz predicts that "some kind of provision for enterprising the earning and learning of a living, for interweaving employment and self-renewal, is going to have to be recognized as the essential condition for an effective career as worker, citizen, or human being".

A host of trends are encompassed by the need Shane describes as "how to remotivate youth to feel that life is good, that it is worth living, and that it can bring enduring satisfaction". Many of the problems of today stem from what this statement implies; some young people seek solutions in fads, cults, drugs, or deviant life-styles. The educational institution will play a significant part in building new values and purpose, but the next several decades will be marked more by questions and searching than by answers and solutions.

If we translate the societal trends into guidelines for counselling and guidance, a general picture of increased pressure for services emerges. The need to make the most use possible of human and material resources leads to a greater concern for individual awareness of potential and opportunities. Material resources will be carefully used by those who are sensitive to the needs of others and are aware of the importance of sharing rather than thinking only of themselves.

The increasing interdependence among nations could enhance concern for problems that are common to different cultures and bring guidance workers in different countries closer together to pool strategies and techniques. Developing and underdeveloped countries can profit from learning about what is done in other areas if they have the opportunity to adapt principles and strategies for local uses. It would be well to avoid an attitude that what is done in technologically advanced countries is best for others. A cooperative approach to unique needs of each culture would be true implementation of the spirit of guidance.

Many of the cutbacks that appear to be inevitable will very likely cause disruptions in established patterns of travel, recreation, and day-to-day living. New modes may actually be growth-producing-there may, for example, be less dependence on commercial entertainment-but the changes may call for difficult adaptations.

The changing age of the population has obvious and important implications for guidance. Not only will there be a shift to include expanded services for those in their middle and later years, but new types of help will be needed, e.g., assisting mid-life and older persons with educational and work planning.

The changing world of work offers some of the most direct implications for guidance and counselling of any aspect of life. Even though efforts are being made to adapt work to individuals and to develop new patterns of work hour and sharing jobs, the central problem of finding meaning and fulfillment will demand increased attention. Perhaps a combination of meaningful leisure activities and income-producing work will be needed. Whatever the eventual solutions, it seems that some kind of human development services both the workplace and in the community will be needed.

The changing world of work offers some of the most direct implications for guidance and counselling and aspect of life. Even though efforts are being made to adapt work to individuals and to develop new patterns of work hours and sharing jobs, the central problem of finding meaning and fulfillment will demand increased attention. Perhaps a combination of meaningful leisure activities and income-producing work will be needed. Whatever the eventual solutions, it seems that some kind of human development services both in the workplace and in the community will be needed.

The increasing need for accountability and making the most productive use of resources will make education give additional emphasis to helping all pupils understand and utilize their full potential. Questions are being raised about the assumed benefits of large schools, and there is a shift emerging that emphasizes compulsory education, not just compulsory attendance. These and other trends imply that help will be needed to make the school a place for learning and development attuned to the needs of the individual and the community.

The task of helping youth to find challenge, meaning, and stimulation in school programs, work, and productive community life is made even more demanding by the changing social and economic conditions. This is a school-community problem that demands the best efforts of practically everyone, but it is one in which guidance personnel have a unique opportunity for effective leadership and service.

A brief and general review of major trends slights a multitude of specific issues, problems and directions of critical significance for guidance workers (e.g. licensure, ethics, preparation, and affirmative action), but it gives the backdrop against which they will be worked out. Moreover, the major trends contain an formation of an increasing need for guidance and counselling for helping all individuals in lifelong growth and development and to give guidelines for dealing with the specific questions and problems.

Fresh Approach

A major point of this book is that new strategies, techniques, and technology are vital of effective delivery of services today. The future will make even greater demands on the creativity and inventiveness of guidance workers. Two factors support this prediction-accountability and financing. From the counsellor's point of view, the major reason is to provide better-quality help to more people, improving the quality of life ranks above the demand for hard evidence of effects and adjusting to cope with financial limitations. But the realities of the situation require a consideration of the most effective use of personal and material resources to achieve desired goals. Tomorrow may usher in strategies that are unknown today.

The past few years have witnessed a proliferating of approaches, technology, and strategies. Some are destined for a brief meteoric life before falling into oblivion. Others are sure to become major styles of guidance in the future. The problem that counsellors face is how to tell the difference. There is no quick or easy way; research and evaluation provide the most valid answers. Intuition may seem a trusty guide, but it is often so entangled in personal commitment to an approach or enthusiasm for a cause that its value is doubtful.

Moreover, the attitude that what is new is good and what is old is bad leads to a distorted view that inhibits a thoughtful and perceptive selection of the most effective means. This naive position, coupled with a tendency to partially try out and quickly dispose of new approaches, not only creates discontinuous development but often relegates to the scrap heap potentially valuable methods and materials. There is much faddishness in U. S. guidance, abetted by an affluence that permits spending of enormous sums on new developments that are discarded even before rigorous testing can be completed. This luxury is fast disappearing. It will take careful evaluation and use of both the old and new to fashion the guidance of the future.

Productive elements that will gain additional use in the years ahead are reflected in earlier chapters. Consultation is one. Together with psychological education and "giving guidance away", it represents a new taking shape for many years. Paraprofessional and computers also have great potential. The needs survey, a new label for holding guidance close to what the public wants, is obviously here to stay. It has never disappeared since the concept of guidance first surfaced at the turn of the century, but since then it has fallen on hard times. Accountability is of course not new; the only surprising things is that it took so long to emerge as a major consideration in the helping services. A number of other strategies have been endorsed in the preceding pages; the movement toward lifelong learning and guidance, and integrating the school with the community and workplace are the most significant. The separate elements are not new, but the synthesis brings into being a strategy of tremendous importance.

One front along which the profession advances does not involve large scale movements nationwide in scope-it is in the day-to-day work of the counsellor who may, for example, develop a better way to help a counsellee explore goals, make decisions, and carry out plans, or devise a new mode of working with groups of pupils or parents. It could be any of the multitude of things the counsellor does. Shared with colleagues, these activities have a ripple effect that eventually makes a difference in school guidance.

Reflections on programs naturally lead to speculation about the practice of guidance five, twenty, or thirty years ahead. What will it be like? Is it possible to look into the future with any certainty?

Some trends appear to be fairly clearly indicated by current developments. One of these is licensure. There almost certainly will be some type of widespread provisions for licensure, which will have an impact on school counsellors. Effects will be felt more definitely by those in non-school settings, however, as it is predicted that employment in an educational institution will enable the counsellor to practice regardless of licensure status.

Accountability will be given more attention in all settings. Evidence of positive effects will be needed to ensure the continued existence of school guidance services as well as to maintain support for programs in other settings. Moreover, counsellors will be expected to expand services with little additional financial support.

The counsellor's role will be more clearly defined, partly because of accountability and partly because of the use of new strategies such as outreach and psychological education, which give the work a visible structure and purpose.

Increasing attention will be given to the needs of special groups, like mid-life and older persons, minorities, the handicapped, and women. Moreover, we will see at least the beginning of the implementation of lifelong learning and school-community cooperative approaches.

Changes in public education, particularly the expanded infusion of career education, will make the school a more dynamic and realistic learning environment. At the same time the "basics" will be increasingly emphasized. All of these changes will offer counsellors opportunities to serve in new ways and to build a solid position in education.

More processes and personnel will be utilized to expand the reach of guidance services. Paraprofessionals are one example, particularly peer counsellors. After their slow start in the past decade, computers will be used with increasing frequency.

As school budgets are examined, questions will be raised about the necessity for guidance services. The predicted outcome, however, is that there will be an increase in the support for services because they offer ways to deal with the most pressing school and community problems.

The impact of the social, economic, and political trends described will have a more pronounced effect on guidance and counselling than in the immediate future. It is predicted that more definite patterns of those trends given for the next five years will have emerged. e.g., licensure regulations will be crystallized, career education will be the major mode in public education, and guidance roles will be more clear-cut and more widely understood. Computer technology will be used, and counsellors will have much more time to devote to the personal, effective, and decision-making needs of youth.

Lifelong education and school-community cooperation will be realities, and counsellors will work with all ages in both school and community. There will be increases in the number of counsellors needed; preparation standards will provide for differential staffing, with high levels of technical and human-relations competency for those in supervisory positions. At the same time there will be increased attention to prevention of problems and the provision of easily available community-wide services. School counsellors will be regarded as logical persons to coordinate all school-guidance and pupil-personnel services, and will provide leadership community-wide.

Planning for Days to Come

Disregarding the gloomy projections of those who question the likelihood of civilization lasting into the 2lst century—such apprehension would have been equally appropriate in any approach of recorded history—it is not only possible but essential to look ahead to try to discern a reasonably accurate, if tentative, outline of the shape of guidance Leaders in the field, such as Berdie, Harris, Morgan, and Walz, show a substantial consensus about major developments in the future.

Four characteristics stand out. First, the counsellor will go where people are; outreach will be major strategy, and there will be considerable use of support persons. Marple describes a thought provoking fantasy of the future in which "Friendship Centers" alter the lives of people nationally and internationally. But typically, no clear-cut definition of the arrangement of such a center is given; but the implication is that location and type of housing will be of less importance than what happens in the community.

The second major prediction is that services will be available lifelong; the school-age emphasis will have disappeared. Guidance will be provided over the whole range of individuals and groups; no social strata or subculture will be favoured over any other. Along with this breadth, helping agencies and institutions will collaborate far more than they do today, and guidance workers will have a more comprehensive knowledge of and better working relationships with, colleagues in other settings.

Much of the counsellor's work will emphasize prevention; while crisis help will be provided, the major thrust will be the change agent's task reducing or eliminating destructive features of the environment that generate problems.

The counsellor's increased versatility will require a sound background in theory, research, and techniques, the quality of preparation will rise. Facilitating personal development, building effective working relationships, and gaining an in-depth understanding of various cultures will be given higher priority. Preparation programs will utilize input from the school, the community, and the working world, and measure student progress on the basis of competency.

Other aspects of the role in the years ahead involve legal status, ethical practices, professional organizations, and counsellor's supply and demand Prospects are good for increased professional status and the attendant legal and ethical responsibilities. Professional organizations will again induce employers to upgrade hiring standards. Some form of licensure will be in operation; counsellors will participate in setting qualifications and examining applicants. It is very probable that counsellors will be completely in charge of this process.

Expansions in the directions predicted here—lifelong service, and broad applications in life areas-will mean that the demand for counsellors will exceed the supply. Notwithstanding changes in support at the federal and state levels, and increased competition for available funds, the need for counsellors is bound to increase by leaps and bounds.

Additional Reading

Bhaskara Rao, Digumarti (1994). *Scientific Aptitude,* New Delhi: Ashish Publishing House. ISBN 81-7024-658-X.

Bhaskara Rao, Digumarti (1995). *Animal Kingdom.* New Delhi: Discovery Publishing House. ISBN 81-7141-274-2.

Bhaskara Rao, Digumarti (1995). *Batracology.* New Delhi: Discovery Publishing House. ISBN 81-7141-279-3.

Bhaskara Rao, Digumarti (1997), *Scientific Attitude.* New Delhi: Discovery Publishing House. ISBN 81-7141-308-0.

Bhaskara Rao, Digumarti (1996). *Scientific Attitude vis-à-vis Scientific Aptitude.* New Delhi: Discovery Publishing House. ISBN 81-7141-308-0.

Bhaskara Rao, Digumarti, Editor (1996). *Encyclopaedia of Education for All,* 5 Volumes. New Delhi: APH Publishing Corporation. ISBN 81-7024-759-4 (set).

Vol. I *Education for All: The World Conference.* ISBN 81-7024-760-8.

Vol. II *Education for All: The EPA-9 Summit.* ISBN 81-7024-761-6.

Vol. III *Education for All: Quality Education for All.* ISBN 81-7024-762-6.

Vol. IV *Education for All: Planning and Monitoring.* ISBN 81-7024-763-4.

Vol. V *Education for All: The Indian Scenario.* ISBN 81-7024-764-0.

Bhaskara Rao, Digumarti, Editor (1996). *Global Perceptions on Peace Education,* 3 Volumes. New Delhi: Discovery Publishing House. ISBN 81-7141-319-6.

Bhaskara Rao, Digumarti, Editor (1996). *National Policy on Education*. 2 Volumes. New Delhi: Anmol Publications Pvt. Ltd. ISBN 81-7488-323-1.

Bhaskara Rao, Digumarti, Editor (1997). *Care the Child*, 2 Volumes. New Delhi: Discovery Publishing House. ISBN 81-7141-394-3.

Bhaskara Rao, Digumarti, Editor (1997). *Education for the 21st Century*. New Delhi: Discovery Publishing House. ISBN 81-7141-389-7.

Bhaskara Rao, Digumarti, Editor (1997). *Reflections on Scientific Attitude*. New Delhi: Discovery Publishing House, ISBN 81-7141-319-6.

Bhaskara Rao, Digumarti, Editor (1997). *Success Story of a Primary Education Project*. New Delhi: APH Publishing Corporation. ISBN 81-7024-850-7.

Bhaskara Rao, Digumarti, Editor (1997). *World Food Summit*. New Delhi: Discovery Publishing House. ISBN 81-7141-386-2.

Bhaskara Rao, Digumarti, Editor (1998). *Adolescence Education*. New Delhi: Discovery Publishing House. ISBN 81-7141-432-X.

Bhaskara Rao, Digumarti, Editor (1998). *Community and School Nutrition Education*. New Delhi: Discovery Publishing House. ISBN 81-7141-435-4.

Bhaskara Rao, Digumarti, Editor (1998). *District Primary Education Programme*. New Delhi: Discovery Publishing House. ISBN 81-7141-396-X.

Bhaskara Rao, Digumarti, Editor (1998). *Earth Summit*, 2 Volumes. New Delhi: Discovery Publishing House. ISBN 81-7141-435-4.

Bhaskara Rao, Digumarti, Editor (1998). *National Policy on Education: Towards an Enlightened and Humane Society*, New Delhi: Discovery Publishing House. ISBN 81-7141-426-5.

Bhaskara Rao, Digumarti, Editor (1998). *Reforming School Education*. New Delhi: Discovery Publishing House. ISBN 81-7141-403-6.

Bhaskara Rao, Digumarti, Editor (1998). *Teacher Education in India*. New Delhi: Discovery Publishing House. ISBN 81-7141-406-0.

Bhaskara Rao, Digumarti, Editor (1998). *World Summit for Social Development*. New Delhi: Discovery Publishing House. ISBN 81-7141-420-6.

Bhaskara Rao, Digumarti, Editor (2000). *Education for All: Achieving the Goal*, 3 Volumes, New Delhi: APH Publishing Corporation. ISBN 81-7648-152-1.

Vol. I *The Global Consensus*. ISBN 81-7648-155-6.

Vol. II *Mid-Decade Review Reports of Regional Seminars*. ISBN 81-7648-154-8.

Vol. III *Issues and Trends*. ISBN 81-7648-155-6.

Bhaskara Rao, Digumarti, Editor (2000), *International Encyclopaedia of AIDS*, 11 Volumes in 13 Parts. New Delhi: Discovery Publishing House. ISBN 81-7141-6 (Set).

Vol. 1 *Introduction to HIV/AIDS*. ISBN 81-7141-523-7.

Vol. 2 *HIV/AIDS—Issues and Challenges*, 2 Parts. ISBN 81-7141-524-5.

Vol. 3 *HIV/AIDS—Socio Economic Realities*. ISBN 81-7141-524-3.

Vol. 4 *HIV/AIDS—Law Ethics and Human Rights*, 2 Parts. ISBN 81-7141-526-1.

Vol. 5 *AIDS and NGOs*. ISBN 81-7141-527-X.

Vol. 6 *AIDS and Home Care*. ISBN 81-7141-528-8.

Vol. 7 *STD Case Management*. ISBN 81-7141-529-6.

Vol. 8 *HIV/AIDS Prevention and Care—Teaching Modules for Nurses and Midwives*. ISBN 81-7141-530-X.

Vol. 9 *HIV Prevention Education for Education for Educational Institutions*. ISBN 81-7141-531-8.

Vol. 10 *Instructional Modules for AIDS Education*. ISBN 81-7141-532-6.

Vol. 11 *School Health Education to Prevent AIDS and STD—A Package for Curriculum Planners*. ISBN 81-7141-5338-4.

Bhaskara Rao, Digumarti, Editor (2000). *International Encyclopaedia of Science and Technology Education*, 11 Volumes. New Delhi: Discovery Publishing House. ISBN 81-7141-548-2 (Set).

Vol. 1 *Science and Technology Education*. ISBN 81-7141-568-7.

Vol. 2 *Science Education in Developing Countries*. ISBN 81-7141-570-9.

Vol. 3 *Organisational Structure of Science*. ISBN 81-7141-570-9.

Vol. 4 *Science Education in Asia and the Pacific*. ISBN 81-7141-571-7.

Vol. 5 *Science and Technology Education for All*. ISBN 81-7141-572-5.

Vol. 6 *Values, Ethics, Talent and Girls in Science and Technology Education*. ISBN 81-7141-573-3.

Vol. 7 *Popularization of Science and Technology Education*. ISBN 81-7141-574-1.

Vol. 8 *Science, Power and Society*. ISBN 81-7141-575-X.

Vol. 9 *Information Technology*. ISBN 81-7141-576-8.

Vol. 10 *Teacher Training in Science and Technology Education*. ISBN 81-7141-577-6.

Vol. 11 *Teacher Training in Science and Technology: A Curriculum Framework*. ISBN 81-7141-578-4.

Bhaskara Rao, Digumarti, Editor (2001). *Distance Education in Different Countries*. New Delhi: APH Publishing Corporation. ISBN 81-7648-229-3.

Bhaskara Rao, Digumarti, Editor (2001). *Decentralised Management of Education (Management of Education in Panchayati Raj and Municipal Bodies)*. New Delhi: Discovery Publishing House. ISBN 81-7141-617-9.

Bhaskara Rao, Digumarti, Editor (2001). *Electrochemistry for Environmental Protection*. New Delhi: Discovery Publishing House. ISBN 81-7141-619-5.

Bhaskara Rao, Digumarti, Editor (2001). *Global Educational Studies*. New Delhi: Discovery Publishing House. ISBN 81-7141-616-0.

Bhaskara Rao, Digumarti, Editor (2001). *Global Synthesis of Educational Assessment*. New Delhi: Discovery Publishing House. ISBN 81-7141-613-6.

Bhaskara Rao, Digumarti, Editor (2000). *International Encyclopaedia of Human Rights*. 7 Volumes in 13 Parts. New Delhi: Discovery Publishing House. (Royal Size). ISBN 81-7141-567-9 (Set).

Vol. 1 *International Instruments of Human Rights*, 2 Parts. ISBN 81-7141-595-4.

Vol. 2 *Regional Instruments of Human Rights*. ISBN 81-7141-604-7.

Vol. 3 *Human Rights and the United Nations*, 2 Parts. ISBN 81-7141-605-5.

Vol. 4 *Fact Files of Human Rights*, 3 Parts. ISBN 81-7141-605-3.

Vol. 5 *Study Stories of Human Rights*, 3 Parts. ISBN 81-7141-607-3.

Vol. 6 *International Meetings on Human Rights*, 2 Parts. ISBN 81-7141-608-X.

Vol. 7 *Professional Training in Human Rights*. ISBN 81-7141-609-8.

Bhaskara Rao, Digumarti, Editor (2001). *Jomtein Decade of Education*. New Delhi: Discovery Publishing House. ISBN 81-7141-618-7.

Bhaskara Rao, Digumarti, Editor (2001). *Nuclear Materials: Issues and Concerns*, 2 Volumes. New Delhi: Discovery Publishing House. ISBN 81-7141-611-X.

Bhaskara Rao, Digumarti, Editor (2001). *World Conference on Education for All*. New Delhi: APH Publishing Corporation. ISBN 81-7141-274-9.

Bhaskara Rao, Digumarti, Editor (2001). *World Conference on Higher Education*, New Delhi: Discovery Publishing House. ISBN 81-7141-610-1.

Bhaskara Rao, Digumarti, Editor (2001). *World Conference on Science*. New Delhi: Discovery Publishing House. ISBN 81-7141-612-8.

Bhaskara Rao, Digumarti, Editor (2003). *Inspiring Experience in Teacher Education*. New Delhi: Discovery Publishing House. ISBN 81-7141-656-X.

Bhaskara Rao, Digumarti, Editor (2003). *International Studies in Education*, 3 Volumes, New Delhi: Discovery Publishing House. ISBN 81-7141-647-0.

Bhaskara Rao, Digumarti, Editor (2003). *Military Conversion: Impact on Science and Technology*, New Delhi: Discovery Publishing House. ISBN 81-7141-578-4.

Bhaskara Rao, Digumarti, Editor (2003). *United Nations Millennium Summit*. New Delhi: Discovery Publishing House. ISBN 81-7141-632-2.

Bhaskara Rao, Digumarti, Editor (2003). *World Assembly on Aging*. New Delhi: Discovery Publishing House. ISBN 81-7141-637-3.

Bhaskara Rao, Digumarti, Editor (2004). *World Conference on Human Rights*. New Delhi: Discovery Publishing House. ISBN 81-7141-661-6.

Bhaskara Rao, Digumarti, Editor (2003). *World Education Forum*. New Delhi: Discovery Publishing House. ISBN 81-7141-639-X.

Bhaskara Rao, Digumarti, Editor (2004). *Education Employment and Human Resource Development*. New Delhi: Discovery Publishing House. ISBN 81-7141-681-0.

Bhaskara Rao, Digumarti, Editor (2004). *Successfully Schooling*. New Delhi: Discovery Publishing House. ISBN 81-7141-677-2.

Bhaskara Rao, Digumarti, Editor (2004). *European Education and Teachers*. New Delhi: Discovery Publishing House. ISBN 81-7141-702-7.

Bhaskara Rao, Digumarti, Editor (2004). *Teachers in a Changing World*. New Delhi: Discovery Publishing House. ISBN 81-7141-694-2.

Bhaskara Rao, Digumarti, Editor (2004). *Learning to Live Together*, 4 Volumes. New Delhi: Discovery Publishing House.

Vol. 1 *International Conference on Learning to Live Together.*

Vol. 2 *Globalisation and Living Together.*

Vol. 3 *Curriculum for Learning to Live Together.*

Vol. 4 *Science Education for the Contemporary Society.*

Bhaskara Rao, Digumarti (2004). *International Guidelines on Open and Distance Education*, New Delhi: Discovery Publishing House.

Bhaskara Rao, Digumarti, Editor (2004). *Adult Learning in the 21st Century*. New Delhi: Discovery Publishing House.

Bhaskara Rao, Digumarti, Editor (2004). *Educational Practices: Research and Recommendations*. New Delhi: Discovery Publishing House.

Bhaskara Rao, Digumarti, Editor (2004). *Chernobyl: Never Again*. New Delhi: APH Publishing Corporation.

Bhaskara Rao, Digumarti, Editor (2004). *Virology and Immunology*. New Delhi: APH Publishing Corporation.

Bhaskara Rao, Digumarti, C.A.P. Swami and B.S.V. Dutt (1997). *Self-Evaluation in Student Teaching*. New Delhi: Discovery Publishing House. ISBN 81-7141-374-9.

Bhaskara Rao, Digumarti and B.S.V. Dutt, Editors (2003). *Education: Programmes and Policies*. New Delhi: APH Publishing Corporation. ISBN 81-7648-470-9.

Bhaskara Rao, Digumarti and D. Naresh Kumar (2004). *School Teacher Effectiveness*. New Delhi: Discovery Publishing House.

Bhaskara Rao, Digumarti and D. Sridhar (2002). *Job Satisfaction of School Teachers*. New Delhi: Discovery Publishing House. ISBN 81-7141-652-7.

Bhaskara Rao, Digumarti and Digumarti Pushpa Latha (1994). *Achievement in Biology*. New Delhi: Discovery Publishing House. ISBN 81-7141-264-5.

Bhaskara Rao, Digumarti, C. Sridevi and K. Vijaya (1995). *Achievement in Social Studies*. New Delhi: Discovery Publishing House. ISBN 81-7141-281-5.

Bhaskara Rao, Digumarti and Digumarti Pushpa Latha (1995). *Achievement in English*. New Delhi: Discovery Publishing House. ISBN 81-7141-283-1.

Bhaskara Rao, Digumarti and Digumarti Pushpa Latha (1994). *Achievement in Science*. New Delhi: Discovery Publishing House. ISBN 81-7141-280-70.

Bhaskara Rao, Digumarti and Digumarti Pushpa Latha (1995). *Achievement in Mathematics*. New Delhi: Discovery Publishing House. ISBN 81-7141-278-5.

Bhaskara Rao, Digumarti and Digumarti Pushpa Latha, Editors (1998). *International Encyclopaedia of Women*. 5 Volumes. New Delhi: Discovery Publishing House. ISBN 81-7141-410-9.

Vol. 1 *Status of World's Women*. ISBN 81-7141-494-X.

Vol. 2 *Women, Education and Empowerment*. ISBN 81-7141-498-1.

Vol. 3 *Women Challenges and Advancement*. ISBN 81-7141-497-4.

Vol. 4 *Women and Family Health*. ISBN 81-7141-497-4.

Vol. 5 *Women and International Action*. ISBN 81-7141-498-2.

Bhaskara Rao, Digumarti, Digumarti Pushpa Latha and Digumarti Harshitha, Editors (2001). *Biological Warfare*. New Delhi: Discovery Publishing House. ISBN 81-7141-597-0.

Bhaskara Rao, Digumarti, Digumarti Pushpa Latha and Digumarti Harshitha, Editors (2001). *Women as Educators*. New Delhi: Discovery Publishing House. ISBN 81-7141-602-0.

Bhaskara Rao, Digumarti and Digumarti Harshitha, Editors (2001). *Education in India*. New Delhi: APH Publishing Corporation. ISBN 81-7141-207-2.

Bhaskara Rao, Digumarti, Digumarti Pushpa Latha and Digumarti Harshitha, Editors (2001). *Assessing Learning Achievement*. New Delhi: Discovery Publishing House. ISBN 81-7141-601-2.

Bhaskara Rao, Digumarti, Digumarti Pushpa Latha and Digumarti Harshitha, Editors (2001). *Energy Security*. New Delhi: Discovery Publishing House. ISBN 81-7141-598-9.

Bhaskara Rao, Digumarti, Digumarti Harshitha and K.R.S.S. Rao, Editors (1999). *Advanced Biotechnology*. New Delhi: Discovery Publishing House. ISBN 81-7141-516-4.

Bhaskara Rao, Digumarti and K.R.S. Sambhasiva Rao, Editors (1996). *Current Trends in Indian Education*. New Delhi: Discovery Publishing House. ISBN 81-7141-311-0.

Bhaskara Rao, Digumarti and K. Vijaya (1995). *A Text Book of Evaluation*. Ambala Cantt: The Associated Publishers.

Bhaskara Rao, Digumarti and N.V.M. Mohana Rao (2002). *Problems of Mentally Handicapped Children*. New Delhi: Discovery Publishing House. ISBN 81-7141-645-4.

Bhaskara Rao, Digumarti and S. Chandra Mohan (2002). *Sports Management*. New Delhi: APH Publishing Corporation. ISBN 81-7648-467-9.

Bhaskara Rao, Digumarti and Sk. Johni Basha (2004). *Teachers' Population Education Awareness*. New Delhi: APH Publishing Corporation.

Bhaskara Rao, Digumarti, V.V. Rao, V.V. Lakshmi and V.V. Krishna, Editors (1999). *Status and Advancement of Women*. New Delhi: APH Publishing Corporation. ISBN 81-7648-169-6.

Babu, P.C., Author and Digumarti Bhaskara Rao, Editor (2004). *Flowers of Wisdom*. New Delhi: Discovery Publishing House. ISBN 81-7141-695-0.

Bhagya Lakshmi, Lingineni, Author and Digumarti Bhaskara Rao, Editor (2000). *Reading and Comprehension*. New Delhi: Discovery Publishing House. ISBN 81-7141-543-1.

Bhuvaneswara Lakshmi, Gadde, Author and Digumarti Bhaskara Rao, Editor (2000). *Attitude Towards Science*. New Delhi: Discovery Publishing House. ISBN 81-7141-541-6.

Devraj, T.A.S., Author and Digumarti Bhaskara Rao, Editor (1997). *Trace Analysis of Uranium and Thorium*. New Delhi: Discovery Publishing House. ISBN 81-7141-375-7.

Durga Rani, K., Author and Digumarti Bhaskara Rao, Editor (2000). *Educational Aspirations and Scientific Attitudes*. New Delhi: Discovery Publishing House. ISBN 81-7141-555-55.

Dutt, B.S.V. and Digumarti Bhaskara Rao (2001). *Empowering Primary Teachers*. New Delhi: Discovery Publishing House. ISBN 81-7141-615.2.

Ediger, Marlow and Digumarti Bhaskara Rao (1996). *Science Curriculum*. New Delhi: Discovery Publishing House. ISBN 81-7141-321-8.

Ediger, Marlow and Digumarti Bhaskara Rao (2000). *Teaching Mathematics Successfully*. New Delhi: Discovery Publishing House. ISBN 81-7141-552-0.

Ediger, Marlow and Digumarti Bhaskara Rao (2001). *Teaching Science Successfully*. New Delhi: Discovery Publishing House. ISBN 81-7141-600-4.

Ediger, Marlow and Digumarti Bhaskara Rao (2001). *Teaching Social Studies Successfully*. New Delhi: Discovery Publishing House. ISBN 81-7141-596-2.

Ediger, Marlow and Digumarti Bhaskara Rao (2002). *Philosophy and Curriculum*. New Delhi: Discovery Publishing House. ISBN 81-7141-631-4.

Ediger, Marlow and Digumarti Bhaskara Rao (2002). *Improving School Administration*. New Delhi: Discovery Publishing House. ISBN 81-7141-633-0.

Ediger, Marlow and Digumarti Bhaskara Rao (2002). *Elementary Curriculum*. New Delhi: Discovery Publishing House. ISBN 81-7141-658-6.

Ediger, Marlow and Digumarti Bhaskara Rao (2003). *Language Arts Curriculum*. New Delhi: Discovery Publishing House. ISBN 81-7141-657-8.

Ediger, Marlow and Digumarti Bhaskara Rao (2004). *Teaching Language Arts Successfully*. New Delhi: Discovery Publishing House. ISBN 81-7141-678-0.

Ediger, Marlow and Digumarti Bhaskara Rao (2004). *Teaching Mathematics in Elementary Schools*. New Delhi: Discovery Publishing House. ISBN 81-7141-687-X.

Ediger, Marlow and Digumarti Bhaskara Rao (2004). *Teaching Science in Elementary Schools*. New Delhi: Discovery Publishing House. ISBN 81-7141-709-4.

Ediger, Marlow and Digumarti Bhaskara Rao (2004). *School Curriculum and Administration*. New Delhi: Discovery Publishing House. ISBN 81-7141-709-4.

Ediger, Marlow and Digumarti Bhaskara Rao (2004). *Modern Elementary School*. New Delhi: Discovery Publishing House.

Ediger, Marlow and Digumarti Bhaskara Rao (2004): *Relevancy in Elementary Curriculum*. New Delhi: Discovery Publishing House. ISBN 81-7141-751-5.

Ediger, Marlow and Digumarti Bhaskara Rao, (2004). *Teaching Social Studies in Elementary Schools*. New Delhi: Discovery Publishing House.

Ediger Marlow, B.S.V. Dutt and Digumarti Bhaskara Rao (2004). *Teaching English Successfully*. New Delhi: Discovery Publishing House. ISBN 81-7141-707-8.

Harshitha, Digumarti and Digumarti Bhaskara Rao, Editors (2004). *Educational Innovations*. New Delhi: Discovery Publishing House.

Indira Devi, Author and J. Prasanth Kumar and Digumarti Bhaskara Rao, Editors (2004). *Values in Language Text Books*. New Delhi: Discovery Publishing House.

Jayasree, Kandi, Author and Digumarti Bhaskara Rao, Editor (1999). *Correlates of Socialisation*. New Delhi: Discovery Publishing House. ISBN 81-7141-517-2.

John Babu, Chikati, Author and T.J.R. Prasad, G.M. Madhukar and Digumarti Bhaskara Rao, Editors (1996). *Problem Solving in Mathematics*. New Delhi: APH Publishing Corporation. ISBN 81-7648-273-0.

Lalitha, T., Author and K.S. Prabhakaram, D.S.N. Sastry and Digumarti Bhaskara Rao, Editors (2004). *Educational Philosophic Beliefs*. New Delhi: Discovery Publishing House. ISBN 81-7141-765-5.

Madhu Bala, Jampala, Author and Digumarti Bhaskara Rao, Editor (2004). *Adjustment Problems of Hearing Impaired*. New Delhi: Discovery Publishing House.

Marja, Talvi and Digumarti Bhaskara Rao, Editors (1996). *Educational Leadership and Social Changes*. New Delhi: Discovery Publishing House. ISBN 81-7141-320-X.

Nirmala Jyothi, M., Author and Digumarti Bhaskara Rao, Editor (2003). *Non-detention Systems in School Education*. New Delhi: Discovery Publishing House. ISBN 81-7141-654-3.

Prabhakaram, K.S., Author and Digumarti Bhaskara Rao, Editor (1998). *Concept Attainment Model in Mathematics Teaching*. New Delhi: Discovery Publishing House. ISBN 81-7141-424-9.

Prasanth Kumar, J., Author and Digumarti Bhaskara Rao, Editor (1998). *Effectiveness of Distance Education System*. New Delhi: Discovery Publishing House. ISBN 81-7141-437-0.

Prasanth Kumar, J., Author and G. Sundara Rao and Digumarti Bhaskara Rao, Editors (2000). *Open University Student Support Services*. New Delhi: Discovery Publishing House. ISBN 81-7141-550-4.

Ramatulasamma, K., Author and Digumarti Bhaskara Rao, Editor (2002). *Job Satisfaction of Teacher Educators*, New Delhi: Discovery Publishing House. ISBN 81-7141-655-1.

Rama Krishnaiah, D., Author and Digumarti Bhaskara Rao, Editor (1998). *Job Satisfaction of College Teachers*, New Delhi: Discovery Publishing House. ISBN 81-7141-438-9.

Rama Kumar Ratnam, M., Author and Digumarti Bhaskara Rao, Editor (1998). *Dukka: Suffering in Early Buddhism*. New Delhi: Discovery Publishing House. ISBN 81-7141-653-5.

Rathaiah, Lavu and Digumarti Bhaskara Rao, Editors (1996). *International Innovations in Education*. New Delhi: Discovery Publishing House. ISBN 81-7141-359-5.

Ramesh, Ganta and Digumarti Bhaskara Rao, Editors (1998). *Environmental Education: Problems and Prospects*. New Delhi: Discovery Publishing House. ISBN 81-7141-423-0.

Rathaiah, Lavu and Digumarti Bhaskara Rao (1997). *Achievement Correlates*. New Delhi: Discovery Publishing House. ISBN 81-7141-385-4.

Reddy, Sudhakar Y., Author, and Digumarti Bhaskara Rao, Editor (2003). *Creativity in Adolescents*. New Delhi: Discovery Publishing House. ISBN 81-7141-659-4.

Reddy, M.S., Author and Digumarti Bhaskara Rao, Editor (2004). *Creativity in College Students*. New Delhi: Discovery Publishing House. ISBN 81-7141-697-7.

Radramamba, B., Author and Digumarti Bhaskara Rao, Editor (2003). *Problems of Teaching*. New Delhi: APH Publishing Corporation. ISBN 81-7648-462-8.

Sanjeeva Rao, P.C., Author and Digumarti Bhaskara Rao, Editor (1996). *A Text Book of Geology*. New Delhi: Discovery Publishing House. ISBN 81-7141-313-7.

Satya Narayana V., Author and Digumarti Bhaskara Rao, Editor (2001). *Physical Education, Social Attitudes and Leadership Qualities*. New Delhi: Discovery Publishing House. ISBN 81-7141-593-8.

Srinivasulu Reddy, M., and K.R.S. Sambasiva Rao, Authors and Digumarti Bhaskara Rao, Editor (1999). *A Text Book of Aquaculture*. New Delhi: Discovery Publishing House. ISBN 81-7141-482-6.

Srinivasa Rao, Mandalapu, Author and Digumarti Bhaskara Rao, Editor (2004). *Achievement Motivation and Achievement in Mathematics*. New Delhi: Discovery Publishing House. ISBN 81-7141-674-8.

Vanaja, M. Author and Digumarti Bhaskara Rao, Editor (1999). *Inquiry Training Model*. New Delhi: Discovery Publishing House. ISBN 81-7141-515-6.

Vanaja. M. and N. Sneha Latha, Authors and Digumarti Bhaskara Rao, Editor (2004). *Student Shyness*. New Delhi: APH Publishing Corporation.

Valeri V. Koustiouk, Author and Digumarti Bhaskara Rao, Editor (2002). *A Text Book of Cryogenics*. New Delhi: Discovery Publishing House. ISBN 81-7141-642-X.

Valeri V. Koustiouk, Author and Digumarti Bhaskara Rao, Editor (2004). *Refrigeration and Environment*. New Delhi: APH Publishing Corporation.

Veena Kumari, Balusu and Digumarti Bhaskara Rao (1996). *Operation Black Board*. New Delhi: Ashish Publishing Corporation. ISBN 81-7024-711-X.

Veena Kumari, Balusu, Author and Digumarti Bhaskara Rao, Editor (2000). *Psycho-Social Correlates of Achievement*, New Delhi: Discovery Publishing House. ISBN 81-7141-547-4.

Vanaja, M., Author and Digumarti Bhaskara Rao, Editor (1999). *Inquiry Training Model*. New Delhi: Discovery Publishing House. ISBN 81-7141-515-6.

Venkata Rao, P. and Digumarti Bhaskara Rao (1989). *A Text Book of Zoology—Junior Intermediate*. Guntur: Vignan Publishers.

Venkata Rao, P. and Digumarti Bhaskara Rao (1989). *A Text Book of Zoology—Senior Intermediate*. Guntur: Vignan Publishers.

Venugopala Rao, K., Author and Digumarti Bhaskara Rao, Editor (2000). *Teacher Morale in Secondary Schools*. New Delhi: Discovery Publishing House. ISBN 81-7141-551-2.

Vidya, C., Author and Digumarti Bhaskara Rao. Editor (1996). *A Text Book of Nutrition*. New Delhi: Discovery Publishing House. ISBN 81-7141-309-9.

Vidya Bharathi, D., Author and Digumarti Bhaskara Rao, Editor (2000). *Educational Philosophies of Swami Vivekananda and John Dewey*. New Delhi: APH Publishing Corporation. ISBN 81-7648-309-9.

Books in Telugu Language

Bhaskara Rao, Digumarti (1986). *Dhrushya Sravana Bodhanapakaranalu* (Audio Visual Teaching Aids). Guntur: Nagarjuna Publishers.

Bhaskara Rao, Digumarti (1993). *Jeevasashtra Bodhana* (Teaching of Biology). Guntur: Nagarjuna Publishers.

Bhaskara Rao, Digumarti (1995). *Vignanasasthra Bodhana* (Teaching of Science) Guntur: Nagarjuna Publishers.

Bhaskara Rao, Digumarti (1997). *Vidya Manovignana Seshtram* (Educational Psychology). Guntur: Creative Press.

Bhaskara Rao, Digumarti (1998). *DSC Study Material*. Guntur: Nagarjuna Publishers.

Bhaskara Rao, Digumarti (1998). *Upadhyayudu Vidya*. (Teacher and Education). Guntur: Nagarjuna Publishers.

Bhaskara Rao, Digumarti (1998). *Vidya Drukpadalu* (Prespectives of Education). Guntur: Nagarjuna Publishers.

Bhaskara Rao, Digumarti (1999). *EdCET Teaching Aptitude*. Guntur: Nagarjuna Publishers.

Bhaskara Rao, Digumarti (2001). *Bharata Samajamulo Upadyayudu Vidya* (Teacher and Education in Emerging Indian Society). Guntur: Nagarjuna Publishers.

Bhaskara Rao, Digumarti (2001). *Bhoutika Sastra Bodhana Paddathulu* (Methods of Teaching Physical Science). Guntur: Nagarjuna Publishers.

Bhaskara Rao, Digumarti (2001). *Jeeva Sastra Bodhana Padhathulu* (Methods of Teaching Biology). Guntur: Nagarjuna Publishers.

Bhaskara Rao, Digumarti (2001). *Vidya Manovignana Sastram* (Educational Psychology). Guntur: Nagarjuna Publishers.

Bhaskara Rao, Digumarti (2003). *Patsala Yajamanyam/Paripalana* (School Management and Administration). Guntur: Nagarjuna Publishers.

Bhaskara Rao, Digumarti (2004). *Vidya Sanketika Sastram mariyu Computer Vidya* (Educational Technology and Computer Education). Guntur: Nagarjuna Publishers.